South Africa:
Land of Hope?

Taffy Gould McCallum

For Mary

With fond regards,

December 1989

AMAGI PUBLICATIONS

AMAGI BOOKS
PO Box 92385 Norwood 2117

First published October 1989

ISBN No. 0–620–14195–6

Printed and bound by The Natal Witness Printing and Publishing
Company (Pty) Ltd, Pietermaritzburg.

For all my South African friends.

May they, one day, come to know one another.

Every age needs men who will redeem the time by living with a vision of things that are to be.

— Adlai Stevenson

Faith is not belief without proof, but trust without reservations.

— Anonymous

ACKNOWLEDGMENTS

I would like to express my appreciation to all those South Africans — unfortunately, too numerous to mention here by name — who facilitated the arranging of interviews and who offered suggestions as to people and books worthy of consideration.

I would like to thank my father, Emil J. Gould; my Smith College classmate, editor Helen Haddad; and one of my former students, Juliana Field, for the time they spent reading over the manuscript and for their perceptive comments on how better to present this extensive material.

Gratitude goes to Edith Kearney, for checking my South African spelling and facts, and to Betty Ann Cowett and Sallie Snyder, for their proofreading and suggestions.

Baie Dankie to Robert and to Margaret Farenham, for their tutelage and support in my study of Afrikaans.

And finally, I offer special thanks to Jane Martin Ghazarossian, for her guidance; to my colleague, Dorlene Shane, for her assistance, encouragement and advice; and to Diana and Isidor Berrill, of Cape Town, who first sparked my interest in and introduced me to their country.

Author's Note:

As a substantial portion of the material presented here consists of direct quotations, the use of American orthography would not ring true to those being quoted or to readers in the English-speaking world outside the United States. On the other hand, to adopt South African orthography in my own narration would strike a false note and, perhaps, smack of affectation to the American reader. Therefore, at the risk of causing some confusion among those most sensitive to language and spelling, I have alternated between the two orthographies, presenting each speaker in his/her native voice. Where names are used (e.g. "Labour Party" or "coloureds"), they are spelled, even in my narrative, as they are found in South Africa. The omission of punctuation after titles and initials also conforms to South African practice.

Following current stylistics, I have used lower case letters when describing blacks, whites, and coloureds. The Reverend Leon Sullivan, in his Code for American companies doing business in South Africa (Appendix VII), capitalizes "Blacks" but leaves "whites" in the lower case. As I have presented the Code in its entirety and exactly as it appears officially in print, I have not deviated from the original in quoting it.

In an effort to ease the conversion of South African *rands* (R) to American *dollars* ($) — to give a general idea of relative costs and values — I have simply divided by two, even though the official exchange rate varies slightly from the resulting figures.

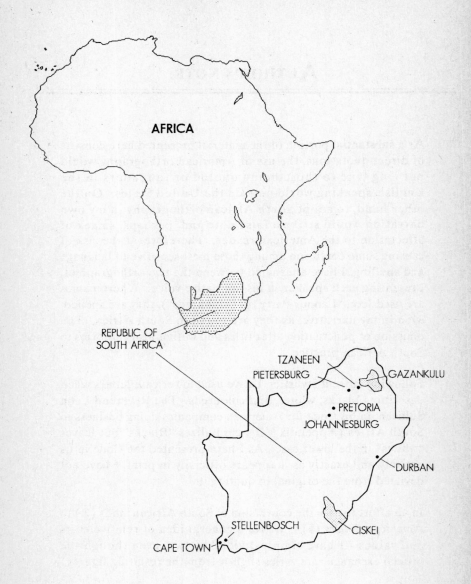

AFRICA

REPUBLIC OF
SOUTH AFRICA

TZANEEN
PIETERSBURG
GAZANKULU

PRETORIA
JOHANNESBURG

DURBAN

STELLENBOSCH
CISKEI
CAPE TOWN

Table of Contents

Chapter 1

IN-PERSON INTERVIEWS
(First-Person Narrations)

Table of Contents
(Continued)

Table of Contents
(Continued)

South Africa: Land of Hope?

Table of Contents
(Continued)

Table of Contents
(Continued)

Chapter 2

Chapter 3

Chapter 4

Table of Contents
(Continued)

Chapter 5

Table of Contents
(Continued)

Appendices

Table of Contents

(Continued)

Table of Contents
(Continued)

Bibliography

Index

INTRODUCTION

Is there hope for South Africa — or is a black-white bloodbath inevitable? From reading the international press and watching American newscasts, it would seem only a matter of time before we learn of yet another conflagration on the world's second-largest continent.

I visited South Africa in 1977 and 1978, and both times I wondered how long the situation there would — or could — last. In the ensuing years, I have followed the South Africa story with great interest. I have read histories and novels, biographies, newspapers, magazines, and an assortment of reports from foundations both "left" and "right." As a newspaper columnist and radio talk-show host, I have tried to gather new evidence and impart information. On three occasions I interviewed representatives of the South African government.

Now I have returned from a third trip to that fascinating and complex country — this time having interviewed some eighty-two South Africans, across the political spectrum and through all population groups.

What I learned was startling. Where, like most people, I expected to find seething anger and a country on the verge of revolution, I found instead frustration, impatience, cynicism, and resolve — but all tempered by a determination *not* to destroy a country that, right or wrong, remains the most economically viable and socially desirable on the African continent.[1]

---

1   Leon Louw and Frances Kendall, *South Africa: The Solution* (Bisho: Amagi Publications, 1986), p. 169.

1

South Africa: Land of Hope?

On my first trip to South Africa, I had already been struck by the difference between expectation and reality. Yes, there was segregation and, yes, there were slums, but I'd grown up in the South: It had not been that many years since *Miami* had had the equivalent of a Separate Amenities Act, and the slums in South Africa were no worse than those in Mississippi, Alabama, Louisiana, or Georgia. The major difference between life in America and life in South Africa was that we in America had begun to strike down our laws of segregation — *de jure* if not *de facto*. South Africa, on the other hand, continued its policy of apartheid, enforcing a code book of laws that, in many cases, could be described only as comic, were it not for the tragedy involved.

My trip was arranged when, in the fall of 1987, the South African Consul General asked if I would like to go back to South Africa to see for myself what changes had taken place and what was happening in that beautiful but beleaguered country. From time to time, he said, the South African Department of Foreign Affairs invites "opinion formers" from other countries to visit as their guests.

I confess I was skeptical: What would I really see and what would be expected in return? As a topic of timely interest South Africa would be high on my list in any case, for future columns and talk shows, but the question remained as to what would be planned for me.

To my great surprise, *I* did the planning. The Consul asked me for the names, places, and categories I preferred and passed them on to Pretoria for arrangements to be made. There were no "understandings" regarding future programs or articles. Under those conditions, I accepted and made the trip in mid-April of 1988.

As it turned out, the South African government arranged about half the interviews I conducted. In some cases they told me point-blank that, were *they* to request appointments with the people I had listed, they would be turned down; I would have to arrange those on my own. In other cases, "liberal" contacts in South Africa recommended people I had not listed, and I made those arrangements as well. At no time did anyone from the South African government try to thwart my speaking with those with an anti-government stance — or even voice surprise at my desire to do so.

2

I did not, it is true, tell all whom I interviewed that I had come to South Africa, this time, as the guest of the government. But I did always say it was my third trip there and that I hoped to present a balanced account of what is going on in the country *now*, rather than confirm a preconceived notion and make a case for either the "left" or the "right." Only one person hoped I would *not* present a balanced account — the attorney representing Winnie and Nelson Mandela. He later also refused me permission to publish our interview in this book.

I am not and never have been an apologist for apartheid. Whatever the original intention, it has become a system that is cruel, irrational, and indefensible. But it is important to note that the British in South Africa have been as much to blame as the Dutch. Where the Dutch passed laws to protect themselves economically (beginning in 1869), the British codified what can only be labelled as out-and-out imperialist colonial racism.[1]

Many people, both here and in South Africa, have asked what the major differences are between the South Africa of today and the one I saw a decade ago. Outwardly, of course, "petty" apartheid is gone. In restaurants, theatres, sportsgrounds, and public transport, South Africa is a fully-integrated society. What remains of "grand" apartheid is primarily the Group Areas Act. This is the Act that determines who may live where — in many cases ignored by both the populace and the government, but nonetheless the outstanding remaining barrier between the present government and non-white South Africa, and the law without whose rescinding South Africa will never be a free and open society.[2]

In human terms, the changes I see are these: Among the blacks (and here I mean all people of color), I sense new self-esteem. They are not arrogant, but neither are they obsequious. Nor do they seem to look at whites with the same suspicion and/or apprehension as was the case in the

---

1   Louw and Kendall, op. cit., p. 32.

2   It must be mentioned, here, that the Population Registration Act is another sticking-point with many South Africans. The classification of individuals by racial groups serves not merely for census-taking but, rather, is frequently used to serve a hidden agenda of racial discrimination.

late 70s. They speak up more — many offering the first "Hello!" They are better dressed, healthier looking, more purposefully active, and generally exhibit a greater sense of well-being. Among the whites, there is a new sense of involvement; no longer are they the detached members of a privileged society. Many English-speakers, a substantial portion of the Afrikaner "Intellectual Community," and — more recently — even Afrikaner National Party government workers now express impatience with a system they see as out-of-date, inhuman, and continued at their peril.

I found it interesting that of South Africans who asked my opinion on this question, be they black or white, liberal or conservative, none disagreed with my assessment.

Some points should be made here concerning the "common ground" on which South African blacks and whites operate — common ground unknown to much of the outside world:

1. There is no debate in South Africa about whether or not "the whites took the land from the blacks." History shows and the United Nations acknowledges that, in simple terms, the whites arrived at the Cape at generally about the same time black tribes were moving south from Central Africa. Both groups lived in what is now South Africa, with no idea the others even existed, so small were the groups and so vast the land. Only when both groups enlarged and spread out did they meet — and fight — over territory. (If *anyone* could lay claim to prior inhabitancy, it would be the "brown" Khoikhoi who, with their cattle, were found in the area at the time the Dutch arrived at the Cape in 1652. The Khoikhoi, for a variety of reasons, died out by the middle of the eighteenth century.[1] For some keen insight into the centuries-old battle for territory and identity by *all* the tribes in South Africa, read the fascinating *White Tribe Dreaming*, by Marq de Villiers.[2])

---

1   Richard Elphick, *Khoikhoi and the Founding of White South Africa* (Johannesburg: Ravan Press, 1975).

2   (New York: Viking, 1988).

4

2. As mentioned earlier, apartheid is not something invented by the present South African government when it came to power in 1948. Rather, it is a set of laws originally codified in the middle of the nineteenth century and going back, in fact, to 1660[1].

3. The problems South Africa faces are not simply black vs white. Among the blacks there are tribal divisions which remain, particularly in rural areas, points of contention. Though urban blacks increasingly think of themselves first as South Africans and second as Zulu, Xhosa, Soto, Venda, etc., the opposite remains true outside the cities. Among the Indians, too, there are divisions, mostly by religion, and the white community still bears the scars of British-Dutch animosity, dating to the early nineteenth century.

4. The outside world's idea that the white minority in South Africa should turn the country over to the black majority is neither a rational nor a well-founded opinion. South Africa has a Third World country living within the borders of a First World country. Black illiteracy stands at seventy-five percent. Of all the blacks with whom I spoke, even in AZAPO—the Azanian Peoples Organization, considered by some other blacks as the "left lunatic fringe"—not one thought blacks were ready to take over the running of the South African government and economy. What they do want is a reasonable place in South African society, and even that translates more as economic opportunity than as voting rights.

South Africa is a complex society, one unlike any other in the world. The question of how to come to grips with its problems occupies almost every citizen every day. As Leon Louw and Frances Kendall point out in their book, *South Africa: The Solution*, few South Africans may know where any of the myriad political parties stand on nuclear energy, economic policy, or education, but everyone knows where they stand on apartheid: Racial politics is all-absorbing.[2]

Although the Border Wars of the 1770s were between Boer and black, and the Zulu Wars of the 1870s were between British and black, in a certain

1   Louw and Kendall, op. cit., pp. 12,31.

2   Ibid, p. 75.

5

sense it may be said that black South Africans have been pawns in an elaborate, strategic, bitter and obdurate contest played out over the past two hundred years between the British and the Dutch. Descendants of both groups are now faced with the dilemma of how to overcome their own differences and deal with a majority population that is, increasingly, politically aware, economically prepared, and socially desirous of integrating into the mainstream of South African life.[1]

The outside world offers quick-fix solutions that are no solutions at all. Often these suggestions come from people who have spent little or no time in South Africa; some of them, I dare say, can barely find the country on a map. The result – among blacks as well as whites – is frustration, bewilderment, and anti-American feeling. (Our lack of knowledge about their country becomes even more embarrassing when one realizes how much they know about us – our history, our culture, our politics, and our geography.)

A few words about how I chose my list and conducted the interviews: I was particularly interested in several specific areas and groups of people. Naturally, it was important to meet with members of all major political parties and population groups. I was also interested in the areas of education and enterprise, and I wanted to visit a "homeland" and an "independent country" – political entities for blacks, set up by the ruling Nationalists wholly within the boundaries of South Africa, and considered by many to be nothing more than puppet manipulations of a racist government. Finally, I wanted to meet students, academics, and religious leaders, the last because of the important place religion holds in the lives of all South Africans.

Where I had specific names in hand, I requested those interviews. As certain individuals were unavailable, alternates were chosen – with my approval. In order to ensure that I was not getting just "the government line," I obtained other names and arranged other interviews through

---

1   Stuart Cloete, in *Against These Three: A Biography of Paul Kruger, Cecil Rhodes and Lobengula, Last King of the Matabele,* describes the history of South Africa in graphic-but-succinct terms: "Nowhere else did three cultures – the ancient barbaric, the religious pioneer, and the modern industrialist – coexist . . . . Not merely three nations, but three worlds warred." (Boston: Houghton Mifflin Company, 1945) p.5.

contacts I knew to be anti-government. My purpose throughout was to determine how a broad range of South Africans view their problems and their future and to learn how much of the story is filtering through possibly biased press accounts.

I arrived in the country with prepared sets of questions – based on my reading and research – for people in the various categories. As mentioned earlier, the list of those I wished to interview doubled as I travelled and, of course, new questions arose even in the course of discussion. There were, fortunately, no time constraints. In some cases, people who thought they would give me twenty or thirty minutes wound up giving me as much as two hours. As they came to realize that I had read, researched, and thought about their problems, they opened up to me, even becoming eager to tell their stories. As the reader will see, façades are not a problem here. South Africans, one and all, are straightforward in voicing their opinions.

In addition to the interviews done in person, I was in touch with another group of South African individuals in writing. In some cases, this was due to a simple lack of time, difficulty of logistics, or conflict in schedules. In other cases, those whose opinions I sought would not or could not meet me face-to-face but agreed to accept my questions in writing. Where anonymity was requested (even by those who met me face-to-face), I have honored those requests.

The interviews – fifty of the eighty-two I conducted – are arranged chronologically. There are two reasons: first, because most people spoke on a variety of subjects; and second, because any attempt to categorize these individuals would be to establish a bias, which I specifically set out to avoid. The complete list of those interviewed and the questions I had formulated prior to arriving in South Africa may be found in Appendices I and II.

One cannot, of course, expect to get the full story of any country's political proclivities in the course of a mere four weeks. In an environment as intricate as South Africa's, such expectation would indicate not only folly but presumption. Research and investigation done prior to my 1988 trip served me well, but only as background. I tried, therefore, to round out my understanding by reading a variety of newspapers during the time I was there and a wide selection of books, magazines, and other publications following my return. For the reader who desires a more complete picture of what large numbers of South Africans are thinking, saying, and doing, the chapters following the interviews should provide an amplification.

It is strongly recommended that the reader spend some time studying Appendices III through IX before considering the interviews. The four population groups and the various political parties to which reference is made throughout the book are described in Appendices III and IV. And as one must have some sense of South Africa's turbulent past, in order to appreciate its present and anticipate its future, I have included a brief historical outline (Appendix V) borrowed from the Louw and Kendall book mentioned earlier. The dismantling of apartheid, listed near the end of that outline, is described in detail in Appendix VI.

Appendix VII contains details of the provisions of the last amended "Sullivan Code," that body of rules and regulations affecting American companies doing business in South Africa, more completely known as the "Statement of Principles of U.S. Firms with Affiliates in the Republic of South Africa."

In the absence of any interviews of members of the African National Congress — based outside South Africa — the reader will find, in Appendix VIII, details of the ANC's "Constitutional Guidelines for a Democratic South Africa" — the amended Freedom Charter. First presented by the ANC in 1955, the Charter was amended in 1988. Following publication of the amended version, the *Weekly Mail* — one of South Africa's leading anti-apartheid newspapers ("the paper for a changing South Africa") — offered leaders of the country's major political parties the opportunity to comment on the 1988 changes. Excerpts from those comments are included, following the "Guidelines."

Finally, Appendix IX presents the Bill of Rights drawn up by members of the KwaZulu/Natal Indaba, the multi-racial legislative body discussed in detail in the interview with Peter Badcock, in Durban.

It is my hope that, on learning what a broad cross-section of South Africans think about their country and their future, readers will form an educated opinion as to the role they and *their* country should play in that future — an opinion based on fact, rather than on three-inch headlines or sixty seconds on the evening news.

South Africa is on the lips of the world. Legislative bodies from the Far West to the Far East debate her politics and their role in her future. Few people hear more than what one or two "celebrity leaders" on either side of the apartheid issue think about what is happening there. But South Africa is a complex country with complex problems, and no matter how many people one meets, there is always another opinion waiting to be heard.

We dare not confine ourselves to the voices of only the most strident.

Chapter 1

IN-PERSON INTERVIEWS
(First-Person Narrations)

PRETORIA

My trip began in Pretoria, with a visit to the Bureau for Information of the South African Department of Foreign Affairs, whose officials had arranged my itinerary and asked whether there were any additions or deletions I wished to make to the list of interviews. I did, in fact, add a few names — as I would continue to do throughout my stay. As I said to one official, I did not make the trip to go sightseeing; I wanted to learn what the people were thinking and saying. I did, however — in an effort to broaden my understanding of the country and its diverse people — visit several museums and tribal Art and Culture Centres.

I remained in Pretoria for three interviews, beginning with Herman Stadler, a spokesman for the Security Branch of the South African Police Department. As security is an issue of paramount importance to South Africans of all races, I was especially interested to hear the views of this particular department.

Herman Stadler (white)

The South African Police Force is approximately fifty percent black and fifty percent white, with officers receiving equal pay for equal work. In certain non-white residential areas we have officers serving their own people; in the white areas the police force is mixed.

Our major concerns at the moment are internal security and terrorism. We have strict firearm control laws. All applications are thoroughly screened and licences are granted on merit. Applicants with criminal records, especially records relating to violent crimes, are automatically disqualified. In spite of strict control, large numbers of firearms are stolen each year. In 1987, more than 10,000 were stolen. Very few of our crimes are drug-related, as opposed to the situation in America. We do have a marijuana problem [known here as *dagga*] but practically no cocaine.

The African National Congress, an avowed terrorist organisation that learnt guerrilla tactics and revolutionary warfare in Vietnam, plays the major role in the revolutionary onslaught against South Africa. Policemen, especially black policemen, are subjected to intimidation by the ANC, which has vowed to render the country ungovernable and sees black policemen as sellouts. Many of these policemen have lost their lives in the line of duty, killed by other black people.

Under normal circumstances, when *children* are arrested they are released into the custody of their parents. If circumstances so dictate, however, they are held in a place of safety, together with other juveniles. Unfortunately, many of the children are being exploited by the ANC. It is the black children, in many cases, who are "necklacing" other blacks. [This is the gruesome act of tying a person's hands and legs, then placing a rubber tire around his neck which is filled with gasoline and set on fire, burning the victim alive.] Often these children give us false names and addresses, so we are unable to contact relatives. On other occasions, when we can contact the families, they beg us to keep the children in our custody, to keep them out of further trouble — or simply because the families cannot cope with them. Unfortunately, our attempts at rehabilitating juvenile criminals are not much more successful than any other worldwide attempts at rehabilitating adults.

Next, I travelled to the lovely and impressive Union Buildings, where major governmental offices are housed, to meet with Frank Land, Director of the USA Section in the Department of Foreign Affairs. This department handles bilateral relations and is always interested in gleaning new information from visiting journalists. In addition, naturally, it hopes to dispel any erroneous preconceived notions one may have about the country. (At the end of my trip I met once again with Department officials, to see which if any of those preconceived notions had been confirmed or altered.) This interview seemed to set the tone for my entire visit. It quickly became obvious that no punches would be pulled, yet neither was there any hesitancy to give forthright descriptions of what was going on in South Africa.

Frank Land (white)

You Americans certainly have a strange way of treating your friends. South Africa has supported you and the West in international conflicts, while the Russians vow to run you into the sea. Yet you send billions of dollars in aid and technology to help the Russians but increasingly want to isolate us. We understand there are differences in approach between the more pragmatic Reagan Administration and a hostile Congress where the legislation originates. The Administration, through "constructive engagement," seeks to influence South Africa through positive measures such as funding projects in our country. But that approach – though effective – has not prevailed, and the bottom line is that Congress has imposed sanctions legislation which has put a brake on the very progress they insist upon our achieving.

It's a shame that your sanctions and disinvestment schemes have not only *not* accomplished what you thought they would but, in addition, have caused tremendous anti-American sentiment in this country, which we never have had before. The ultra-right is now more anti-American than anti-British. They say, "The more we change, the more sanctions are imposed; so why bother changing any further?" That right wing has grown in strength. The moderate and even liberal whites, in the meantime, are bewildered that you can be so misguided, and the moderate blacks are shocked and upset that you have deserted them. Ironically, while the West has imposed sanctions our trade with other African countries has increased, as has our political interaction – reflecting our economic interdependence and a more pragmatic political approach.

As to Nelson Mandela, we know he is a symbol to the world and we know what the reaction will be if he dies in jail – though we have also been given reports that the radical young blacks will kill him if we release him, to create a martyr. Nelson Mandela is not a *political* prisoner; rather, he is in jail for the crime of sabotage. [This has been confirmed by Amnesty International.] The government has made it clear that his sentence could be commuted if he should reject violence as a means of political change. But so far he has not done so. [Following a July 1989 meeting with State President PW Botha, Mandela released a statement indicating his co-operation in seeking a peaceful solution to the country's problems. The statement surprised Mandela's ANC followers but delighted most of the rest of the world.]

We released Govan Mbeki – another member of the ANC serving a long sentence – on humanitarian grounds, and we had a backlash from the right-wing conservatives. In addition, radical blacks tried to manipulate him into grandstanding against the government, so of course there are

15

limiting political considerations as well. It's all well and good to want and to try to push reforms ahead, but if—because we move too fast—the National Party should lose office to the right wing, then the whole reform movement would be completely lost. So we must move judiciously. A National Council or "Great Indaba" of black leaders is being considered, and more and more of the discussions in the tricameral Parliament are taking place jointly, so there is progress in joint decision-making—though it may seem too slow for the Americans.

Sanctions and disinvestment, unfortunately, have slowed the reform process considerably. When people begin to suffer economically, or if jobs are scarce, they don't become more liberal; they pull back, instead, to protect themselves. That is why the sanctions legislation should be replaced by programmes to create jobs and so create work for young blacks. Such programmes would allow them to develop the skills they need to negotiate a better deal for themselves in South Africa.

As a former teacher and one who places great emphasis on quality in education, I had made a special point of wanting to speak with someone involved in the planning of black education. I met with Ekhart Posselt, Deputy Chief of the Department of Education and Training, with whom I exchanged a good deal of information. I was also provided with reams of reports, charts, graphs, tables, and other literature so typically produced by education departments the world over.

Ekhart Posselt (white)

This Department concerns itself with the education of all blacks in South Africa. There is no compulsory education; rather, it is *voluntary* compulsory education—meaning that any group that wishes to make its children go to school may do so, but the government does not impose it. Our drop-out rate is, as we understand it, lower than what you have in America.

Our children are trilingual, speaking English and Afrikaans as well as the language of their native tribe. The government sponsors a programme of pre-primary education for ages four to six. At age six, we have a "bridging year," a school-readiness programme to better prepare the students for school. Eighty-nine percent of black children ages six to sixteen are now in school, and though we are building fifteen new classrooms every day, the demand still exceeds the supply.

Our schools are comprehensive in scope. We offer academic courses but also commercial, technical, and home economics tracks, all four giving access to university. We also have a common core syllabus throughout the country. In addition to universities there are technical colleges, which are pre-tertiary, and technikons [trade schools], which offer more practical tertiary courses.

South Africa also has an extensive adult education system where all courses are available free, both day and evening. The students can do an entire twelve-year course at their own pace. Literacy is our primary interest and most adults master three languages in three years. There are also community enrichment courses which teach women how to take care of their children and offer a full range of home economics subjects.

Qualification is the sole determinant of salaries for all teachers. Teaching is highly paid, comparable to other public sector jobs, and attracts the best students. Teacher training schools have three-year programmes. In the past, black teachers were trained with less than twelve years of schooling, but in 1980 a new teacher training course was determined, and by 1992 all black teachers will have had a full twelve years of primary and secondary education plus three years of tertiary teacher training. Trainees get bursaries [scholarships] which they repay by teaching.

The pass rate for black university students is low compared to whites. Studies show that sixteen percent of the population must have a sound education to satisfy the needs of upper and middle management in a growing economy. We must strive to improve black education at all levels so we can reach that percentage. All students take guidance courses in grades eight through twelve which give them information on universities, vocations, and bursaries. Through these courses we can identify the brighter students, whom we encourage to continue on through university. We are also beginning special programmes for gifted students.

South Africa: Land of Hope?

Many people ask about integrated education in South Africa. Of course, there are private schools which are integrated at all levels. However, integrated public education at this point would be *black* education, as seventy-five percent of all school children are black. Since there is a difference between black and white education — in language and culture, for example — trying to place all students in the same school is just not practical. In addition, the white South African students have always gone to separate schools, depending on whether they spoke English or Afrikaans. Those students have little interest in mixing with each other: They play different sports, they sing different songs, and they have different heroes. Even the universities have attracted students based on their language and culture, although that of course has all changed, now, to a large extent.

The government recognises the importance of improving black education and is committed to doing so. Spending has increased over forty percent in just the last few years, and although we have a long way to go we are pleased with the results we are seeing.

*   *   *

PIETERSBURG

Leaving Pretoria, I flew to Pietersburg, in the northern Transvaal—hotbed of Afrikanerdom and the right-wing political parties. Having made a specific request to have dinner at the home of some Afrikaners with children, I spent a fascinating evening with a family whose guest list included fellow Afrikaners, Professor Jan Pretorius and his wife, and a black woman, Mabel Chueu. While the teenage son and his friends support the far-right conservative parties—vowing to fight the changes they acknowledge as inevitable—his parents (who prefer to remain anonymous) were more liberal than I had expected, conceding that their perceptions and perspective had changed over the years. (Afrikaners whose politics fall to the far right were apparently unwilling to comply with my request for hospitality-cum-interview.)

Discussion was lively; there was disagreement, to be sure, but with an impressive lack of animosity, at least among the adults.

Mrs Chueu is known as "Mama Afrika," following her selection, in 1985, as the Outstanding Woman in Africa—recipient of the prestigious Adelaide Ristori Award presented by Italy's Ristori Foundation, for outstanding contributions to community development. By being so honored, Mrs Chueu joined company with Margaret Thatcher, Golda Meir and Indira Gandhi, all former recipients of the Ristori award. A teacher, organizer of women, and one still active in community development, Mrs Chueu is President of the National Council of African Women, Northern Transvaal Region. Her special interest lies in combatting nutritional deficiency.

Professor Pretorius is head of the History Department, University of the North. He has been involved in the education of blacks for the last thirty years.

Mabel Makgole Chueu (black)

We have so far to go, in the education of our people. Seventy-five percent of the blacks still adhere to their tribal culture. The question of one man/one vote that you Americans keep bringing up is not our greatest concern, though even if we had it we wouldn't necessarily elect blacks. We believe in electing only according to merit, not colour.

South Africa: Land of Hope?

Our greatest problem is overpopulation, and for that you can blame our culture. We have always considered children to represent great wealth; now we must make people understand that more children mean greater poverty. By the year 2000 we will have reached the limit of our water resources, and the land just cannot support so many people. In black society pregnancy has been seen as a rite of passage, proof that a girl is not barren. Sex education has no effect. Twelve-year-olds are having children and the families take care of them. Even educated black women have been having multiple children, though we are finally beginning to see a change among the more educated.

The second big problem is illiteracy. Seventy-five percent of the blacks can't read or write: tribal traditions are too strong. We have no hope of ever being able to run a country or even of voting if so few of us are literate. We have very few role models; those blacks who do succeed usually move up and move out. In the homelands some of the Council members have no education and are, therefore, unaccepted by the university students – who, fortunately, are now getting an education. Our duty as members of the National Council of African Women is to make the grassroots people understand that they *need* education. We need *compulsory* education for all blacks, but many of the tribal people don't want their children going to school because they want them to work in the fields. Fortunately, black women are taking the lead and more and more are insisting that their children go to school.

One of the reasons we have no respect for so-called leaders like Tutu, Boesak, and Tambo is that they tell *us* to boycott the schools, while *their* children are in private schools in London. We don't trust anyone who encourages our children to stay out of school. Only the radical blacks accept Tutu. The moderates and the educated blacks keep more quiet, out of fear, so you don't hear much from us. But I guarantee you *we* are the majority of the blacks in this country. We are the ones who are anti-violence, so we must work quietly, behind the scenes. We fear for our lives and our homes being burnt if we speak out, but believe me when I tell you that our numbers are growing. Two years ago, we never could have taken the chance to come here – to a white person's home. We would have been followed and probably killed, by black vigilantes, the Comrades. It was the same with black women who didn't support the boycott of white stores in 1985 and 1986. The radicals control us through intimidation.

20

The moderate element is against sanctions, because it has meant that blacks have lost their jobs. We need those jobs so that peaceful change can come. You Americans must learn to see South Africa as an *African* country, not a European one. We are making changes, but the process is slow because this is basically a primitive country.

We moderates are appealing to the Americans who are concerned with the blacks in South Africa: Assist such organisations as the National Council of African Women with funds to erect educational facilities and for campaigns to fight against the high rate of birth. We don't understand the naivete of the Americans in imposing sanctions. Frankly, we doubt that you really want to *help* us. Tutu and Boesak go abroad to collect money, so *they* don't suffer from sanctions, but the money they collect doesn't go where you think it does. It isn't going to the rural areas, to provide *crèches* [day nurseries] and pre-primary facilities. The rural blacks never see the money you send through Bishop Tutu. It all goes to buy guns and support the violence of the ANC. Whites who encourage us to act against the South African government are suspect. American congressmen say what they do for their own gains. We don't trust any white who says he loves the black man more than whites; it's all politics.

Most people overseas don't understand what the majority of South African blacks want or need. Don't encourage us to hate. We don't expect to have power *now*; we have too much to learn. Grassroots black people need education so they can contribute to this society. We can't rule this country until we are capable. The radicals make more noise and get more money, but they are not helping the grassroots people to improve. We *need* the jobs your sanctions have cost us. We don't want welfare; we see how welfare has ruined the blacks in America. The old adage that says, *"Give* me a fish, I eat for a day; *teach* me to fish, I eat for a lifetime,"* is correct, and South African blacks prefer to fish for themselves.

Stop talking about sanctions and releasing Mandela. Be practical and help us educate the seventy-five percent who are illiterate. You may think that all we want is a fully-integrated society. But we still need black universities. We have different cultural backgrounds and we need different teaching methods. By the time our students graduate, then they will be able to compete equally. But let us educate them in our own way, as we know how.

As to the necessity of the South African government negotiating at some point with the ANC: We moderates don't agree. The ANC refuses to reason; they won't even meet with Chief Buthelezi [the moderate black political leader], because he is trying to reach an accommodation with the government. We are *all* anti-apartheid, but most of us would like things to be settled peacefully. The moderates are ostracised by the ANC and the other radicals, but please let the world know that *we* represent the majority of black South Africans.

Professor Jan Pretorius (white)

The major problems experienced by black students everywhere in Africa are due to the fact that the demands of the twentieth century are essentially those of Western culture, as far as science and technology are concerned, and the university as we know it is a development of that culture. It is no use denying that the African is of a different culture. He is simply not just "an Englishman with a different skin colour."

Thirty years ago we were dealing with the black elite, but with greater democracy and more students the quality has gone down. Overpopulation among blacks is a problem as yet unaddressed. The infrastructure of this country simply cannot cope with the tremendous numbers of people who need jobs, schools, services, and places in universities. One of the areas where we see evidence of this problem is in our library: There are not enough books for the number of students. Government assistance is determined by the number who *succeed*, so the problems caused by overpopulation and too many students clamouring for an education make it more difficult for large numbers to be successful.

In 1985 and 1986 [pro-violence] Black Power groups threatened the very existence of the university. The result is that no students want to participate in student government, nor do any dare to speak out in favour of peaceful change. The whole purpose of a university – a place for the free exchange of ideas – is therefore compromised.

Adding to the complexity of the situation is the question of what laws you apply to a specific group. Do you allow, for example, a claim of

22

"bewitching" or "witchcraft" as a defence? There are tremendous cultural gaps between groups, and that's not just between whites and blacks. During the unrest of 1985 and 1986 in black schools, it became more clear than ever to black leaders that a great number of whites would find it extremely difficult to turn over the country to a group of the population whose approach to education seemed to be illustrated by their children's *burning* of schools rather than attending them.

*   *   *

TZANEEN

The following morning I visited the University of the North, originally for blacks only. The student body, with a male/female ratio of 2:1, has grown from 420 in 1964 to 6200 today. Students enter as early as age sixteen; ninety-five percent of them live on campus, in single-sex dormitories. Indian students live off campus, to be able to prepare their own food. The faculty is two-thirds white, but the president and vice president are black.

All courses are taught in English and the university is open to anyone who speaks the language. There is a large contingent of foreign students. Students may learn Afrikaans, French, German, Latin, or any of five African languages as part of their course of study.

In general, Liberal Arts is the most popular area of concentration, followed by Commerce and Administration, Education, Science, Law, and Theology. The Department of Agricultural Economics trains teachers, extension officers, and managers for agricultural areas.

Because of unrest caused by radicals in 1985-86, students are unwilling to be involved in student government and moderate students no longer speak out on political issues. It was interesting to learn, however, that black students have maintained friendly contact with Afrikaner students they met last year, while visiting Rand Afrikaans University — in Johannesburg.

Associated with the University is the Business Advisory Bureau whose director, Evert van Dijk, is a Dutchman committed to the teaching and fostering of sound business practices among black South Africans. This interview, and others like it around the country, were arranged in response to my interest in the development of a strong black middle class. I have long promoted such development as part of the solution to the cycle of poverty in which many underclass citizens, the world over, find themselves locked.

Evert van Dijk (white)

Our Bureau is designed to promote Small Business Development. Nine other bureaus around the country offer similar programmes, using other university facilities. We have 854 members who, through their dues and with support from large businesses, provided eighty-eight courses for 1778 people last year. Charge for the courses — which are given both at the university and in the actual service areas — is R25 [$12.50] for members and R50 [$25] for non-members.

We have fifteen thousand small business people in our area, with a growth rate of 5.6 percent per year. I believe the [economic] growth rate in the United States is five percent. Formerly, it could take a small businessman up to three years to obtain a licence and to open his business. Because of a ten percent unemployment rate and the recognition that new businesses are desperately needed to put people to work, we have been able to considerably reduce the time it takes to obtain a licence — sometimes to as little as one month.

Our main activities consist of following up on those who take our courses — we make actual visits to their place of business — and helping to implement what they have learnt here. Our motto is "Attitude, Not Aptitude, Determines Life's Altitude." We also counsel new businesses and provide feasibility studies; we will advise against undertaking a business if we feel the project is not viable. In addition we produce a magazine for our members, offering them the latest in business information.

One of our most exciting projects is a complete supermarket, for teaching every facet of the running of that sort of business. We have a loading dock, cash register, refrigerated racks and standard shelving, and a full stock of grocery items. One can learn everything necessary for the successful operation of a grocery store.

Our greatest need is for more classrooms. My theory is that the blacks could build their own classrooms for one-fourth the price the government spends, and we would be clearing the land for agriculture as well. If we sent people out to gather rocks from the fields, we could build schools out of rock — rather than brick — and roof them in the traditional thatch.

Literacy is sometimes a problem, and we encounter cultural differences and superstitions. In advertising, for example, colours have different meanings for different tribes, and customs differ. The Zulus are the most business-inclined. Some of the northern tribes are less assertive, though our local Lebowa Bakeries was the first black-owned company on the Johannesburg Stock Exchange.

Our Junior Business Awareness Program is opposed by the radicals, as they equate capitalism with apartheid, but the moderate blacks — by far the majority — recognise that capitalism is their salvation. We also have to deal with black-on-black discrimination; wages paid by blacks are very low. And few co-operatives are successful because blacks are accustomed to co-operating only socially, not in business. We are trying to teach these new businessmen the importance of supporting their own communities.

We underestimated black interest in education in this country. In fifty years, there will be one million blacks in universities, so we must be able to offer good education and good jobs: South Africa has a potential three million ANC insurgents, because of unemployment. Our progress has been remarkable, considering where we started. It's very exciting to be here, and I'm quite optimistic.

My meeting with Dr and Mrs Lindsey Milne was not for an interview, but I include them here for the information I acquired from them on how they run Westfalia Estate (which produces some of the best avocados in South Africa!) Following my return to the United States, Dr Milne sent me a copy of a videotape which more fully explains the whole concept of Westfalia and how it began.

Mrs Milne was, at the time of our meeting, about to become ordained as a Deaconess in the Anglican Church. She felt certain that Bishop Tutu was misunderstood and misquoted — that he does not, in fact, support Communism or violence, in spite of the fact that he supports the ANC, which advocates both.

South Africa: Land of Hope?

Dr and Mrs Lindsey Milne
Westfalia Estate

In 1929, Westfalia Estate was purchased by Dr Hans Merensky, a humanitarian, conservationist, and entrepreneur whose basic theories dealt with the importance of realizing the potential of all individuals. Upon his death in 1952, this Estate — with other estates he had set up throughout South Africa — became a part of the Merensky Trust, administered through a Foundation. The Westfalia Estate, located in Tzaneen — the "fruit basket of South Africa" — has one of the largest avocado farms in the world but is involved as well with forestry and water conservation. It also serves as a "window on the modern world" for unsophisticated (unskilled) black South Africans, who are inducted into a world of technology and scientific farming in an atmosphere that emphasizes dignity, pride, responsibility, decent wages, excellent facilities, and a new language.

The Estate employs approximately one thousand blacks, who live on the 20,000-acre property. While providing employment and housing, the Milnes also have set about teaching their employees how to be self-governing. In addition to the attention given to literacy and home economics skills, workers are taught about democracy, voting, running a meeting, running a town, economics, management, and banking. They also have been helped to establish two viable schools, with a total of five hundred pupils.

Women are an important part of the Westfalia society and are given lessons in child rearing, nutrition, and home industries. Wives of senior management assist the wives of workers, after hours, to learn crafts such as clay-modelling, knitting, and sewing. Men are developing mechanical, agricultural, and management skills, and they are given the opportunity for "self-building" projects, where the materials are supplied and they build their own recreational facilities.

The Westfalia management philosophy is one of participative management and shared responsibility. The Herzberg tenets of personnel motivation are applied in practice at every level of management, resulting in highly-motivated workers who take pride in the achievements of the farming enterprise. Their personal concerns, too, are of importance at Westfalia: When a study showed that South African blacks are more comfortable communicating while sitting around a fire, the decision was made to continue putting stoves in the houses but a *fireplace* in the meeting halls.

With the stated theory that "only the best is good enough if you want to be competitive," good work is rewarded by praise, bonuses, promotions, and improved quality of life. There is concrete evidence at Westfalia that Dr Merensky's theories were on the mark, and it is the action and determination of South Africans such as Dr and Mrs Milne that make me optimistic about South Africa's future.

*   *   *

GAZANKULU

The issue of "homelands," in South Africa, is one that is hotly debated — both in and out of government circles. Knowing that facile opinions are formed from scanty information, I set as a high priority a meeting with the leader of one of those homelands — hoping to hear the story from those most directly affected.

The area of GaZankulu became a homeland in 1969, with the Chief Minister as its Chief Executive Officer. The people of GaZankulu — members of the Tsonga tribe — were without a Chief and so sent a delegation to the University of the North, to ask Professor Dr HWE Ntsanwisi to lead them. He took a cut in salary and was forced to send his children away to boarding school, but he accepted the position.

The Tsongas are considered to be among the most industrious of all the blacks in South Africa. They have never before had their own homeland, having always been slaves of other tribes. Here, owning their own homes for the first time, they have never burned a house or a school or school bus, and the residential areas are beautifully landscaped and well kept. Residents have the choice of living in traditional kraals (a group of huts) or in modern houses with running water, plumbing, and electricity. The more affluent citizens live up on the hill, in homes custom-designed by professional architects. Two-car garages hold vehicles that are well cared for, and citizens' pride in their community is obvious. Residents of the kraals alone have contributed over R3.5 million ($1.75 million) to community development.

Seven hundred whites live in GaZankulu, of whom 105 work for the government. Twelve thousand of the 675,000 blacks in the homeland work in government service. It is a totally mixed society, with no race problems and very little crime, a fact attributable to the tribal traditions.

Members of the GaZankulu Youth Movement are active in a positive way. They learn construction skills, farming, irrigation, and animal husbandry. Now owning their own nursery, they supply fruit trees to the elderly as a community service project; remaining trees are sold to raise money for other endeavors.

Forty factories, run by the GaZankulu Development Corporation, provide good jobs in a variety of consumer goods manufacturing plants, as well as training in marketing and management. In one plant, the physically handicapped learn to make carpets. There is also a teachers' training college and a very active and successful marketplace.

There were no signs of this homeland being used as a "dumping ground" for blacks or for the exploitation of its residents, as some of South Africa's critics have averred.

I met with the Chief Minister in the Council chambers. In addition to his position in GaZankulu, Professor Ntsanwisi serves as President of the National Cultural Movement, Ximoko xa Rixaka.

Professor Dr Hudson William Edison Ntsanwisi (black)

The Minister of Finance, Barend du Plessis, is accurate when he says that an equal opportunity for the accumulation of wealth is a priority of the present South African government, and that they have increased spending on education, social services, development and security for the black population.

The international community thinks sanctions will dismantle apartheid and all people in this country will then share politically, socially, and economically. That is the wrong approach. The *right* approach to helping black South Africans is to give them education and skills, to help this country keep its world standing economically. We *could* share economically were it not for sanctions: We are already acquiring skills and exerting more influence. As the economy expands, there is more cake to share.

Economic progress has slowed down, due to sanctions. Therefore, it will take us longer to improve our status. Our political initiatives have slowed down as a result of the slowdown in the economy. Initiative and reform can only take place when the economy is virile.

World corporations enriched themselves at the expense of the blacks in South Africa. Now the United States companies have sold out to South Africans, and the US has lost its influence. South African corporations never heard of the Sullivan Principles. We black South Africans have not benefitted at all from sanctions; only the whites in South Africa have benefitted. As a result of that exercise blacks are now unemployed and feel great insecurity. If a revolution takes place, who will benefit? With the French and Russian revolutions, change was long and slow in coming. But look at the Industrial Revolution in Britain — it helped people and there were rapid changes. We need an *industrial* revolution here, not a *bloody* revolution.

How am I looked upon by other South African blacks? Am I a puppet of the South African government? Pragmatists participate in the creation of a new South Africa, one that will accommodate all aspirations. Yes, I am looked upon as a puppet by some. Radicals shout slogans. But slogans don't bring about changes. I say, "Apartheid stinks to high heaven," but we must negotiate. I don't care what other people think I am. I worry about what *I* think I am.

The majority of blacks in South Africa don't support the ANC. If they did, the ANC wouldn't have to "necklace" people to make them go along; they wouldn't have to plant explosives to intimidate people. If people agree with you, you don't need to intimidate them.

As to tribal differences, the blacks here don't differ on the main objectives; we all want to share politically. It's in the *means* that we differ. The tricameral Parliament includes everyone but blacks. That is wrong. *All* groups must be represented in a new constitution. The crux of the problem in South Africa is between black and white interests. Blacks want political participation. Many whites reject that idea, but we must create a forum.

One man/one vote is not realistic now. Maybe that will come at some point in the future, but the best place for us to start is with the idea of a federation [independent states joined in a central government]. Then all groups can be represented. Each population group could choose one leader, and the four leaders would share power. We could have eleven national states, the same divisions as we have now. If each state chose four representatives, that body of forty-four would serve as the legislature. The four leaders, representing the four population groups, would serve as the Executive Committee. Black Africans would accept that.

South Africa: Land of Hope?

GaZankulu has chosen to exist as a "homeland" rather than as an independent country because independence is not attractive to us. I'm a South African, and I'm not prepared to abdicate my birthright or my share of the South African economy and natural resources, or to separate myself from the mainstream of South Africa. There would be no gain for the majority of us, only for the top few. Independence is a *choice*. We have no fear of being forced into that position by the South African government. Would we like, at some point, to do away with the homelands? No. Homelands are part and parcel of South Africa. Here, blacks have a say in their own government.

We have a great problem with overpopulation and lack of education. We are making some progress with overpopulation, but it is a slow process. When a black man has no sports grounds, no swimming pool, no tennis courts or soccer fields, his recreation is in the bedroom. Education is the key to our upliftment. But blacks must do it for themselves; the whites can't do it for us.

The Group Areas Act can go to hell! The reality is, there wouldn't be that much change if it were rescinded. But affluent blacks could live anywhere they want. There wouldn't be much change because, basically, people like to live among their own kind. But we want to know that we *can* live anywhere we can afford. Here, those who prefer to live in *kraals*, as they have for centuries, are free to do so; others choose to live in brick houses with electricity, televisions, and indoor plumbing.

It's like the liquor laws. Everyone was so sure when they made it legal to sell liquor to blacks that we would see drunk blacks all over the place. In fact, *fewer* blacks bought liquor after it was made legal than bought it before! The same thing happened when they did away with the prohibition against interracial marriages. Everyone expected a rush of them, but there have been very few. "Grey" areas — allowing some areas to be mixed, even as others are still restricted to blacks or to whites — are OK as a first step. Let people get used to the idea of mixed neighbourhoods and see how well they can work. Separate-but-equal in education is not acceptable. But, yes, we *would* be willing to integrate one grade at a time and to take twelve years to do it. We are going to try that, here, next year.

In the urban areas there is less tribalism among blacks. The conflict in the cities is promoted by the politicians. As the older, more rigid whites die out, we expect to have an easier time with younger, more adaptable people, but the Conservatives indoctrinate their children – so we may not find them dying out after all. It is the radical whites, the ultra-right, who stand to lose the most with an integrated society. They are the blue collar workers, the farmers, and the uneducated who fear losing their jobs to competent blacks. But "Adapt or Die" is still the slogan of the Nationalist Party.

It is true that many whites in South Africa have been unaware of the terrible conditions in which the blacks have lived, because they were never exposed to it. They kept to their own communities and never came to see ours. Now that they have been *made* aware of those conditions, more of them are acting to change them. That gives us hope for the future. The international community doesn't realise there are forces for change in South Africa. At this point, we cannot tell who will win the next election. If the Conservative Party wins, we will all be back at square one. But the blacks won't revolt successfully now. We just don't have the technology yet to fight the eleventh strongest military power in the world [the South African army]. Anyone who tells the black South Africans that he can win a revolutionary war will be not a general but a murderer.

I would like to send this message to the blacks in America: I am a black South African leader in one of the non-independent national states. I abhor apartheid because I believe it is discriminatory, divisive, immoral, and evil. As far as that is concerned I share the same view with men like Bishop Tutu, but there are certain things which I don't share with him at all, and I don't apologise for it.

I believe in articulating the aspirations of our people. I don't believe in disinvestment and sanctions as a means of dismantling apartheid. I believe that the best way to dismantle apartheid lies in the acceleration of the economic advancement of the black man. In training him in skills which will enable him to exert influence on the economy of this country, with his preponderance in numbers he'll be able to exert control. He will do this by way of keeping South Africa's economic and commercial world standing and thus guarantee a bigger economic cake for all to share. In this way we will be able to correct the imbalances that exist in the sharing of wealth and education and of other political and economic opportunities in this country.

I don't believe that isolation and sanctions will solve that. What I've realised is that sanctions have brought, in their train, unemployment, insecurity, poverty, and violence . . . sanctions have been counter-productive. They haven't reached the white man but have impoverished the blacks. The whites have bought the American corporations at take-away [bargain] prices. Sanctions have diminished American influence in South Africa. They have diminished the influence of the Sullivan Code and also retarded the reform initiatives which were taking place.

The lunatic right fringe is gaining more momentum than heretofore. This is a sad time for South African blacks, and I urge black Americans to change their minds and fight for the economic advancement of the black man in South Africa. For instance, in the United States itself in the 1960s, when I was studying at Georgetown University, the American blacks — especially the men — felt emasculated because they were unemployed. But with the opening of universities and the integration of schools, the state of affairs has since changed. Black Americans occupy important positions in Congress and in the State Department, and they have been able to exert influence and take pride in being Americans without having fought a second War of Independence.

So we would urge that, instead of taking away American influence from South Africa, you use that influence to bring about change. When the Monroe Doctrine failed, it was Roosevelt and Churchill who brought the old and new worlds together to fight against Hitler. And when Germany was conquered, it was not isolated. The Marshall Plan rebuilt it, not by isolation but by its presence. And what black South Africa needs today is the presence of the Western powers, with their technological and economic know-how.

*   *   *

CAPE TOWN - STELLENBOSCH

The next four days were spent in Cape Town and Stellenbosch, where I conducted twenty-eight interviews. Parliament was in session, allowing for access to members of all the major political parties, in addition to those in my other areas of concern. The politicians are presented first, in alphabetical order, by party. (It should be noted here that my attempts to interview leaders of the ultra-right political parties were rebuffed; they refused to grant meetings to anyone who does not speak Afrikaans. I am now studying the language, in preparation for my next trip there.)

Corné Mulder (white)
Conservative Party

We are not afraid of change; it is a question of direction. White voters are not sure what the government is going to do. There are too-vivid memories of Rhodesia. This [National Party] government has a credibility problem: It makes changes without telling the people. It talks old ways but does new things; it lies to the people.

The strength of our party consists not just of the twenty-three seats we hold now but of the forty-seven, even up to sixty-three, that we might take in the next election. We feel our support is growing, as uncertainty over South Africa's future increases. Not all our members are in the upper age groups; traditional National Party members are harder to change. But we say to the young people, "We are not talking about what South Africa will be in *five* years; we're talking about what it will be in *thirty* years."

There are no women members of Parliament in our party, but we are interested in women's issues such as separate tax structures that will be fairer to women.

Most of our support is among the rural whites, although we had our biggest majorities ever in the urban areas in the last election. We know we'll never attract the rich professionals; we appeal to the lower income, non-professional whites. We don't, of course, know whether the blacks will go along with what we are trying to do, but the Nats haven't got so far with the blacks either. The Nats see power-sharing as a solution, but there are few success models. Look at Ireland, Lebanon, Cyprus, and Rhodesia.

South Africa: Land of Hope?

You can't *share* power without *losing* power. Black leaders actually support us, in secret. To the coloureds, partition [each population or tribal group to have its own homeland and government] might be a good solution. They have told us, "If we're not successful with the Nats, we might join you."

We offer the non-white South Africans this: The Nats say, "You can come in, but you come in as a second class citizen; whites will keep power and control." But that's unfair and won't work. So *we* say the solution is to go for partition; make the country smaller, with its parts interwoven economically. We would be like India. The whites would elect a white parliament in Cape Town and the blacks would elect a black parliament in the homelands. Each of us would govern ourselves and have our own president. Who decides who gets what land? We will give them back their historic homelands and the surrounding areas. There will be freedom of movement and no segregation. People will have residential rights but not political rights.

As for the Group Areas Act, we would go for Home Rule within the white-controlled areas. We ask the young people of this country to look ahead thirty years. Do they want to live under a black majority government and president? There is the risk of a one-party state, where whites *may* be tolerated. But we can't promise the whites they will have any rights. We don't have a constitution like you do, where people are guaranteed rights that cannot be taken away. The South African constitution can be amended at any time, by the ruling party. It is not sacred. It's logical to give blacks rights, but what about white survival? The outside world doesn't understand. They think South Africa is the United States. South Africa has a constitution problem *and* a black/white problem.

There is no example of success in all of Africa. Federation hasn't worked, because no one wants to recognise the old colonial borders. Black governments have not been moderate; even those that started out that way later turned radical. If the West wants that, that's unacceptable to us. Ironically, if we can sell our idea to the rest of Africa, the Americans will go along. Will the rest of Africa accept it? Only if the majority of South African blacks do. But will the Xhosa accept the Zulu? [South Africa's

38

two largest black tribes] We don't think the whites are better; we are just different. And remember, the Afrikaner has no place else to go.

Americans don't understand our problem. They think blacks and whites here are like blacks and whites there. The South African coloureds are closer to the American blacks than the South African blacks are. The coloured language and sub-culture are the same as the Afrikaners' — just as the language and basic culture in the United States are the same for blacks and whites. South African blacks, on the other hand, are tribal; they are not like the coloureds. But the ratio of coloureds to whites in South Africa is 1:2, while the ratio of blacks to whites in the United States is 1:10. Non-whites, in South Africa, outnumber whites by a margin of almost 6:1. That makes a big difference.

Reverend Edward Jacannathan Mannikam (Indian)
House of Delegates

I am a South African of Indian extraction — a church minister, first, and a Member of Parliament, second. In spite of my Hindu background, I joined the Dutch Reformed Church at age twenty-two, hoping to reform it from within. I rebelled against the Church's influence in government policy. Now I find myself suspected by both sides: The Indians suspect me for having joined the Dutch Church, and the Dutch suspect me for my radical thinking, as being a Communist.

Church reforms did not begin until 1980, reaching their peak in 1985 when the Church announced that apartheid was *not* divinely or scripturally sanctioned. Apartheid is now used only as a lame excuse. Eternal principles cannot be compromised, but here religion is being used for political purposes, as it was by Hitler and Khomeni.

The South African Council of Churches is to the blacks as the Dutch Reformed Church is to Afrikaners — both political. Religion equals politics in South Africa, and has throughout our history. As the government bans the ANC, the ANC uses the SACC. Rascals who have never been to church are suddenly wearing crucifixes, using the Church as a political front organisation. They are wolves in sheep's clothing. Moscow says, "Use the clergy, the children, and the unions. Become a 'good Christian'; use it for our purposes."

South Africa: Land of Hope?

The blacks are a nation, but the coloureds are only a nation in the making; they are human-made. In two hundred years, South Africa will be coloured. We are a nation in the making, like Brazil. The Indians in South Africa have faced great discrimination and so have become a self-help community. We were more discriminated against by the English than we are by the Afrikaners. We have a good relationship with the coloureds, because we have a "cosmetic relationship"! That goes for the Cape coloureds; the Natal coloureds are more white, which is worse. Our relationship with the blacks is only fair; there is much suspicion between us. Most of the Indians have remained in Natal, where we first arrived and where the blacks are of the Zulu tribe. But the Zulus believe the Indians are an obstacle to Zulu progress. Albert Luthuli [first head of the ANC] many years ago said, "The master is white, the dog is black, and the chain that holds the dog is Indian. The dog, in anger, will always bite the chain, but that will only hurt the dog. Then the master will shoot the dog."

As to our participation in the tricameral government [see Appendix V], remember that the Indians have always suffered discrimination in South Africa. First we were forced to live in Natal. That immediately made us anti-government; we were the forerunners of political agitation. Ghandi's Indian African Congress became the African National Congress which became the Congress of Democrats. Indians formed the South African Communist Party and are still a factor in it. Their numbers are unknown, because they are underground. Indian children are now the newest radicals; they felt the greatest discrimination. They don't know the whites, but they see the blacks as their friends. The whites are the enemy, and their Indian parents are stooges and sellouts. We had a South African Indian Council but we wanted parliamentary representation. We didn't worry about the technicalities — we thought we'd beat them at their own game. That was the pragmatic approach; but what about the blacks, who were excluded?

We did some soul searching. The blacks became even angrier, as they saw the whites lining up the coloureds and Indians against the blacks. On the other hand, if we refused and stayed out we'd get nothing. It was a *Catch-22* situation. We spoke up for the blacks — the twelve million urban blacks, that is, not those in the independent countries or the homelands — but the whites said to us, "Take it or leave it." So we took it, under protest.

All hell broke out amongst the blacks, bringing on the riots, the State of Emergency, and sanctions. That was the stupidity of the Nationalist Party. It would have made all the difference in the world if even only a few blacks had been included. They could have extended the life of this Parliament ten years. Even the State of Emergency would have been accepted, and Germany, France, England, and the United States would have poured money in to help us. We would have had clout against the ANC. The tricameral government has worked well. We are already debating jointly, so we are really more one than three, but we are moving without the blacks.

The Group Areas Act must go—completely. We won't have that much movement of people, even after it is rescinded. The idea of "own" affairs [categorizing issues as pertaining to specific population groups, individually] is nothing more than the constitutional entrenchment of apartheid. We see that as a serious problem. Everything must be considered "general" affairs [pertaining to all South Africans, equally]. The majority of white South Africans are behind the president, but the longer we delay in making real changes, the more we are at risk: The far right and the far left will continue to gain. If the Conservative Party comes in, South Africa will be a wasteland. The military can contain Africa, but it cannot contain internal terrorism. If the majority of South Africans can consolidate, we can move ahead. Then the president can say, "The *people* told me to do this." He would no longer be the head of a *party*; he would be the head of a *people*. PW Botha has had as his motto, since 1977, "Adapt or Die." He wants to be part of the solution, not part of the problem, to ensure his place in history.

We are at a crossroads. One way will take us to the high road and prosperity. We can become the most powerful industrial, technological, and economic region in the whole of Africa. We must come out from the mud we're stuck in—that is, right-wing conservatism. That doesn't mean we act to please the left-wing radicals. But we must address the political aspirations of the urban blacks of this country.

First, we must release Mandela immediately. I have no fears of repercussions. If there are any, they will only last a month or so, then die their own death. He won't be a political king. History has proven that. History doesn't move backwards. The past is related to the future, but

South Africa: Land of Hope?

Mandela is seventy. If a superpower like Russia had the courage to release Sakharov and Russia hasn't turned capitalist, then why is South Africa afraid to release an aged, ailing man who doesn't want to offend the ANC? The immediate release of Nelson Mandela will give South Africa immediate credibility in the world to which South Africa belongs, to show that she upholds Western values and that she upholds the Roman-Dutch law on which her system is based.

Second, the Group Areas Act should be dumped in the first ash heap, where it belongs. The Mount Nelson Hotel, where we are now having dinner, was restricted to me five years ago. Today, any black, coloured, or Indian hobo can enter and use any of its facilities. But we observe that my wife and I are the only non-whites in the room. Years ago there was a hue and cry about the Nico Malan Theatre being for whites only. A petition signed by thousands of people of all colours was drawn up and I was one of the signatories of that petition, which was presented to the Administrator of the Cape Province. The Nico Malan was opened fifteen years ago, yet only last year did my wife and I step inside, to see Pieter Dirk-Uys [the political satirist]. I can cite instance after instance of various discriminatory laws that have been repealed, but no earthquake has taken place in South Africa. People tend to protest when they are legislatively barred from certain areas.

It is natural for people to gather and to live with their own kind. Freedom of association also means that people associate with people of other cultures voluntarily. We have had enough bloodshed, turmoil, grief, and separation for the last three hundred years, so before we go to the low road of wasteland and destroy ourselves in the process, let us prove to the world, in the words of our national anthem, "Bondsmen only to the highest and before the whole world free."

And to my American friends, we thank you for your love, your concern, and your interest in our country. Your historical development is similar to ours. You started your country because of religious persecution, and so did we. You created a black problem by importing slaves from Africa; we inherited a black problem. We erred legislatively. We are now paying heavily for the errors of the past. We confess from the bottom of our hearts that we have sinned before God and man in regard to the oppressive legislative programme that we have had against people of colour. We have categorically and openly stated it through no less a person than our State President, who said in 1985 at the opening session of Parliament, "Apartheid is outdated." We condemn apartheid as a heresy. We have now started legislative programmes to undo all the wrongs we have done. We have repealed more than one hundred oppressive statutes. There is only one left, and that is the Group Areas Act. And we can promise you that it is on its way out. The walls of this Act are now cracking.

During the times of our discriminatory legislative programmes, you and your multi-national companies enjoyed all the profits in this land of milk and honey. You made billions because of our oppressive legislative programmes. When we sucked dry our labourers of colour, in terms of their wages, your profits and balance sheets soared because legislation was on your side. But it deeply hurts us that because of our legislative reform programme — as a result of which a labourer is worthy of hire irrespective of his race, colour, or creed — and because your profits were slipping down fast, you — in the name of disinvestment — started pulling out of our country, to the extent that you even totally ignored President Reagan's "constructive engagement." When you made money you believed in constructive engagement, and it shocks us that you have now become sanctimonious hypocrites and reject the very philosophy that your president expressed.

Let it be known to you, I am not a puppet of the South African government. I am only a loyal South African citizen who has suffered under the oppressive legislative programmes of the South African government, aided and abetted by your multi-national companies. I condemn apartheid openly — and with all the contempt that it deserves — publicly, without fear of being arrested or detained. However, my loyalty is to the land that gave me birth. When my country calls for us to defend her against Moscow and its satellite allies, we want you Americans to know that South Africans — about ninety percent of them — will forget the infighting that is taking place now and will rally around our president and shed the last drop of blood for our motherland. And we will *never* hand this country of ours to the Communists on a golden plate. History will record that we South Africans did this because of our patriotism and our love for our country, and we want you Americans to know that history will also record that you, as a leading Western nation in

43

the world, are contributing to a path that Moscow has committed itself to, if you continue with your vicious vendetta against us.

May I, in conclusion, remind you that even if it means reducing our country to a wasteland, we will do so — in case you are of the opinion that out of fear we will run to you for assistance. Our pride will not allow us to do that, because we genuinely believe that the reform we have started in our country is a genuine reform that will put South Africa on the high road of progress and stability. If you would like to join us on that high road, we welcome you.

Patrick McKenzie (coloured)
Labour Party

Do the recent proposals made by State President PW Botha represent hope or rubbish; are they real or a sham? This is the first time in three hundred years that people other than the whites are part of the South African government. You must also remember that all so-called coloureds and blacks in South Africa are political in their thinking.

I am the youngest Member of Parliament. I was one of the leaders of the 1976 Soweto riots in the Cape. After the 1980 uprising I was sent out of the country because the security police were looking for me. Then I had to view my options. At that time the white South Africans were very clever: No blacks or coloureds were conscripted into military training. I could have led a violent revolt, but that would have led to the destruction of my people. I was not needed in prison; I was needed outside, with the masses, working for change. My constituency, Bonteheuwel, is the most radical of the Cape Province. It is a sub-economic area, and all the past boycotts and riots in the Cape started in my constituency.

But my feeling today is that we haven't yet fully explored the non-violent options. I often quote Martin Luther King with regard to the non-violent struggle. In 1983 I entered the system. My reaction to the excluding of the blacks from the tricameral system is this: One at a time is better than none. The ANC has been trying to organise in Bonteheuwel, but thus far they have been unsuccessful. We in Bonteheuwel are sandwiched between two black areas, and the relationship between blacks and coloureds is a good one because we are all oppressed. We have mixed residential areas and schools.

The so-called coloureds and whites in South Africa are actually the same, except for colour. Where the blacks are tribal, the coloureds are urban and more affluent. But even the tribal blacks could have joined to form a legislature in 1983. When survival is at stake, they can work together. But I still see the three-part legislature as a beginning, even though it excludes the blacks.

Riaan Eksteen was recently sacked as the head of the South African Broadcasting Corporation, for not being a patsy to the government. He devoted too much airtime to the fight between State President Botha and Allan Hendrickse, the head of the [coloured] Labour Party and a Cabinet Minister. That fight was about the opening of the beach in Port Elizabeth, which until recently was a whites-only beach. We coloureds defied the ban — that beach *used* to be ours — and PW Botha was angry at Hendrickse's actions. Hendrickse then resigned from the Cabinet, and the President's Council has now lost credibility, as there is no one representing the coloureds. To date, no one yet has filled that position.

The Nationalist Party cannot ignore the Conservative Party. The standstill in progress in this country is due not to sanctions but to the gains by the CP. As long as blacks and coloureds are not part of any new deal, the NP will continue to be attacked by both sides. If the Nats are prepared to move away from apartheid and the CP, we will support the president. I believe the majority of whites will go with the NP. The Conservative Party gained because of uncertainty and instability. When there is uncertainty people tend to go with stability. Everyone fears a new Rhodesia. If PW can spell out what his future plan is, he will be supported — if it is for total equality.

Non-whites are prepared for a slow process for reform — ten years is not unreasonable — as long as our aspirations are met. We don't want a radical change overnight. But the Group Areas Act must be rescinded — and not gradually. You won't, in any case, see a great exodus of blacks, moving from where they are now. It's all a question of economics; most blacks can't afford to live in the white areas. But those who can afford to should be able to do so. One of the reasons people fear change in this country is that they don't really know each other; the Group Areas Act has kept them apart. It is important that they see how well the mixed areas are working so they will have less fear.

As for sanctions, I am totally against them. Regarding Tutu and Boesak, I must tell America that there is another side to the story. Sanctions are *not* helping the blacks in this country. I don't agree with the idea of "own" and "general" affairs. All policy should be based on what is good for all South Africans, not for the members of any given group. I see the trade union movement as a politically positive force, as a platform for the blacks. But just as the ANC was hijacked by the Communist Party, the unions are being hijacked by the ANC.

Moderate blacks in this country are afraid to speak out — and here I mean all non-whites. When I signed my name on the register as a Member of Parliament, I signed my death warrant; my children and my wife have already been threatened. But I am staying in the same house in which we have always lived, and because of my love for South Africa and for Cape Town I am prepared to put my head on the block for them. The Communist style is always to hold back the leaders. Well, I refuse to be held back.

We are also making inroads with birth control among the coloured population and have reduced the average number of children per family from 2.4 to 1.6. The white rate is approximately 1.2 and the Indians also have stabilised their population. But the black birth rate is still very high and has shown no drop.

I would like to say this to the Americans, and especially to black Americans: Invite more moderate non-whites to America. America should see South Africa as its friend, but it should see South Africa as African, not European. We are Africans — but we are aligned with Western values. Our countries should see each other as brothers against the onslaught of Communism. The Cape, as a strategic position for the West, has as much importance as the Panama Canal. Sanctions are hurting the wrong people; they should be rescinded immediately. And don't believe everything you read in your newspapers. I have actually seen foreign journalists and cameramen stage "riots." They also lie about what is really happening and what life is like here. One journalist, for example, wrote a story about our children — saying they are kept behind fences, in "concentration camps." Well, I will show you that fence and you will see that it is designed to keep our children from running out onto the highway — as any good neighbourhood would protect its children. That journalist had his cameramen *place* the children with their noses against the fence, just to make a story. That infuriates us. We need your help, but we don't need the lies.

Pieter Schoeman (white)
National Democratic Movement

In June of 1987, after the general election, I became impatient and disillusioned with the Progressive Federal Party and joined Frederik van Zyl Slabbert at Dakar to meet with the ANC. I had no illusion that the violence would end, but I wanted to hear what the ANC had to say. I went to the Dakar meeting as an Afrikaner, not as a member of any political party. That meeting did have an influence on my decision to resign from the PFP [Progressive Federal Party] and become one of the founding members of the NDM [National Democratic Movement]. I would say that the information shared was selective on both sides. There was not much comforting about the meeting, except that we did identify common ground and express the need for future talks. The ANC is still convinced that capitalism and apartheid are synonymous, although ironically the original architecture of apartheid was one of development.

We questioned the effects of the ANC's strategy of violence, as a result of which blacks have lost jobs, vigilantes have taken over, schools have been boycotted, and the whites in general have hardened their attitudes to such an extent that there has been a right-wing backlash. Our comments were at first met with silence; then an intensive debate followed, on the use of violence and the ANC's perspective of the armed struggle.

We also wondered about Soviet and Communist involvement in the ANC. We were told that blacks are nationalists, first, and socialists, second. Yet the ANC sees the welfare state as the perfect ending to apartheid. It wants to overthrow the whole system of South African law which it identifies with apartheid injustice. But you must remember that these people live well in London and direct the revolution from there. Apartheid has also become the bogey of all that is wrong. A hard analysis of Third World economics and not Marxist sloganeering should be on the agenda.

We had a better discussion on economics than on politics. In the South African context, namely a Third World country within a First World country, a social market economy seems only reasonable. Thabo Mbeki, their leader, is an economist who says they learnt their lesson in Mozambique: You can't change things overnight and suddenly nationalise everything.

We also knocked heads with the ANC over the question of a universal franchise. We want to make it possible for the Third World to move into the First World, but while they are still Third World, a process different from traditional Western democracy is necessary. One group of blacks met with government officials of Senegal to discuss constitutional affairs; that was a meeting of blacks with blacks. The Senegalese were realistic about a multi-ethnic society and told the ANC, "Everything you've discussed, we tried—and it didn't work." For that reason the Senegalese have amended their constitution to allow veto rights and minority representation. I had the impression that Mbeki understood this.

How did the Dakar meeting come about? Van Zyl Slabbert said to Mbeki, "You don't really know the Afrikaners," and Mbeki replied, "I'd like to meet them." Mbeki later admitted it was a real eye-opener; the blacks had thought Afrikaners were all fascists. So it is important that members of the ANC meet Afrikaners. By the end of the meeting with the ANC there was a feeling of goodwill, and we cleared up a great deal of misunderstanding. The sad fact is that it is much easier to meet *them* [from London] than the Comrades [vigilantes] in our own black townships. Now we must work at getting all the people in South Africa to meet each other; we must open avenues and seek new ideas and communicate them. As Mbeki said, even the "experts" lose contact at times because of outside pressures and influences.

South Africa is not a classless society, but unfortunately class and society happen to coincide. The Afrikaner is very skeptical of PFP [English] liberalism. Nelson Mandela is a symbol to blacks—and the accepted leader—although Oliver Tambo calls the shots.

University of Stellenbosch students are naive to think that a strong move by the Conservative Party will force a coalition amongst all the other parties: The differences between the Nats and the liberal opposition parties are just too great.

The Group Areas Act will not be rescinded soon. "Grey" areas will appear, little by little, and then ultimately the Act will be scrapped. But "grey" areas will be counter-productive if they are marked by tremendous overcrowding — four families to a house — and the market economy is distorted. South Africans are not racists; we should not be equated with the Nazis. There is basic goodwill here, and there is lots of common ground. The irony is that the National Party and the UDF [United Democratic Front] basically want the same thing. But people will vote for those they think can win.

My argument against Helen Suzman's idea of a set-up similar to the United States is that there may be no "state" where the whites are the majority. The white electorate has a subconscious fear of black domination. So it is essential to address these white fears and come to grips with the present untenable situation, which tries to entrench white minority rule. The Natal Indaba might work because that grants ethnic representation. Group thinking remains a very strong motivating force.

Our ultimate blueprint has not yet even been conjured. Fear is the greatest factor affecting us all. And in addition to fear, the blacks also suffer from suspicion; we all lack trust in one another. In South Africa, symbols can cause conflict. We don't have a sacrosanct constitution like the Americans. To the Americans, the Constitution is almost a religious document.

My message to the American public is this: We could do so much if we could get the process going. This is a take-and take situation [everyone can win]. You must recognise that progress has been made and that we must be encouraged — especially from abroad — to speed up the process of change, in order to achieve true democracy.

Sheila Camerer (white)
National Party

The Nationalists, who until recently were mostly Afrikaners, have in the past never had more than one woman Member of Parliament at a time in their ranks. Since May 1987, they have had four. [This has now increased to five.] I am English-speaking, as is another of the women, who is Jewish. Two are Afrikaners. The men in the party started off referring to us as "our roses" and tended to treat us like porcelain dolls and patronise us, but not anymore, now that they have become used to so many women around the National Party committees. They expect us to talk about consumer issues, but we also speak on law and order. As a lawyer, I am on the Justice Standing Committee and speak on justice and prisons. The rugby players of the Party tend to dominate the Defence and Law and Order debates, however. Finance is an area in which I would like to specialise and I am now trying to take on more of those issues. Recently, I was elected secretary of the White Affairs Budget Caucus group. More and more women are running for office, but in this country one must be nominated by one's own party before one can stand for election. That means that those who run on the party ticket are already well aware of what the party platform is. The nominating process, therefore, becomes of primary importance.

Our party is moving away from placating the Conservative Party. We are spelling out what whites can expect. And the only way to a secure future is to share power. Our party is no longer in an unassailable position, so we are having to be more specific about our plans for the country.

Ideally, the Group Areas Act should be rescinded, but if it were, the danger is that this would substantially strengthen the Conservative Party. What many people fear is a decline in health standards. They don't really want twelve people cramming into a house designed for four or six. At present the Group Areas Act is unenforceable — and has been so since 1982. Permits are freely given to non-whites to move into white areas. If no one complains, the area becomes integrated. Mixed areas, or "free settlement areas" as they will be known, will be established soon. [The Free Settlement Areas Bill was approved in early 1989.]

It seems that no matter what we do or change in this country, there will be no let-up from the rest of the world until we have one man/one vote. We accept that black leaders must be part of the decision-making process, but this country is simply not prepared for one man/one vote at this time. The American attitude seems to be, "Don't confuse me with the facts." Black moderates have gone to the United States and have attempted to speak with members of your Congress, but they weren't even given the courtesy of a meeting. They were told, "South African black moderates are pawns of the South African government and we consider them irrelevant."

We have established the principle of "own" affairs for each race group and "general" affairs which apply to all. However, groups can be considered regionally, rather than by colour [race groups]. The schools present a different problem, since until ten years ago there was a substantial difference between standards of education offered to the different race groups. This is all changing rapidly and the government has instituted a ten-year programme to achieve parity among the race groups. There are many private English schools but no private Afrikaner schools. Afrikaner schools are always government schools. Some government English schools have asked for their schools to be racially mixed, but the government has said, "No, there are enough avenues for mixing already." The private English-language schools are racially mixed.

Can South Africa exist in a state of "permanent transition"? I think not. We must have an end point; a goal must be specified. We have made a great move forward recently and I expect that to continue. We are seeing a "rapprochement" between people of different colours in this country, especially in the urban areas.

Helen Suzman, who has been lionized the world over for her brave stand against the odds and for freedom for all South African citizens, left a Parliamentary session to give me a few minutes of her time. In truth, after thirty-five years of honing her position, Mrs Suzman can give you in twenty minutes what some others may take an hour or more to spell out. In May of

1989, Mrs Suzman announced that she would not seek re-election but, rather, would retire from Parliament at the end of the then-current term.

Helen Suzman (white)
National Chairman, Progressive Federal Party

I wish I could convince the American public and the Congress that sanctions and disinvestment are counter-productive. White South Africans are buying up the American businesses and the blacks lose out on social responsibility programmes that are reduced. I have just returned from another trip to America, and I can tell you it is frustrating to find that if one is against sanctions one is suspected of being racist.

There *is* change in this country, and it is not all cosmetic. The abolition of the Pass Laws and the recognition of black trade unions are substantive changes. Eighteen percent of university students at Wits [University of the Witwatersrand] and Cape Town universities are now non-white. We [the PFP] are in favour of a "mixed" economy, a combination of free enterprise and social welfare. Capitalism cannot be identified with apartheid, as the radicals are saying. We are in favour of a Federal Parliament — one House — and a federal system based on geographical areas, not colour. We must use negotiation, not force; discuss, not dictate.

One man/one vote is inevitable, but with safeguards — just as, for example, the make-up of the United States Senate protects minority rights. Utah has two senators and so does California. An independent judiciary and a Bill of Rights provide further checks and balances against the excessive use of power by the majority.

I was not part of the group that went to Dakar and met with the ANC, but we *must* speak with these people. My party is against violence — from whatever quarter it emanates.

I do not have more hope for this country than I did six years or even six months ago because of the gains made by the Conservative Party. I am worried that some of our supporters will move over to the National Party and the Nats will move to the CP. But we applaud all change and moves forward, as we always have.

Adrienne Koch (white)
President's Council

A great many people in the Cape Province would like to secede and go it alone. Of course, we in the Southern Cape are a long way from the real problem – the huge influx of blacks from inside and outside our borders into the cities. We are having problems, but not to the same extent as some of the other large metropolitan areas. We must work to protect the black moderates, to keep the country stable. Having blacks in the Cabinet represents a significant leap. The crimes of the Sharpeville Six were committed against moderate blacks. That's what you get with mob violence. We must protect the moderates and keep the rule of law. This is a starving continent. The black man in Africa – with the exception of a few, often corrupt leaders – is far worse off today than he was under colonial government.

The AWB [far-right Afrikaner political party] is frightening. Eugene Terre'Blanche is a former actor and playwright. He is a terrific speaker, a Hitler-type crowd hypnotiser. The rise in the Conservative movement is a white backlash to sanctions and what is seen as the total unreasonableness of the world. As far as Mandela is concerned, we fear that if he is released there will be huge, organised, uncontrollable crowds to meet him – and bloodshed and violence. When Lenin arrived at the Finland Station in Russia, it triggered off riots and a Bolshevik Revolution, violent revolution. The moderates were smashed. The radicals at Cape Town University won't even let Helen Suzman speak – and she's their champion.

We should take a lesson from the United States and its dealings with the Shah of Iran. Look what happened when he tried to push reform too far too fast. But we realise we are now walking alone. We can no longer count on America; you have become unreliable. You encourage us, then withdraw when the going gets tough. You should, rather, be helping us to build black housing; that would make you popular and do some good. We are not just going to lie down and say, "We've sinned; take the country." We *are* willing, to a large extent, for economics to take over, but the whites, coloureds, and Indians are all terrified of being completely overwhelmed by the vast number of blacks.

53

South Africa: Land of Hope?

We are not a nation of racists; it would be more truthful to say we are a nation of snobs. We want to keep up our standards, protect civilisation. Most of us see no reason to mix on an equal footing with uneducated farm labourers. Remember, this country is a mixture of First and Third Worlds. However, we are realising more and more that colour is not the problem; standards are. We are adjusting our attitudes, constantly making changes. Relationships which used to be difficult between the English and the Afrikaners are definitely improving. Changes taking place today are not due to external pressure, though that pressure did help get it started.

University of Stellenbosch Students (white)

*The opinions of students and professional academics are always of interest. The world already knows what **radical left** students think, but what about those raised in the traditions of Afrikanerdom?*

It is said that the University of Stellenbosch — an Afrikaans- language university — has produced more upper-echelon South African government officials, throughout its history, than any other university in the country. I went out to that University and met with a group of students. There was no consensus, but neither was there any lack of conviction; the discussion was lively and could have continued for days.

The students present were Gawie Botma, editor of the school newspaper; Hein Brand, of the Political Research and Dialogue Committee; Neil Shaw, of the Theatre Committee; Jaco Strauss, Vice-Chairman of the Student Representative Council; Barrie Terblanche, reporter; and Carla van der Spuy, a Student Affairs representative. All of these students are white; non-white students refused to participate, knowing I had come to South Africa as a guest of the government and choosing "not to lend validity to the discussion." I hope that, on reading this book, they will regret that decision.

We began with a general discussion based on my questions, following which I offered each student the opportunity to send a message to America.

Of 8500 students at the University of Stellenbosch, ninety-eight percent are white, with 400-500 coloureds, a few Indians, and a few blacks. Non-whites receive bursaries [scholarships] from the Department of Education or from private corporations. Admission is actually open to all South Africans, but there remains a desire to maintain Stellenbosch's Afrikaner Christian character. There are students from other countries and there are no significant problems as a result of integration. The residence halls are still segregated; black residence halls are co-ed. Most of the students want "open" or mixed residence halls; some prefer a "local option," meaning each hall will decide for itself. When a poll was published, showing sixty-six percent of the students in favor of mixed halls, there was a backlash from the black students — who felt the [majority] whites should not be the ones making the decision.

The students made much of the fact that in spite of their Afrikaner upbringing, their politics are quite liberal — considering themselves enlightened but admitting that, while they may be seen as liberal by Afrikaner standards, there are many in South Africa who still consider them right of center. In defense, these students consider those at the University of Cape Town strictly radical: No freedom of speech is granted by students at UCT, as even Helen Suzman was denied the right to speak there. According to the Stellenbosch students, the moderate student movement will support the present South African government in the long run, but moderate students want to end apartheid and end it now. These students see black students as their friends and try not to be paternalistic, but it sometimes causes a strain on both sides, as this relationship is a new one to all concerned.

Politics are very important on campus, though the black students don't join in on debate. The Black Students Organisation says it doesn't want to foster the liberal image of the university, that it doesn't want the outside world to think things are better than they are. There is a feeling, among these white Afrikaner students, that "young Turks" in South Africa get taken in by their own political party, that by the time they are in a position of power they already have joined the establishment — with the result that there is little chance that anyone with new ideas will have much effect. The Group Areas Act, in their opinion, must be rescinded immediately. "Grey" areas accomplish nothing.

I quoted and asked their opinion on a report that says eighty-five percent of white South Africans are anti-apartheid. They generally agreed that "apartheid" must be more specifically defined: Few, they believe, want the lower schools integrated, but integrated housing could be accomplished "with sufficient propaganda" promoting it. In the absence of fully-integrated housing, the "homelands" have served a purpose — providing factories, jobs, and government experience which have benefitted the blacks as a transition. Now, however, it is time to do away with them.

They see a government based on a regional federation as the only acceptable plan and would like to see policy based on regions, rather than on ethnic divisions. There seemed general agreement that the Conservative Party cannot win; if it starts gaining too much, all the other parties will join together to defeat it. But they admit that the National Party doesn't want a coalition government; it wants to rule alone.

As for the State of Emergency, one student opined that most everyone thinks things are better because they don't read or hear about what's bad. Some students think things actually are better, while others believe things are just "simmering." The brain drain and the youth drain are of concern to these young people, who believe that apartheid can be reformed.

Some interesting distinctions were made between the blacks and the coloureds: "The coloureds are Afrikaners, so we relate to them easily. They have our same language and culture, which is more important than the colour of their skin. But because they have been ostracised for so long, they have lower self-esteem than do the blacks, who have their own culture." Indians, who live mostly in Natal, are basically unknown to the Cape students.

This group is disturbed that the ANC resorts to bombings and feels that, were the government to lift the ban on all "illegal" organizations, the ANC position would become more moderate and "South Africans would stop killing South Africans." They are equally convinced of the counter-productive nature of sanctions, as they harm the wrong people. "Economic viability is important to any country, especially for education," said one student, continuing, "I don't understand how the United States can be called a free-market country if the government can dictate to corporations what they can and cannot do. We see sanctions as the ultimate hypocrisy on the part of your Congressmen."

Another student put it in more specific detail, as the others nodded in agreement: "Be honest in your attempts, America. Don't use us to promote your own careers, like Ted Kennedy. What I'd like to see America do is to learn more about what's really happening in this country. Americans present fresh ideas, so you are effective in establishing contact among different groups.

Sanctions are bad, ineffective. Many institutions not associated with the government are doing positive things to bring people together, such as IDASA [Institute for a Democratic Alternative for South Africa]. It is important that communities get to know and understand each other. The government is often opposed to these attempts, but Americans should support them. Leave your preconceptions and ideology at home and just help us get to know one another. Sending money and guns to the ANC through Bishop Tutu is counter-productive. Be constructive. Give money to the uplifting of the black communities, not to political organisations. Promote capitalism. We are concerned about the Communists in the ANC."

Professor Sampie Terreblanche of the University of Stellenbosch is, I learned subsequent to our meeting, one of South Africa's most widely-known and highly-respected academics. He is also something of an activist: In October 1988, I learned of his joining a delegation that met with ANC and Soviet Union officials, in West Germany; the following month, I read his name as one of the founders of a new, liberal, Afrikaans-language newspaper [see p. 164]; and by January 1989, he had become an advisor to the newly-formed Democratic Party. His April 1988 comments follow.

Sampie J Terreblanche (white)
Professor of Economics, University of Stellenbosch; Chairman of the Discussion Group '85 at the University of Stellenbosch

The University of Stellenbosch is not as conservative as it used to be, though it is basically still pro-establishment. But after close association with the Nationalist Party, I have now broken away, having become either enlightened or overexposed! I began to realise that we were defending a losing cause. Although I bear almost the same name, I am at the opposite end of the political spectrum from the Terre'Blanche of the Conservative Party. Actually, among Afrikaners, there are only about four hundred names which you will see over and over again. If you go back far enough you will see that we are all related. It does, frequently, cause identity problems—especially in cases such as my own.

South Africa: Land of Hope?

South Africa is the only "New Europe" on the African continent. We would have had greater success with double the number of whites; the situation would have been more manageable. We were never a colony of Holland; rather, we were a colony of the Dutch East India Company, so we actually developed by mistake, without help. As opposed to the rest of the world, for instance, no universities were started, and few people came here. Harvard was founded in America in 1636, sixteen years before the Dutch even arrived at the Cape. The first University College here was founded only in 1829 — after the English took over.

During the fifty years before World War I, fifty million people left Europe for "New Europes." Thirty-five million went to the United States, but fewer than 250,000 came to South Africa — in spite of our gold and diamonds and Britain's victory in the Boer War. Why didn't the 365,000 British troops who came here to fight in that war stay or return? Why did we receive so few immigrants over the years? Because we had no navigable rivers; people were less inclined to cross the Equator; agricultural conditions were not that good; it was the first time many of them saw blacks; and they had difficulty with the hot days and cold nights. [Those British soldiers, during the Anglo-Boer War, became known as *"Rooinekke"* ("Rednecks") for the effect of the sun on the back of their necks. Many present-day Afrikaners continue to derogate English-speakers by this name.] Of the 600,000 Boers in South Africa at that time, almost ten percent of them died in that war. Compare that to America's losing 55,000 men in Vietnam. With three million Afrikaners here, today, do you think they are prepared for 300,000 to die? Too ghastly to contemplate!

Why did I break with the Nats after serving as a consultant? In 1985, when this country truly seemed on the brink of revolution and the atmosphere was extremely tense, we formed a discussion group at the University to come up with some new models and solutions. It was that group which first proposed the idea of a National Council. In 1986 we presented a memorandum on "perceptions." We found the Nationalist Party guilty of major misperceptions such as 1) that a solution to South Africa's problems is possible without the ANC; 2) that Moscow is behind all the anti-government activity against South Africa; and 3) that "we can go it alone," without the rest of the world. These types of misperceptions are an indication of conceptual blockages developed after forty years in power. We have a government unable to break away, one with no new thinking and an inability to correctly identify the problems in South Africa. The memorandum was ignored because this government tries to convince foreigners that the situation is not as bad as it seems; but it is. To the Nationalist Party it is considered a sin to be pessimistic, because — as Solzhenitsyn said — the truth is never popular. The academic's problem is how to get through that shield and not be killed as the messenger.

Allow me to respond to those three misperceptions; I will take the first two together: We must negotiate with all relevant groups. Admittedly, there is a problem of violence. The ANC must renounce violence, but the government must acknowledge *structural* violence, or at least bring it into the discussion. There are world models where violent groups have been part of a negotiated solution. The South African Communist Party is also a factor; which faction will lead? As to the ANC Freedom Charter, that rhetoric is to be expected. But we must understand that the ANC views violence as a bargaining chip.

There are moderates among the blacks, as well as radicals. But as long as the State of Emergency and apartheid exist, all blacks who participate in discussions with the government will be seen by the radicals as Uncle Toms. Black support for the ANC comes mostly from the Xhosa: They are anti-Zulu and, therefore, anti-Buthelezi. According to a government poll, the breakdown among blacks shows twenty percent who will not negotiate, thirty percent who will negotiate, and fifty percent who are still uncommitted. The "Securocrats" in our government see only an attempt at a total onslaught against whites, against Christianity, and against apartheid. They are obsessed by the notion of security. This is the image you have of all South Africans, created by the media and by left-wing circles in Washington and in Europe. They blur the truth.

As to South Africa's ability to "go it alone," we *can* go without the United States, but we cannot go without the whole world — especially not without the UK [Britain] and West Germany. One-third of everything we produce is exported, and one-third of everything we use is imported. Our government's defiant attitude towards the rest of the world is not productive. We are adept at sanctions-busting, but that is expensive.

South Africa: Land of Hope?

With a slower growth rate, confidence in South Africa will be undermined; that will affect trade, investment, and banking.

The United States Congress insists on sanctions because of your country's own unsolved civil rights problems. In truth, if you really wanted to help the black South Africans, you would help us to expand our economy. That is how blacks will prosper. Sixty percent of white workers are Afrikaners in the Civil Service. The economy must expand to create new jobs, or those whites will thwart progress. A revolution, here, could not succeed without outside interference. But the situation is still serious because of the deteriorating economy. From a growth rate of 5.5% during 1960-1973, we have now fallen to a rate of 2%. In per capita terms, we are simply becoming poorer. We are in a siege economy, with "stagflation," and we face continued impoverishment due to overpopulation.

The Conservative Party exists in what we call "the maize triangle," the rural areas. From the 1930s through the 1970s, the government pampered white farmers. In 1978 the debt situation was such that, with their crop yields, it took farmers eighteen months to repay their debt; now it takes five years. That means those debts will never be repaid, for with international isolation they will become poorer and poorer.

South Africa is caught in a *Catch-22* situation: On the one hand, we cannot afford *not* to abolish apartheid and *not* to give blacks direct representation in Parliament; but on the other hand, given the decline in our economy and in our tax capacity, we cannot afford to give them direct representation in Parliament because they will exert unbearable pressure to spend more on the blacks.

The government must make a commitment to change over time. Apartheid capitalism must become democratic capitalism, but even a twenty-year growth period will not render us able to support a complete welfare state. We must accept a welfare-oriented capitalistic system, and white living standards will have to decline. Unfortunately, as in the United States, capitalism and ethics seem mutually exclusive, but one must decide whether it is more important to increase per capita income or to have a nation of happy faces. There is no question that the system must be rectified in South Africa. Apartheid must be abolished, but over time. We cannot have sudden abolishment, but we must have a strong government with a strong commitment, blacks in Parliament, foreign investment, and economic growth.

What sort of time frame is acceptable and reasonable? Twenty years, perhaps, with support from the world — with a Marshall Plan-type of aid programme. It must be a credible programme with visible results. Mutual trust is the most important ingredient. There is really a great basic goodwill in this country; our ordinary, everyday relations are remarkably relaxed. Foreigners have difficulty understanding and accepting this. That goodwill is remarkable, but time is running out. That goodwill won't last forever, if change is not forthcoming.

Rural Foundation For Human Resources (white-organized)

Continuing in my quest to discover what is being done to provide meaningful work and a decent standard of living for South Africa's black population, I visited the Rural Foundation for Human Resources, also located in Stellenbosch. As I found in other parts of the country, those involved in the process are both committed and enthusiastic — and justifiably proud of what they already have accomplished. The Foundation, formed in 1962, is a private, non-profit organization formed to upgrade the quality of life of South African farm workers.

The services of the Rural Foundation are available where a minimum of three hundred families will participate. This often means that not all of them work on the same farm. The organization reaches workers on three levels: management, including the forming of trade unions; working life, including training in specific skills; and social life, including sports facilities, women's clubs, youth clubs, and day-care centers. Foundation funding comes from three sources: ten percent private, twenty-five percent from the farmers, and sixty-five percent from the Department of National Health and Population Development, the last with no strings attached. Some six million people — twenty-percent of South Africa's population — live on the country's sixty thousand farms. This includes 1,270,000 farm workers and 5.5 family members per worker.

Farmers decide to join the Foundation and contribute to it, but it is the workers who set the priorities. The Foundation is active all over South Africa and also serves migrant workers who own property in the homelands but return annually to the same farm for additional work. As farmers recognize that happy workers are more productive, more and more of them join the Foundation. Housing on the farms is provided by the farmer — of a style chosen by the workers — but the workers often do the actual construction. Water, electricity, food, transportation, and medical care are included as workers' benefits, and farmers generally also hire workers' wives. Three thousand farmers are currently on the waiting list, as the Foundation searches for additional funds.

Most popular programs include skills training, literacy courses, community centers, clinics, and teacher training for pre-school children. In its first year of operation, the pre-school simulation program saw an increase from fifty-three percent to eighty-four percent in the pass rate of its students subsequently entering school.

In a tradition-bound, male-oriented society such as South Africa, where attitudes towards women have generally been summed up by the expression "kirche, kinder, und kuchen" (church, children, and kitchen), I was naturally interested in the place of women in today's South Africa. I spoke with Margaret Williamson, Editor of the Women's Section, **The Argus** *newspaper.*

Margaret Williamson (white)

Women in South Africa are more accepting of change than are the men; there is more in common among those with husbands and children. Professionals also tend to be more open to change, as are those who have travelled outside the country. When I was at university, in the 1950s, we were afraid to have coloured friends. Even later, only those who were social workers were able to maintain friendships with people of colour. Now, of course, one can have friends of any colour and not worry about what anyone else thinks or says. Changes have come about in South Africa not because of outside pressure but from a general liberalisation of the South African people. We resent pressure from those who have never even visited this country. Many of them don't want to believe the truth; they just want to impose their ideas on us, whether or not those ideas are suitable for our situation.

It is true that many South African whites lived in a sort of cocoon and were—believe it or not—totally unaware of how the blacks were living in the homelands or even in the squatter camps. They may have read about it, but they never saw it. For a long time, they never even read about it. As the facts were publicised and more people became aware, things started happening. The whites in South Africa do care—many of them, anyway—and they are doing something about it. It is a slow process, too slow for many, and unfortunately many people have chosen to leave, fearing a bloody revolution. The real estate market has not fallen as a result of the numbers who are leaving. Many, in fact, wait to leave until the house is sold, so there is not really a sense of urgency about it. The most concerned are probably those with sons who are approaching the age of military service.

Most of the Jewish families, who tend to be liberal, have sent their children to other countries. We are suffering a brain drain and a youth drain, and that is our greatest tragedy—all those bright, good, young people leaving and taking their talents elsewhere. Some come back, especially those who went to Australia. But many of those who have emigrated—Jews and non-Jews, young and not-so-young—still keep a house or a flat [apartment] here. They all *want* to come back. Life cannot be easy for them, away from South Africa. Not only do they leave a life-style, but they go to a new place with no family and friends for support.

Most white South Africans are more conscious of *class* than they are of race. The racial part of it was an issue in the early years of this country, but now it's more the feeling of, "How much do I really have in common with my milkman?"

Women have always been discriminated against, here. A single woman cannot obtain a housing loan. Even a married woman, whose company offers a better housing deal than her husband's, cannot apply with her company; only her husband can obtain the loan. Among teachers, a married woman cannot have a permanent post, as her first allegiance must be to her husband. Many men and women live together without marrying, for professional as well as tax reasons.

South Africa: Land of Hope?

Complaints about censorship centre more around violence than sex, both in the newspapers and on television. We would never allow anything like your "raunch radio" in this country, but our main complaints centre around the frequent and tremendous violence, especially on television. Television could be a greater force for good – but, then, that is a complaint all over the world. A lot of our television comes from America. Blacks and whites commonly are shown together, even on programmes which originate here.

The liberalisation of this country is definitely gaining momentum. There are great numbers of people working together for a fully-integrated society that will give everyone equal opportunities. The attitude of the whites has totally changed. I'm very optimistic, and I think women will continue to play an important role in making it work.

*Women have, indeed, been instrumental in implementing much of the change that already has taken place in South Africa – and in encouraging even more substantial change. As described in the magazine **South African Panorama**,[1] the women's organization, Kontak, "was established twelve years ago by a group of Afrikaans women in the Witwatersrand area [in and around Johannesburg] who decided to make a positive contribution towards the establishment of closer contact between people of divergent cultures and religious faiths." As the article's author points out, "the organisation was unwittingly established shortly before the country was to enter one of the stormiest decades in its history. [Yet] throughout the subsequent period of unprecedented unrest and large-scale social upheaval, of political stress and economic uncertainty, Kontak survived and succeeded in building bridges between people with widely-divergent lifestyles and attitudes.... Kontak has grown steadily and expanded countrywide. At present there are twenty-six branches in different parts of South Africa, while membership and the establishment of new branches [continue to] grow. Kontak believes that personal acquaintance with each other is of cardinal importance at a time when new demands that call for considerable adjustments are being made on all the inhabitants of the country."*

---

1   "Getting to Know You," (October 1988), pp. 1-2.

Among the South African women caught up in the cause of promoting cross-cultural relationships is Cape Town interior designer Shirley Kaplan — wife, mother, grandmother, and now President of the South African Delegation for Friendship Among Women. Her story follows.

Shirley Kaplan (white)

Our salvation will come from the basic goodwill that exists in this country and from our sense of humour. Women-to-Women groups are always effective.

There are wonderful examples of individual companies in South Africa, working to improve our society. For instance, a major insurance company gave away a free trip abroad to its highest achievers. It was a totally mixed group which travelled together, getting to know each other as human beings. It was very successful. When I heard about the Delegation for Friendship Among Women, I invited the Secretary-Treasurer — from St. Paul, Minnesota — to come to Cape Town. It was a catalyst for people to mix. I gave a cocktail party for her, and half of the people there were black and coloured. That was May 1987. In September 1987, I took a delegation of South African women to the United States — one black, one Indian, one white, and one coloured. We were accompanied by a young Italian woman who works for the South African Broadcasting Corporation and had asked to join us. We travelled to Chicago, St. Paul, Oklahoma City, Los Angeles, Santa Barbara, Houston, Detroit, and New York, spending three days in each city, four functions per day. We were constantly interviewed by American newspapers and radio and television.

The black woman was forty years old, with three children. Her husband runs a bus company. The Indian woman, also in her forties, runs a multi-racial cooking school. She and her husband, an anaesthesiologist with three white partners, live in a white area and have done so for years. Since there were never any problems, they never moved. The white woman, again of the same age, is an academic — outspoken, to the left in her politics, with a specialty in trade unions. Finally, the coloured woman, in her sixties, runs a senior citizens' home for the deprived.

An amazing camaraderie developed among us as we travelled and got to know each other, and we couldn't wait to share the experience in South

65

Africa. The only hostility we met in America was from some black women in Chicago, who softened after we spoke with them. American women are very warm.

Most Americans, men and women, were quite surprised that we could and would travel together. Most Americans don't know anything about South Africa except sanctions. The people in Detroit told us, "We have the same problems you do." The Detroit blacks were very warm and understanding and were interested in sharing ideas. We realised that the problems we have are not with the American people, but rather with the American politicians.

The reaction, when we returned to South Africa, was incredible. Articles were printed with photographs showing all of us together. All over the country, women wanted to get involved. Women are mothers first; they can understand other women's point of view. The Bureau for Information and the National Party were both impressed with the results of the trip. And we have had requests from other countries to visit them—even from Canada, which is highly anti-South Africa. A group in Washington, D.C. is waiting to meet us; Barbara Bush is a member of the American Delegation for Friendship Among Women. We are also helping multi-racial schools with their social events. It is this kind of thing that will change South Africa, that *is* changing South Africa right now. If you help us, it will happen faster.

Visit to Crossroads and Khayelitsha

The "shanty towns" of South Africa have been filmed, photographed and discussed more than any other feature of this troubled land. I went to see Crossroads, on the outskirts of Cape Town. As with later visits to Soweto and Alexandra — both outside Johannesburg — the reality was to alter my preconceived notions.

Information and comments were provided by George Stamelatos, Administration Officer of the Community Services Department of the Western Cape Provincial Administration. We walked and rode through Crossroads and Khayelitsha — the former a squatters' settlement, the latter a new town being developed by the South African government to house the increasing numbers of rural blacks moving to the cities.

Crossroads has been the site of tragedy and unrest, as one of the camps bulldozed by the army some years ago, but none of that was apparent, on my visit.

The original squatter camp appeared spontaneously in 1975 and consisted of shanties constructed of whatever materials could be scavenged. The people who came here came in search of jobs; their presence and their housing were illegal. Today there is no more "influx control" and the people who are here — whole families — have formed a municipal body and town committees. (The current Town Secretary, a white South African training the residents in the art of democracy, is himself being trained by the blacks as an herbal witch doctor.) The government has now levelled the shanties and replaced them with army tents. Word spread that if you lived in Crossroads you would get a house, so what was open space in 1975 and had 23,000 people by 1978, became — with New Crossroads across the street — 100,000 by 1981. It is difficult to get a true count of the residents of Crossroads because the blacks who live here count only adults as "people," but all of them are of the Xhosa tribe. There are nine political groups, ranging from radical to conservative. The 1985 riots were between the two factions; the conservatives won.

Now there are three distinct areas: the army tents (temporary housing); a section of what can be described only as make-shift houses; and the newer section, with homes made of concrete or a recently-developed material consisting of woven fiberglass bags filled with sand, cement, and lime, which hardens as brick and can then be plastered and painted. In each of the areas I was struck by how well-kept the houses and the people are. They also have a new hospital, theatre, and school, with three additional schools under construction. Many of the residents are building their own homes with government loans.

The government housing consists of two bedroom/one bath homes, with running water but no electricity. Electricity may be requested — and there is a whole section of homes with it — but thus far few of the residents have made the request. Government loans are generous: A thirty-year mortgage can be obtained for R20 ($10) a month. If you earn R600 ($300) per month you will pay 3% interest; otherwise the government will subsidize the loan. The total cost of the home is R7000 ($3500). Within two weeks of the announcement of the housing plan, five hundred people had signed up to buy homes. Not

67

everyone in Crossroads is poor; some of the houses will be far more elaborate than others. Many will be built on a self-help basis (do-it-yourself).

The decision to build Khayelitsha was made in 1983, when Crossroads got too big and property was allocated by the government to build a new town. (By 1987 another 180,000 people had arrived, to live in Khayelitsha.) Here one purchases "site and service" and then chooses a house to build there. For R2000 ($1000) one can buy a 300 square meter plot (3240 square feet). Private developers offer models and architects design custom homes for those who can afford them. Apartment houses are considered unacceptable and unworkable to the Xhosa people, as most are rural and need time to adapt to crowded urban living. Furnishings also may be purchased "on time." As in most areas, the millionaires live up on the hill; but the "middle class" area went fastest, where houses sell for R65,000 ($32,500). Many of these homes feature Italian tile baths, built-in kitchens, and two car garages. In the most modest areas, running water and serviced outhouses (i.e. with running water) are provided. Total housing payments never exceed twenty-five percent of one's take-home pay. The houses can be rented for R20 ($10) per month.

The remaining army tents and shanties serve only to temporarily house those who have come to Cape Town and are awaiting proper housing. As sanctions have slowed the economy, jobs have become more scarce. Adult education centers are busy and many people find themselves living in conditions inferior to what they had in the homelands. An interesting sidelight to this was the introduction of native-language radio and television, through which black South Africans have been bombarded with advertising and enticements to come to the cities. It raised expectations and a desire for cash that have, admittedly, caused some confusion among those who took the bait.

The Crossroads Training Centre teaches skills and finds jobs for the residents. Specific skills courses may be requested and job creation schemes abound. Many men are employed in construction in Crossroads and Khayelitsha. A center for legal and social help and the Khayelitsha library are nearby. The ride into Cape Town takes from ten to forty-five minutes, depending on the part of the city to which you are travelling. Transportation is available by bus, train, or combi-taxi (van).

According to Stamelatos most everyone in South Africa expects changes to the Group Areas Act soon. Already there are mixed areas about which no one complains and towards which the government turns a benign eye. Contemporary black women, he says, can be likened to the Boer women in the early years of this country: He sees them as industrious, steady, determined, fair, more successful than their male counterparts — and the group most likely to lead the black South Africans to improve their quality of life.

Finally, he makes this statement, "to the gloom and doomers who leave: Go and don't come back. Those of us who stay know what's wrong and are doing something about it."

Having learned of an Afrikaner medical student who had just returned from studying in the United States, I imposed upon him for a few minutes of his time. He prefers to remain anonymous, but his brief comments underline the hazards of our making knee-jerk recommendations for those in other parts of the world.

Anonymous Afrikaner Medical Student (white)

I have just spent six months in the United States, and I am impressed by how everyone, there, is an *American* first and then whatever else he or she is, second. And the blacks consider themselves Americans like everyone else. I even met Jewish students I didn't know were Jewish until a discussion came up about it. In South Africa the Jews are a separate group. They keep very much to themselves, with their own schools and social groups. I have Jewish friends, here, but I wouldn't think of dating a Jewish girl. I don't think she'd accept if I asked her. [For more details on the Jewish community, see the comments of Professor Anthony Arkin, p. 103.]

I found no animosity towards me as a South African, in America. The animosity seems to come only from the Congress. The Americans I met were just interested in what my day-to-day life is like, here.

Most South Africans — certainly the Afrikaners — see those who emigrate as deserting the cause, as traitors and cowards. The English can "go home" but South Africa is the Afrikaners' only home, and they will stay to defend it. New English immigrants to South Africa tend to be people on the far right, so they are swelling the ranks of the Conservative Party. In some ways I think this country has actually benefitted by the gains in the Conservative Party; it has frightened everyone and forced the government off centre.

My friends and I have been discussing apartheid since we were in primary school. In high school we really became interested in politics. Those of us who are moderate and to the left are fed up with waiting: Most students think full integration is inevitable, and I think most of the adults think so, too — so why not get on with it? The brain drain and the youth drain are more of a concern to the older people. The students are basically optimistic about our future, but we want things to start moving. The South African people are still flexible, though as part of a world-wide collective white guilt, part of their frustration is the feeling that they are not allowed to feel proud of being South Africans. I have built up a defence mechanism that says, "I am neither proud *nor* ashamed to be South African; I am a Citizen of the World."

One cannot have a conversation about South Africa without broaching the subject of sanctions and disinvestment. There is no middle ground, nor is anyone dispassionate about the subject. I met with an oil company executive who presented me with facts and documents outlining the position taken by literally everyone I met, in South Africa, with the exception of Nelson Mandela's attorney and the officials of AZAPO, representing the radical far left.

The executive quoted here has asked to remain anonymous. Further discussion of sanctions will be found in Chapters 3, 4, and 5.

Anonymous Oil Company Executive (white)

American companies in South Africa have had an unfair burden placed on them. They have been given the responsibility of setting right all the evils of this country, which of course is an impossible task. The most devastating effect of your sanctions is that the United States no longer has business or political influence here. With the Sullivan Code and American business adhering to it, there was movement forward in this society. In fact it accomplished what your own Civil Rights leaders did not achieve – action, not just rhetoric. The Sullivan Code was the most effective instrument for change that has been seen in this country. But even as Sullivan was fulfilled, the United States Congress tightened the noose.

Why did Sullivan work so well here? It had teeth in it. It demanded an annual report – audited independently – which indicated money, manpower, investment, and the results achieved. Companies received annual ratings. Some American companies chose not to join but even they were later locked into the system and had to perform. The down side of Sullivan is that there was much wasting of money and considerable freeloading. We were attempting to give American solutions to non-American problems: First World solutions to Third World problems. Consequently, in some cases the term "social justice" was taken as an OK for civil disobedience.

Reverend Sullivan was neither economist nor businessman. Twelve percent of our payroll had to be invested equally in four categories: education, housing, social welfare, and social justice. There was no tax relief for these expenditures, so naturally dividends and profitability were affected. Just the cost of manpower, alone, was inordinately high: Top management people were assigned – for their expertise, counselling and guidance – to administer these programmes. That extended the working day of executives who had their company jobs to do as well. There is no other country in the world where these kinds of requirements are mandatory for the right to do business. There is no other country where American companies have to pay this price to trade.

Another weakness of Sullivan was that American companies competed for "brownie points" and were therefore easy victims of doubtful projects. The money had to be spent, so it was spent – but poorly. There was no consolidation of the enormous amounts of money being spent, with the result that there was duplication, triplication, and cancelling out of each other's projects due to a lack of co-ordination. From 1976 through 1986, $290 million plus manpower plus in-kind services were poured into South Africa – all by the American companies that were forced to do so by your government. These companies never challenged Sullivan constitutionally, because it would have been too embarrassing to admit to the obscene profits being made from this country; it was easier to agree to pour a few million dollars back into South Africa. But many South African companies had been making this sort of contribution for years – Barlow Rand, Anglo American, South African Breweries, and Premiere, to name a few.

The truth is that no American company has actually pulled out of South Africa; they have just changed the way they do business. Kodak now repackages its film in Italy before selling it here; Coca Cola still gets royalties, the major part of its profits. But America and American business no longer command respect or credibility. Your Congress' new double taxation scheme was put together by political opportunists who have succeeded only in isolating American business and causing the meltdown of American influence internationally.

The companies in South Africa that were committed *pre*-Sullivan to creating a more equitable society are continuing *post*-Sullivan to fulfilling those commitments. The signatory association members still meet regularly to discuss South Africa's problems and to work together. On the other hand, those foreign companies that have replaced the Americans – owned by the Japanese and the Europeans – make no investment in this country. They don't contribute one cent to the upliftment of the blacks.

If you wonder how so many blacks can be affected so quickly, consider this: There is a multiplying factor of *nine* in South African black communities. That means that for every black person who loses a job, nine others are affected. That is the trickle-down effect of your sanctions and programmes.

What do I see in South Africa's future? We have great concern but always the hope for a peaceful settlement. It will be a rough ride, but I do not foresee a revolution; the South African army is too powerful. Our greatest concern at the moment is that the right lunatic fringe will develop into a Ku Klux Klan. The Conservative Party is scary. Two things are slowing down our reforms: the radical right wing and a lack of acknowledgment – from the United States and others – for the reforms that already have taken place. The apartheid system is so entrenched it permeates everything, so it will be difficult to dismantle. But it *is* being dismantled and you Americans must understand and acknowledge that. The key to South Africa's future is not one man/one vote; it is economic freedom. We will never achieve our political freedom without economic freedom for everyone. The deregulation of passenger transport is a perfect example. We now have 85,000 black taxi owners who have bought taxis and are operating as entrepreneurs. But these taxis were all bought through Japan; not one is American. General Motors and Ford are now non-entities in South Africa. The hassle factor became so great for American companies that most of them said, "To hell with it." But many of them are still collecting commissions and agency fees.

The real future for South Africa lies in the new education for black children, starting from the earliest stages. At this point black high school graduates still require two years of "bridging" before they are ready for university work. It is unfortunate, but the old education system in this country was designed to make bricklayers out of potential [black] physicians, so they were disadvantaged from the beginning. In spite of this we created a level of black management. But black managers were brought into a totally new environment which clashed with their old culture. Their greatest problems came at the end of the day when they went home: The insistence on integrated housing put an even greater burden on them, as they were then attacked by both sides. But as for performance — compared to whites — they both take just as long to train.

Many of us still here are trying to help make a new South Africa happen. We could use your help.

[For some specifics on what the Sullivan signatories contributed to social programs in South Africa, see the comments of Adriaan Botha, Executive Director of the American Chamber of Commerce, p. 200.]

see the comments of Adriaan Botha, Executive Director of the American Chamber of Commerce, p. 200.

*   *   *

CISKEI

The next several interviews took place in the independent country of Ciskei, a country of 800,000 people and 9000 square kilometres (3510 square miles) wholly within the borders of South Africa. Along with Transkei, Bophuthatswana, and Venda, (together known as the TBVC countries), Ciskei is considered by many to be a "sham country" because of its dependence on South Africa. As such, it is not recognized by the United Nations, in spite of the fact that — according to Donald S. McAlvaney, editor of the "McAlvaney Intelligence Advisor" — the four independent TBVC countries have stronger economies, larger populations, more land, and more freedom than thirty-three other African countries or fifty United Nations members.

The whites who work in Ciskei have a missionary zeal about what they are accomplishing, as blacks and whites work side-by-side to foster growth and education. Because of a favorable tax structure and the industrious nature of the Xhosa people who populate the country (this is their traditional homeland), many international companies have offices and factories in Ciskei. The country's literacy rate stands at seventy percent, the highest in black Africa and almost triple the rate of the rest of black South Africa.

Ciskei has been independent since 1981. The interviews began in Bisho, the fast-growing, modern capital and site of a new international airport which can accommodate 747s.

Headman Somtunzi (black)
Deputy Director-General of Information

President Lenox Sebe has succeeded here because he has the interest of the people at heart. I first met him when he came to my school as a school inspector, when I was in Standard Six [junior high school]. He left an impression on me because he taught us a geography lesson and asked us good, hard questions; he made us think and reason and do correlations between countries. He also understands black history.

Most of the people who live in Ciskei are very traditional; they wouldn't want to go to work in Johannesburg. New people come here all the time because of our economic reforms and our tremendous economic growth. We have more schools here than are found in any other independent state, even though we are smaller. We see the self-governing states as a means to an end, as part of an ultimate confederation for South Africa. We can't run a country without the know-how, and the self-governing states are providing us with that know-how. We continue to learn.

The ANC has difficulty attracting members in Ciskei because the message of capitalism has gotten through. We understand that revolution brings only hardship. The more affluent among us must help the others. Blacks in Ciskei feel change in South Africa is inevitable, but we are looking for it to be peaceful. We believe in Constructive Engagement, because we have seen it work.

Wonga Fundile Tabata (black)
Deputy Director-General, Department of Foreign Affairs

We have always been a proud, independent nation. When our chiefs were defeated by colonial forces in the nineteenth century, the colonial system was applied in Ciskei. Later, we were part of a compromise, forced to become part of South Africa. We fought nine frontier wars with the British. Those conflicts taught us that armed struggle is not an acceptable strategy in our situation. Now we have regained our independence without an armed struggle. Now we are masters of our own destiny.

This structuring is not new in Africa; we are the same as Lesotho, which was granted limited autonomy under British rule. Where Lesotho opted for independence through a constitutional process in 1966, we did the same in 1981. The international community sees us as puppets of South Africa, pointing to the aid it provides. But ask the international community this: Ciskei receives technical aid, but so does Mozambique; is Mozambique a puppet? Lesotho receives technical aid from South Africa; is Lesotho a puppet? Angola receives aid from the Soviet Union; is Angola a puppet? Why does the United Nations recognise all those other countries but deny recognition to us? The principle of interdependence applies everywhere. Our historical ties with South Africa are not denied. That South Africa is a regional power is also undenied. Our people work in South African mines along with people from many other nations. Only those who haven't been here think we are puppets. We are no different from other independent African countries.

Call us a puppet if you like, but come to Ciskei and look at our stability and progress. We are not recognised by the United Nations because of its feelings towards South Africa, but how many coups have been instigated *here* by foreign powers? We have a president elected by the people. Ninety-nine percent of Ciskeians voted for independence. Our National Assembly is made up of elected members, and we have a two-party system; the losing party claimed to represent the views of the Black Consciousness Movement. We also have a dual system of citizenship with South Africa, so that independence should not be a disadvantage.

Why do we not join Transkei [an adjacent independent state], as we are so close? Although we are both Xhosa-speaking, we have always been separate. It was the son of a Xhosa king in Transkei who established his own kingdom, many years ago, to form Ciskei. Ciskei has never had a military government. Military governments are a product of instability, which is what you see in Transkei. Only the southern part of Transkei is made up of Xhosa people, now, and we co-operate with that group. But Transkei is a sovereign state, and we respect its sovereignty.

How do the "homelands" differ from the independent countries? It's a question of authority. Authority is limited in the homelands; they cannot negotiate loans outside South Africa. There are also limitations to their development. We are free to formulate foreign policy and make economic reforms, whereas the homelands need legislative approval from the South African government.

Many of the reforms now taking place in South Africa were originally introduced in Ciskei — especially concerning independent small businesses. Ciskei has attracted industrialists from all over the world. Along with South Africa and other independent countries formerly of South Africa, we are a part of the Secretariat for Co-operation in Southern Africa, for economic development. This organisation concerns itself with taxation, economic incentives, labour matters, and agricultural development — no different from the organisation which has Lesotho, Zimbabwe, Angola and Mozambique as its members. They copied us.

We want people to know that industrialists should come to Ciskei. The cruelty of American sanctions and disinvestment causes more trouble than apartheid. The sanctions affect African people [blacks] more than South

Africa does. We are the backbone of the economy; we have nothing to sell but our labour. If you close off jobs, we have nothing. We understand the anger of the international community against apartheid; it is abhorrent. We don't accept it either. That's why we emphasise that Ciskei will be an open country. Blacks and whites, here, are living and working together in peace. But we cannot accept the disinvestment strategy as a means of destroying apartheid. It will only bring on a revolution, as the jobless will have nothing of value to protect. The result would be chaos.

As far as PW Botha is concerned, we must wait and see. There must be change in South Africa, and the independence of individual states must not be used as an excuse to deny political rights to blacks throughout South Africa. It was our President Sebe who suggested local authorities for urban blacks.

In the meantime, come to Ciskei and see what is being accomplished!

Joe Rowles was born in King Williams Town, making him a white Ciskeian. A former teacher, he started a bank training school in Zambia before returning to Ciskei. His wife, he says, "is the brains behind the administration of the Ciskeian Small Business Corporation."

Eunice Tunyiswa, known as "Mrs T," was born in Transkei but is married to a Ciskeian. She specializes in dealing with women, who represent seventy-five percent of those who apply for loans and have a business failure rate of Zero. She is famous for her speeches to women, in which she encourages them to tell their husbands to stay home and take care of the house and children so the women can go to work and make money.

Mr and Mrs Rowles and Mrs Tunyiswa run the Ciskeian Small Business Corporation.

Joe Rowles (white), Director
Eunice Tunyiswa (black), Deputy Director

The CSBC was established in 1982 by President Sebe. The idea was to identify people with certain skills and encourage them in "cottage industries." This is the "informal" sector of business, including hawkers and people in service industries. We provide workshop space for those who need it, throughout the country, and – without any publicity at all – we average three applicants per workshop. The idea is to foster job creation and loan finance without red tape. We have made over six thousand loans in five-and-a-half years. Loans are unsecured, yet our failure rate stands at an incredibly low 1.5%. Our intention is to encourage and teach good business practices. Borrowers pay interest of 12% – one percent per month, payable monthly on the remaining balance as of the last business day. Money is usually kept for only three months, as working capital; six months if it's for capital and equipment. Business counselling and marketing skills are also our concern.

So high is the quality of work produced in this country that whatever can be produced can be sold. Much of it is sold on contract. The CSBC offers training school classes based on the skills needed. Capitalism has definitely caught on: After five-and-a-half years, there are 233 small workshops and 1653 small businesses. 3700 jobs have been created and, in the last thirty-six months, 1017 knitters have been trained. [Textiles are an important part of Ciskei industry.] Much of what they produce is exported overseas, but that market has been hurt by sanctions and disinvestment. Ciskeians feel great frustration that money pours into Zimbabwe, which is Communist, while Christian capitalist Ciskei loses out.

As businesses outgrow the small business category and require more money – over R10,000 [$5000] – to expand, we send them over to the Ciskei Peoples Development Bank. The business class, in this country, definitely serves as the role model for young people. We have a very strong middle class.

Housing loans are available to anyone with assets. Land qualifies as an asset and the house serves as security for the loan. Some Ciskeians build many houses and rent them out to others. Anyone can buy land from the government. Normal loan rates are 12 1/2% to 13% for a house. Prime

79

rate for commercial loans is 13%; standard rate is 16%, approximately the same as rates in South Africa. Interest is paid on savings accounts at 7%, up to R10,000 [$5000], and at 8% over that amount.

Ciskei is the best example of what South Africa could be. Blacks here are much further along than those in the United States and Canada.

Neville Williamson (white)
Industrial Marketing Manager, Ciskei Peoples Development Bank

There are two main sections to our bank – the Small Business Division, to assist Ciskei nationals in their commercial operations, and our Worldwide Investment Section, where – under strict rules – we offer loans for working capital to those with skills who wish to bring employment opportunities to Ciskeians. As subsidies and concessions abound, we always run the risk of attracting the wrong people coming here for the wrong reasons. That is why our qualifying rules are so strict. But we have gone from forty-seven to 181 factories in this country in five years, with a failure rate of under six percent. We make a report to the government once a year, but we are not political nor are we controlled by politics. We feel a moral responsibility in this country: Once you have given a man a job you must help him keep it. Therefore, we are interested in attracting only business people who have the intention of staying in business in this country.

Of major importance to us is our "after care" system, a system of following up on those to whom we give loans – to supervise and advise them, to aid them through management consulting. We raise money through hotels which we build and run until we find qualified operators; through interest on loans; and through the Development Bank of Southern Africa. Casinos in our hotels provide extra income for education, *crèches*, and old-age homes. Ciskeians pay no income tax if they make less than R8000 [$4000] per year. That means that eighty percent of Ciskeians pay no tax. There is also no corporate income tax: The world's fastest growing economies all feature no corporate income tax. Businesses do pay a fifteen percent withholding tax on internally-distributed funds, and the government levies a twelve percent sales tax on goods other than food and medicine. To give you an idea of costs, a man can buy a horse for R20

[$10], a cow for R200 [$100], or take a 50km [30 mile] taxi ride for R3 [$1.50].

Twenty years ago this was a strictly tribal society. Today Ciskei is a tribal democracy, pulling away from the Third World. The President runs the country with a Committee of Ten and an Economic Advisory Council. There is no royal lineage, here. The people chose Lenox Sebe, author of books on African nationalism and a strong proponent of meritocracy. The outside world thought Ciskei was not viable for independence, but the Ciskeians have made it go. The income base has been expanded and they are less and less dependent on South Africa.

To the Americans I would like to say, try and understand what's going on here. This is a country that deserves your support. 4500 workers lost their jobs in one day, when sanctions were imposed. You should be *encouraging* investment, not discouraging it.

Anonymous Afrikaner Working in Ciskei (white, mid 20s)

I come from a dyed-in-the-wool traditional Afrikaner family. My family and friends were surprised and angry about my working and living here, until I explained to them what is happening and how well we are doing. As people understand, they accept.

South Africa is changing from within, outside the political sphere. Blacks and whites grew up as Africans together. After the separation of school, we have come together again. We accept each other and work together.

I used to be a member of the National Party but I don't vote anymore. I would rather make a difference with how I live my life.

I have confidence that all South Africa will come together. There are more of us who want it to happen than there are of those who are fighting it.

South Africa: Land of Hope?

The area of Dimbaza, Ciskei, was known in 1969 as a "dumping ground" for people who were relocated there by the South African government. Today it is a thriving center of industry. More and more factories open here each year, offering on-the-job training, and employment is available to all who seek it.

I visited Montage Weavers, where I spoke with Ben de Kock and Percy Shaw, directors of the company and both Afrikaners.

Ben de Kock and Percy Shaw (white)

Our workers are ninety-nine percent Christian Xhosas, so we hold church services each morning before work. All our supervisors are Xhosa, as is our designer, Nondumiso Tiso—a native Ciskeian.

With the implementation of an incentive scheme where workers are paid for what they produce, our productivity has increased sharply and the workers are much happier. Some of them work right through their tea break, to earn more money. One woman arrives in the morning before we open the doors and stays until we leave, usually late in the evening. She is saving to buy a house. Our building is rented from the Peoples Development Bank, and we consider that our biggest asset is the people who work for us. We foster team spirit and feature a Personality of the Month.

Wages are higher here than in South Africa but we don't have to contend with labour unions. We could get cheaper labour in South Africa but we would get the problems along with it. Sixty percent of our workers have been here for over eight years.

Practically all of these people are illiterate. They are using their traditional weaving skills and we offer on-the-job training. The more skilled workers operate the machines. It is important for the world to understand that illiteracy does not mean stupidity. The Xhosa come from an oral tradition where reading and writing were not learnt or needed. We accommodate this fact by using schematic and colour-coded information cards. These women are fast learners and competent workers. With the money they earn, they buy land and build houses. They have what they consider a very nice life, a life of stability.

The biggest problem in Ciskei is not the government but foreigners who come here and try to pay slave wages, a situation we encounter a lot with companies from the Far East. We believe in treating our workers well. We provide fresh bread for the tea breaks and subsidise a vending machine, so they can buy soup or a drink for 7¢ [3½¢]. Four times a year we have a big *braai* [barbecue] for all our employees.

There are opportunities in our factory for anyone prepared to work. We won't hire school-age children but we will take them when they finish school. We don't discourage any adult who wants to work; a job will always be provided at whatever her level of competency. Our success is seen in the fact that Montage weavings are shipped to countries all over the world.

I'd rather be a black in Ciskei than a black in America.

Rob and Alison Sayers (white)
Project Manager and Dairy Factory Manager
Keiskammahoek Irrigation Scheme

The Keiskammahoek Irrigation Scheme was started in mid-1976 with several aims in mind: food production; job creation; settlement of middle class Ciskeian farmers; human advancement of Ciskeians; the development of a national dairy herd; the efficient use of natural resources; development of a growth centre; and improved nutrition for the people of Ciskei. We have a total of 1591 hectares [3941 acres], of which 791 [1959 acres] are developed — that is, under irrigation. Two dams provide the irrigation through a gravity feed, eliminating the need for electric pumping.

Farmers are selected from people in the district. Originally, eighty-one farmers were given four hectares [ten acres] each; however, it was later decided to choose the best twenty-seven among the farmers and to give them each twelve hectares [30 acres] to farm. Each hectare will support one cow, initially, increasing to the stage where three to four cows per hectare are supported. The farmers are financed by the Ciskei Agricultural Bank, and the milk produced is marketed through the Keiskammahoek Dairy Factory.

Through improvement in methods, techniques, and management, we have increased production from eleven litres per cow per day, in 1985, to 17.5 litres in 1988. This is said to be the highest yield for this type of farmer in the Third World.

In the Keiskammahoek commercial dairy herd, production has increased from eleven litres per cow in 1985 to 19.5 litres in 1988. All together this gives us four million litres per annum. Milk is sold to schools, hospitals, and stores, with the surplus sold to United Dairies.

Farmers are trained in the husbandry, nutrition, and health of animals; pasture and crop management; fertilisation and irrigation; and bookkeeping. For their own use and for sale, they grow maize, ryegrass, kikuyu, lucerne, and vegetables. Farms are worked by family units, with some farmers hiring extra help in certain seasons. A dairy herd is run on behalf of eighty members of Gxulu Co-Op, whereby the members hire cows from K.I.S. but can purchase the cows through an in-kind exchange in six years. Management is provided by K.I.S. and dividends are paid to the farmers. A thriving town centre attests to the success of the project.

[The Sayers came to Keiskammahoek three years ago, after farming in the Matabeleland region of Zimbabwe.]

Professor Norman GK Holiday (white)
Doctor of Political Science, University of Fort Hare

The University of Fort Hare is the oldest black university in Africa. Most of the well-known black leaders were educated here. "Staged" and trumped-up press accounts of violence on this campus have angered many of the students and faculty, as we feel it has sullied the name of a fine university.

Where American blacks are American and share a culture with white Americans, South African blacks are of nine different cultures and South African whites are of two different cultures. In addition, there are great differences between urban and rural blacks, who don't understand each other. Ours is a fully-integrated university, socially as well as academically. This is a true meeting place of the cultures.

Most of us cannot understand the furore of the outside world over the independent states. They are unquestionably independent. Yes, they are dependent on South Africa for certain things, but then look how many countries in the world are dependent on the United States and England.

If the Conservative Party comes to power, we will have a crisis in this country. We would not be able to force them out in under two years. A coalition government is possible; we have had that before.

We have made a mistake in forcing the ANC underground. Ghandi warned the people in 1910. He said, "If you form a union, don't leave out the Natives." The ANC started out as a peaceful organisation; they tried to negotiate but were spurned. In the 1950s they went underground and the Communists were waiting for them with open arms. There is no way the ANC can get away from Russia now—just like the Cubans and the Angolans.

*   *   *

DURBAN

From Ciskei I travelled north to Durban, in the province of Natal. It is in and around this coastal city that the majority of South Africa's Indian population lives. I first met with three members of that community and gained insight into the business, culture, and politics of 600,000 of South Africa's citizens.

Having visited small business development centers in a homeland and in an independent country, I was curious to see whether as much was being done for non-whites in South Africa proper. At the business development center in Durban the beneficiaries include both Indian and Zulu men and women. (The KwaZulu homeland also is located in Natal.) Adhir Singh has been associated with the Small Business Development Corporation since its inception in 1981. He holds the position of Assistant General Manager and is responsible for finance and advice to small business undertakings located in Natal.

Jugadhusan Devar is an ex-broadcaster of Indian cultural programs in South Africa and is at present engaged in cultural promotion work in the Department of Education and Culture in the Indian house of Parliament, the House of Delegates.

Mike Abel, officially with the New Republic Bank Ltd, may more accurately be called an "ombudsman", as human resources specialist, part-time preacher, and founder of the Association for Free Learning.

*While in Durban I also was able to further my knowledge of the Chief Buthelezi-led political party, Inkatha, and the multi-racial legislative body, the KwaZulu/Natal Indaba, and it was here that I gained new insights into South Africa's Jewish community. Finally, at the suggestion of one of the University of Stellenbosch students, I contacted Khaba Mkhize — editor of the black newspaper, **The Echo**, and one of two black journalists with whom I spoke on this trip.*

Adhir Singh (Indian)

Our purpose here is to assist — irrespective of race, sex, or religion — small business people and those who have the potential to be small businessmen.

Without Acts or red tape we offer rental space open twenty-four hours a day, a mentor programme, and the rental of equipment.

The trade unions put pressure on us not to allow people to stay here too long or to employ other workers, but our interest is in getting these people into the business world. Both Indians and Zulus have a strong merchant class. Our centre is totally open and multi-racial and economic merit is the sole determinant for granting loans. All of the population groups in South Africa now work for and hire all the others. Economics is the key to doing away with racism.

The trade unions in Natal are quite strong and active. The moderate union — under the Zulu Chief Buthelezi — says, "We won't strike because workers need their wages to live. We will work to settle our political differences around the conference table, not by staying out of work." The other unions look down on the moderate unions for this.

In addition to skills and management, we offer a range of financing programmes for the diverse forms and varying levels of sophistication of the businesses requiring assistance. The bulk of our funds go to the expanding of already-established businesses. In this section the average loan is R61,000 [$30,500] and our failure rate is low. On start-up and less sophisticated businesses, our failure rate is relatively higher. Work, as we know it, is new to black men: Traditionally they were the hunters and the women did all the work. Indian men don't mind working for a woman, but among the blacks that causes more problems.

Jugadhusan Devar (Indian)

The Indians have been in South Africa for 128 years, but only recently have they begun teaching Indian languages in South African schools. We have five language groups: Tamil, Hindu, Urdu, Gujarati, and Telugu. There are also several different religions within our community: Hinduism, Islam, Christianity, and — to a lesser extent — Buddhism.

The Urdu and the Gujarati had a tradition in India as tradesmen and merchants, and the majority of them have become very successful businessmen in South Africa. The others came to this country as immigrant workers. The most positive changes we have seen in recent years are in economic advancement, following improvements in education and the end of the Job Reservation Act [which set aside certain jobs for specific population groups]. Indians always have helped their own community and have become socially more aware, so we have been able to move forward, perhaps, more than the other non-white groups in this country.

The animosity that has existed between the Indians and the Zulus has lessened considerably. In my opinion there is no longer any animosity. Credit goes to the Zulu Chief, Dr [Mangosuthu] Gatsha Buthelezi, who has very good intentions and strives to promote harmony all around. The Zulus are considered by the other blacks to be the most dynamic of the black tribes. Dr Buthelezi's leadership is making a strong impact in South Africa.

We are most anxious to see the end of the Group Areas Act, but we don't think a lot will change, nor do we anticipate problems when it is rescinded. People basically like to live among their own kind and there is a lot of goodwill among the people in this country, in spite of all that may be implied to the contrary.

We are against the ANC's policy of violence, favouring instead peaceful negotiations. Negotiation is the only constructive solution. Unfortunately there are Indian radicals as well as black radicals, and they cause just as many problems.

Our women have made tremendous strides in the professions and in business and have moved away from the hide-bound traditions which are now outmoded.

We look ahead with faith and in goodwill and hope for peaceful progress and general happiness for everyone in this beautiful land of bounty and sunshine.

Mike Abel (Indian)

Blacks in this country — that is, blacks, coloureds, and Asians — are suspicious of the government's stated intent to make changes. They don't see positive forward movement in reforms, and the movement they do find is relegated to peripheral issues rather than to total integration or civil liberties. We concede that the Conservative Party has served as a brake-force on the government and we understand the growing concern about violence, but when all else has failed the blacks see violence as the only option. Forcing the UDF underground was a mistake. Bishop Tutu gives a subtle espousal of violence, as opposed to Martin Luther King. Tutu instigates and incites in a Christ-like manner but he dances closely with the Devil.

To understand the extent of support for the ANC, you must separate the methods from the goals. The majority of black youth support the ANC's violence, but among the middle-aged, fewer than half, and among the elderly very few. The broad goals of well-being, though universally held, may be more difficult to define – but in any case the ANC is intimidating moderate blacks throughout the land.

The ANC makes no bones about Communist involvement and sympathies, though Russian participation is more covert. There are even American citizens offering Russian arms to the ANC. These are arms that were purposely hijacked by men who are nothing more than mercenaries. They are also diverting arms to the Middle East, Ireland, and the Arab countries.

Indians espouse a safe route; we keep an ear to the wind. Safety for us is with the whites, because – according to radical blacks – the Indians and the coloureds have a limited place in a future South Africa. The Indians would be the first eased out politically and squeezed out economically. If Canada and Australia continue their idiotic policies it will all land in their lap. Do the Canadians really want 600,000 Indians on their doorstep?

I see the Group Areas Act as negotiable, at this stage. Even when it is rescinded you won't see a lot of moving around. Like attracts like, and water seeks its own level. But you must allow the rich of all colours to integrate. When that happens, the Indians will be the whites' kind, benevolent landlords!

The independent states were originally puppets. But power teaches you that you can test your master, and they've done that. The expert wielders of power have gotten more than the master originally planned to give them. I don't consider them puppets; if they ever were, they are now in the process of disentangling themselves. The learning process was necessary. There is nothing derogatory in what I am saying; it's the only way the blacks can begin to have autonomy.

On the question of one man/one vote, one must consider what is acceptable, what is possible, and what is likely. If you worked out voter qualification criteria, would the blacks accept it? Yes, if it were fair, and if you got the right people to promote it. But you must negotiate the same criteria for all groups. Having qualifications would save the whites for a while. The problem is that everyone is talking and advising but nothing is happening. We have enough ideas to take us into the 21st century, but there's no *action*. It is important to *negotiate*, not just discuss.

History is against the whites. You may win the black hearts, but their minds aren't there yet. The whites must establish trust with the blacks. First give them food, shelter, and a sharing of power. The whites must rely on something more than politics; the blacks must be made to realise that running the whites out of the country would leave the blacks nothing. The whites, at this stage, are indispensable, because the blacks don't yet have the competence to run industry, mining, etc. Capitalism is the opponent of apartheid, but that is difficult for the blacks to understand because they equate capitalism with oppression. The radicals see black capitalism as part of the white system. One of the real problems in the black community is that the black fat cats just get fatter; they don't bring in their brothers. They do to each other what they accuse the whites of doing to them.

The coloureds have hardly progressed at all, certainly not as far as the blacks. The coloureds suffer from the "mañana" syndrome — "tomorrow is another day." They have a huge identity problem because they were bastard children. Few of them have made it or have done anything outstanding in any area. The blacks have more cars, per capita, than do the coloureds.

Few women blacks or coloureds surface as leaders, as they are uneducated and are fighting old tribal prejudices against them. By comparison, four in ten Indian women have university degrees; Indian men just don't want them working. The Indians have a saying, "If you have a wise mother at the dinner table, ultimately you will have a wise nation."

Sanctions are justified only if they achieve results. But the slightest movement forward by the government must be acknowledged. The United States keeps moving the goalposts, making it impossible for South Africa ever to satisfy your Congress. Tutu has unleashed something that got out of hand, and others around the world picked it up for their own benefit. This whole sanctions movement no longer has anything to do with what is really happening in South Africa — and the only ones being hurt are the black South Africans. If Americans really want to help blacks in this country, support organisations like the Black Management Forum. It's one of the most credible organisations in South Africa. On a scale of one to ten, black managers are now only at one, but capitalism can help bring blacks into a commercial environment. Put sanctions money to good use: Put blacks into training and business.

There is a lot of goodwill in this country. The true leaders aren't the leaders the world sees. I know that Americans doubt the credibility and independence of those who speak of other than gloom and doom, but I assure you there is another side to the story.

Inkatha is the independent political party headed by Zulu Chief Mangosuthu Gatsha Buthelezi. For this reason, its detractors refer to it as the "Zulu party," in spite of its broader membership. Milicent Gcaba, a member of the Inkatha National Executive Committee — and a Xhosa by birth — expanded on the party's goals and objectives.

Milicent Gcaba (black)

There is no unity amongst blacks in South Africa because we have differing ideologies. Going back to the Pan African Congress, which supported action and violence, and the original ANC, which was against violence, and with all the other organisations which have since formed, there are just too many platforms.

When the ANC was banned there was no voice for blacks for ten years, until the government established the homelands. Yet most blacks were against the homeland policy. This caused great problems for Chief

Buthelezi, who had always been a staunch member of the ANC Youth League: His people wanted him as leader of their homeland, but what would he say to the ANC supporters? A delegation of fifty men went to him to ask him to serve the homeland. Buthelezi felt he could fight the system from within, so — against his ANC loyalties — he agreed to the position. That put a black mark next to his name with the ANC. It also put Inkatha and the KwaZulu government at odds. Inkatha is an independent party, designed to be the voice of the people and to channel their wishes through the party, through Parliament, and to the Central Government. The Party saw KwaZulu [the homeland government] as the baby of Pretoria. But the Inkatha Board was clever: It decided to make Buthelezi the head of the Party. Now he wears two robes and his allegiance is to Inkatha — which, in any case, is the party of most of the people of the KwaZulu homeland.

The ANC and Inkatha are at loggerheads. When Buthelezi went to London to meet with the ANC and agreed to certain principles, the ANC didn't want the agreements published. But Buthelezi wouldn't agree to secrecy. A controversy erupted and other worldwide ANC leaders then disavowed the London meeting.

Buthelezi is for peaceful change, but the ANC says the time for talk has passed. Now it supports violence, with its baby, the UDF. The formation of the South African Communist Party disturbed the ANC's old, dignified way of doing things. The old ideology is losing out, bit by bit, due to Communist influence. There is no longer any resemblance to the old ANC. Now that it is banned, there is no proper way to run the organisation, and now the ANC and UDF have set about burning people and property and causing a general disruption in the country. Only a small percentage of blacks support these actions. The rest are intimidated, so you don't hear from them. The radical students say that no country won its freedom over a cup of tea, but Inkatha's reply is, "What do *you* have to offer? There is much to be gained through negotiations; don't destroy everything."

The young blacks are the most radical, and there is more violence in the cities than in the country. The homelands and the independent countries have far less crime. The ANC is trying to make inroads in the rural areas, but it is having very little success. The tribal chiefs are part of the Central

Committee of Inkatha, and they are more traditional. Black women tend to be more moderate than the men. The ANC is made up mostly of men. Inkatha represents *all* blacks, not just Zulus, as the ANC would have you believe. I am a Xhosa, and we have Swazis, coloureds, and Indians in the party, as well. The UDF says it will destroy participation in Inkatha by others. But even AZAPO, the radical students' organisation that was originally against us, is now conducting talks with us. Black radicals attack successful black businessmen because they see them as sellouts, but it is the successful black businessmen and women who will help move our people forward. The encouragement of black business is part of Inkatha's programme, which also includes politics, agriculture, economics, religion, and self-development. We especially encourage black women: They represent progress. We have set up co-operatives for bulk buying, sewing clubs, and shops. Black women are learning to help one another.

The press says PW Botha has no time for a proud black African, that he will never negotiate with Buthelezi. Both men are politicians; both are suspicious. For four years they didn't speak. But look how things have changed in this country in four years. Negotiations will come.

There is no need for all blacks to agree on Buthelezi. With federation, each group can choose its own leader. The idea is to not destroy any culture; simply treat them all equally. We are a country of minorities. But you should also know that Nelson Mandela sends Robben Island prisoners to see Buthelezi, when they are released. It is hard to know what Mandela thinks; so many other people speak for him. The ANC doesn't really want him out of jail – he wouldn't opt for violence. They would have to kill him.

Our reaction to Helen Suzman and to the whole delegation that met with the ANC, in Dakar, is this: We are not against anyone speaking with anyone else. Helen Suzman has always supported the blacks, so we don't distrust her now. The more discussions take place, the more progress will be made and the more we will understand each other. [Helen Suzman did not attend the Dakar meeting but has always advocated inviting all parties to the bargaining table.]

The independent countries are good and bad. Being anti-apartheid, we object in principle. [Independent countries represent "separate development" — the cornerstone of apartheid.] Buthelezi objects because those people are no longer considered South Africans. But this is a beginning for development; jackals and lions both exist in the jungle. We must use what we are given to develop ourselves, then advance. There was no excuse for "petty" apartheid, but that's no longer even an issue. One of the ironies is that by being persecuted we were forced to develop on our own. We couldn't try on clothes in white stores, so black stores opened. Our job now is to bring ourselves up to standard. We should learn from all this, not just fight. Ciskei and Transkei are perfect examples: Look how far Ciskei has come, while Transkei and its military government are still backward.

Inkatha has always demanded one man/one vote. But whites have many reasons to be afraid. Negotiations are the answer. Blacks cannot run this country on their own; we should have learnt that lesson from the tragedy in Mozambique, when the whites left. We are aware that the blacks cannot run things yet. Negotiation means each side gives up something. That is why we are pro-federation. We must be realistic; the blacks must work to remove fear as an issue and they must realise that they need the whites to stay.

Do I have hope for a solution in the near future? If they could accept the KwaZulu/Natal Indaba, it would be a model. It's already working. Now, if only we could get the government to approve it officially.

How do we react to the Indians and the coloureds? We think they are both sitting on the fence. There are still scars left from 1948-49, when the Indians and blacks were killing each other. But the Indians have made great gains economically. There are lots of Indians in the UDF, but you will see that, when it comes to boycotting business and the schools, it's only the blacks who participate. The Indians are too smart to keep their children out of school or to hurt their own businesses. We don't have any great problems with the Indians or the coloureds at this point, but we were disappointed that they joined in the tricameral legislature. Blacks are learning to support each other, as the Indians do. The coloureds are just recently developed, in spite of having owned their own homes. More blacks own cars than coloureds do.

South Africa: Land of Hope?

The Group Areas Act must go. Different cultures have different ways of living, but there should be no question of boundaries. If boundaries were eliminated there would be no great movement of people. "Grey" areas are at least a beginning, so we accept them. There are already many places in South Africa where people of all colours are living together and getting along. The government ignores those areas as long as no one complains, and no one has. That gives us hope for the future.

The trade unions served their purpose at first, but now they have become too political. They have forgotten what they were organised for. The ANC is penetrating every organisation in South Africa, including religious organisations like the South African Council of Churches. I'll tell you that the community members of those churches don't understand what the SACC is really doing. Who gave *them* the authority to approve sanctions and disinvestment? American blacks who supported Martin Luther King understand our position. Many business people have helped us, but the Tutu propaganda is too strong for us. People who come to South Africa see and understand that sanctions are bad.

Overpopulation is one of our greatest problems. Family planning has little effect on traditional blacks, but customs change as we urbanise. It is more difficult to convince the men than the women; the men see sex as their recreation. In the urban areas, the children sometimes don't even know who their fathers are. It is the women who must be strong, but that is not always easy—with our traditions.

We have some problems with Black Sash, the liberal English women's organisation. We're not against anyone who is trying to help, but they don't always realise that others are helping as well. There are many ways to deal with a problem. Once an organisation affiliates with the ANC and

South Africa: Land of Hope?

South Africa: Land of Hope?

South Africa: Land of Hope?

UDF—as Black Sash has—they are no longer our friend. They seem more interested in being *against* the government than *for* black upliftment.[1]

Blacks are not yet ready for compulsory education. It is more important to stress quality than quantity, right now, as education is not only in school. We don't object to the idea of separate-but-equal, if white teachers can come into the black schools to make them equal. And we are actually grateful for the State of Emergency: At least now our children can safely go back to school. We don't agree with the government's policies of apartheid, and we certainly seek change, but things were so bad with the violence in this country that we needed the control the State of Emergency has provided.

There is much goodwill in this country, and as the whites come to understand what life has been like for us, more and more of them are coming forward to help us. It is far easier for us to work with other South Africans than with people from overseas. South Africans understand each other—even if we are of different colour, culture, and experience. If apartheid were eradicated there would be nothing wrong with South Africa. The younger generations are becoming much more open with each other and they are getting along fine.

It is good for black students to go abroad to study, if they come back. Most of them do come back; America is good, but South Africa is home. Many of them do good things for our people when they return.

Welfare would be the worst thing for blacks. Charity sent to the SACC from abroad will ruin blacks; they will never learn a skill, will never get a job. Look what welfare did to the blacks in America.

---

1   Mary Burton, President of Black Sash, refused to allow her comments to be printed in this book. Her refusal was put into words almost identical to those used by Ismail Ayob—attorney to the Mandelas—in his denial of permission. Both had previously agreed to interviews and each had spent over two hours in conversation. I can only assume they both feared my book was to be strictly pro-government and—like the black students at the University of Stellenbosch—did not wish to be a party to it.

South Africa: Land of Hope?

Our top priority is to just sit down together to negotiate. The settlement may take ten years, but at least if we're sitting down together, that represents progress. PW Botha has taken a stand, but if he goes too far they will topple his government. The next person will have space that was prepared by Botha, so he must be recognised for his bravery. But Buthelezi is against any further discussions without negotiations.

My message to America is this: We know the United States is sending lots of help to South Africa. We appreciate the fact that in the midst of our problems there are people concerned about us. We must, however, persuade you that disinvestment is not good for us. It is the blacks who suffer. By the time the government suffers the blacks will be totally devastated. Money is channelled through the SACC, but that money doesn't go where it is supposed to: Bishop Tutu and Jesse Jackson are not helping us. And books like *Kaffir Boy* don't help either; they are so over-exaggerated. The changes in this country have been tremendous. There is better understanding among all groups. The youth wing of Inkatha has a good relationship even with Afrikaner students, so there is reason for hope. Help us to move forward; don't help to destroy us.

The KwaZulu/Natal Indaba is considered by many to represent the greatest hope for what South Africa could be. Others, more skeptical, say it works only in this area of South Africa, where there is already considerable interaction among races on an equal basis. It is certainly worth further study by the rest of the country — and the world.

Peter Badcock is Communications Director and Executive Committee member of the KwaZulu/Natal Indaba. He is a communications and marketing consultant and author of six best-selling books, including three on war in Southern Africa. A South African by birth, Mr Badcock lived in Rhodesia/Zimbabwe through its transition and served as an officer in the Rhodesian Security Forces.

Peter Badcock (white)

There is a new Great Divide in South Africa, this time between the pragmatic Moderates — including an element within the National Party — and the Right, including a conservative element in the National Party. Now the government has appointed a Delimination Commission, to redraw the voting boundaries and to correct parliamentary imbalances. The rural communities have held an artificially disproportionate sway since 1948, and with today's boundaries the Conservative Party could win. [More than one South African election — including the critical one of 1948 — has been decided not by popular vote but by the favorable weighting of the rural vote, according to David Harrison in *The White Tribe of Africa*.[1]] In the event of a Conservative government coming to power, reform would be still-born and civil war inevitable. We have a constant re-alignment process going on and now even the local elections are being politicised.

People inside South Africa are more confident of peace than those on the outside. This is so because evidence still exists of a majority desire to sit down and negotiate. However, international pressure on South Africa is actually pushing white South Africa to the right, thus reducing the prospects for a negotiated peace.

Indaba was the 1986 brainchild of the Natal Provincial Government and the KwaZulu homeland government. The two groups recognised and acknowledged their interdependence and the fact that their political boundaries were artificial and senseless. Among other examples of bureaucratic duplication, they have six separate educational systems and several different health systems. Invitations were sent out to all organisations in the two areas, which drew thirty-nine delegations. After eight months of polarisation they reached an accord.

The reaction from other South Africans was one of amazement. That representatives of all population groups could have come together and, in eight months, set a course for their mutual benefit seemed incredible. But these other South Africans didn't see Indaba as a formula for all South Africa, because the make-up of the other provinces — Cape, Transvaal, and

---

1   (London: British Broadcasting Corporation, 1981), p. 151.

the Orange Free State — is different. They did, however, accept that the central Indaba principles are applicable to a national solution — and that view is gaining even wider currency as time goes on.

The people of KwaZulu recognise the dangers of confrontation and know that the eventual winner of a bloody battle will inherit only ashes. They thus see compromise as the only solution and see that they must deal with the fear of black rule felt by whites, coloureds, and Indians. Minority rights, therefore, are an integral part of the Indaba principles.

The Indaba proposals are not for the removal of the area from South Africa but, rather, to establish a separate *regional* government, still subordinate to the South African government. KwaZulu as a homeland would cease to exist and the area would have a single legislature. A Bill of Rights also was drawn up [see Appendix IX], but neither this nor the Indaba proposals is yet being considered by the State Government, which must approve *both* before they may be implemented. There is no "home rule" in South Africa; provincial government is subservient to state [national] government. This means that, even if the majority of the people in Natal are in favor of this scheme, they cannot put it into action if the State Government is against it. At this point the State Government won't even allow a referendum on the issue among the people of Natal, but independent research has confirmed that the Indaba enjoys majority support in the region.

Indaba would demand the total abolishment of the Group Areas Act and all other apartheid laws. Its Bill of Rights forbids all discrimination. Naturally, the members of the Conservative Party in Natal are totally against the whole idea of the Indaba, but Natal is traditionally the most progressive province in South Africa. [Residents of the Cape may dispute this statement.]

What is the likelihood of Indaba being approved? The government seems to accept the spirit but they find certain of the particulars as yet unacceptable. There will most likely be some sort of negotiations.

What the people in Natal *do* have is a Joint Executive Authority, which implements the laws made by the State Government and debates areas of common concern. This is a non-legislative group organised by the State

Government — even though four years ago they said they would never allow it to happen. The JEA has an equal number of representatives from KwaZulu and Natal, so it is like a mini-Indaba. Eight of the ten members are non-white [5 blacks, 2 Indian, 1 coloured, 2 white] and it works just fine. This makes it the first Government-inaugurated body in the history of South Africa — with responsibility for a "mixed" region — to be dominated by non-whites.

South African big business enthusiastically supports the idea of Indaba. They want to use Natal to prove or disprove that power-sharing can work in South Africa. Its working would — in addition to impressing South Africans — also undo the logjam and convince the rest of the world.

South Africa needs the support of the rest of the world. We need full bellies and high employment. Indaba is an attempt to avoid confrontation and conflagration. I grew up in Rhodesia and I am trying to help avoid here what happened there. A victory by either the ANC or the CP would mean the same thing, and that's a situation too terrible to contemplate.

Khaba Mkhize (black)
The political position of my newspaper is progressive. We want to make people think, talk, and debate.

The majority of black people under age thirty would support the ANC. If you had a fair election between Buthelezi and Mandela, Mandela would win it. Buthelezi is supported in Natal, but not so much in the other provinces. [This opinion is challenged in polls conducted by the South African Institute of Race Relations.] Urban blacks are split between Buthelezi and the ANC. Among those who pay allegiance to the ANC are "the Comrades" — young, frustrated, radical gangsters. They intimidate their parents, saying to them, "We're trying to fix *our* future. You have failed; please don't stop us. We'd rather die than toe the line." Then, when Comrades boycott their jobs, they tell their parents, "If you don't want to put your life at stake, OK; but don't go to work." The trouble in Pietermaritzburg was caused by the ANC which, although it claims non-violence, employed the usual violent means in trying to force people to stay away from work.

101

South Africa: Land of Hope?

If blacks had equal opportunities, shelter, compulsory education, and medical facilities, then they wouldn't need the ANC. Education among blacks suffers in quality, but quality and quantity are both important. The whites must pay for black education. Is separate-but-equal acceptable? Mixing is not the issue; quality and standards are.

PW Botha's constitution and the ANC Freedom Charter are not so very different. I can understand the ANC's position on violence; they've been trying to just *talk* since 1912. The Boer War was also violent. Apartheid causes violence; it is an evil policy like Nazism. Violence sometimes works for the blacks: The schools that were burnt were replaced by better schools!

Still, there is lots of goodwill in this country, and change is possible without a bloody revolution. A psychological revolution has already started. The National Party today is like the old United Party used to be [more liberal], and the Conservative Party today is like the old National Party [more conservative].

Most blacks equate capitalism with apartheid because they think apartheid protects capital from flowing into black hands. We don't want a *multi*-racial society; that's one that sets given percentages for each population group. We want a *non*-racial society, one where race isn't even considered.

The Group Areas Act still exists but it's becoming a white elephant. It is self-defeating. There is a shortage of housing in this country, especially for blacks, which is forcing a situation where blacks are moving anywhere they can find shelter — as in the Hillbrow section of Johannesburg. White landlords are renting to blacks because they're the ones who need housing and they can afford to pay for it. Everyone gets along and no one complains or does anything to stop it.

The difference between South African blacks and American blacks, as I saw them when I was in America, is this: American blacks live in houses of brick and concrete, while some of *us* live in houses of mud and cardboard. But American blacks live without hope. In spite of everything you may hear, South African blacks live with great hope for and confidence in our future.

102

In all the research and reading I have done on South Africa, I have been struck by the fact that the Jewish population, in all statistical listings, is described as a group unto itself. Whites are categorized as Afrikaners, English, and Jews, in spite of the fact that the country's first Jews were from England. I arranged an interview with Professor Anthony Arkin, head of the Department of Economics of the University of Durban-Westville and Chairman of the Natal Zionist Council. Professor Arkin also contributed to the book, South African Jewry: A Contemporary Survey, edited by his father, Professor Marcus Arkin, of the same university.

Professor Anthony Arkin (white)

At 117,000 persons, Jews account for less than one percent of the total South African population and only two-and-a-half percent of the white population. The large majority of them — eighty percent — came from Lithuania, between 1870 and the 1920s.

The Lithuanians were not industrialised; they were traders, artisans, and scholars. This group would not have adapted to the American industrial society as easily as did the Jews from Poland and Germany. Zionism was strong in Lithuania in the 19th century, however, giving these new South Africans linkage with the world Jewish community — a community with which they felt more at home than in their adopted land where no one else spoke their language, though Yiddish had closer affinities to Afrikaans than to English.

In the 1930s, German Jewish refugees numbering between five and six thousand came to South Africa. These Germans, like the British Jews, more easily acculturated to South African society than had the Lithuanians before them. By the late 1930s, Jews had gone into manufacturing and retailing and had become quite visible in South African society. As in many other parts of the world, Jews entered the professions in numbers disproportionate to their total population.

Nazi-inspired anti-Semitism carried through the 1940s. British clubs also excluded Jews — even as they do today, though to a much lesser degree — so it's no wonder the Jews of South Africa bonded tightly. Politically, the Jews were originally supporters of the United Party – the party of [General Jan] Smuts, the ardent Zionist [and twice Prime Minister of South Africa]. The National Party was a party by and for Afrikaners, and Jews were not even allowed to join until the 1950s. The Jews were deeply concerned when the Nats came to power in 1948; however, as Israel gained its independence without huge waves of Jews arriving in South Africa, tensions eased and the Jews and Nats reached an accommodation. [According to the Arkin book, the creation of the State of Israel "evoked sympathy and respect in the Calvinist Afrikaner," who had always admired Jews as other "People of The Book."[1]]

South African Jews have always been staunch supporters of Israel. In 1948 the Israeli Defence Force had a substantial contingent of volunteer South African Jews, and some of Israel's largest financial donations, today, come from this country. Israel has always taken an anti-apartheid stand, so it was 1972 before South Africa and Israel exchanged ambassadors. Jews had been a thorn in the side of the Nats for some decades, but the Six Day War came and went, the face of Africa started changing, and South Africa recognised Israel as a potential ally. At that point, the Nats began attracting Jews to their party.

Relationships between the Jews and other population groups were marked more by distance than by clashes. The majority of Indians were in Durban, whilst the Jews were mostly in Johannesburg and Cape Town. Jews began funding welfare services for blacks and coloureds but contact remained minimal. In the early years Jews had their own schools, but later some of those were among the earliest multi-racial schools in the country.

Few Jews went into politics[2] or the Civil Service, the latter considered a giant "bootstrap" operation to elevate the Afrikaners. Instead, they stuck

---

1   Stephen Cohen, "Historical Background," and Jocelyn Hellig, "Religious Expression," *South African Jewry* (Cape Town: Oxford University Press, 1984), pp.10, 98.

2   Only one Jew has held Cabinet Rank in South Africa, but there have been several Jewish members of Parliament and, in the early 1980s, the mayors of South Africa's three largest cities were Jewish. (Harry Schwarz, "Political Attitudes and Interaction," Ibid., p. 139.)

to commerce, where thirty percent of them owned their own business, as opposed to seven percent of other population groups. There was far less assimilation of Jews into South African society than in America. Here there is very little intermarriage and the "melting pot" philosophy has never taken hold.

Though there is little overt anti-Semitism evident in South Africa today, I don't anticipate the Jews ever integrating into South African society to any greater extent than they have thus far. I think they're comfortable as they are.

* * *

JOHANNESBURG

The last group of interviews I present, here, took place in Johannesburg and are arranged in the order in which they were conducted. The list is varied and represents a broad range of concerns and viewpoints.

Anonymous Member of ACTSTOP (white)

ACTSTOP, an organisation established to help blacks who were being evicted from "white" areas, was formed in 1978 when a newspaper article pointed out integrated housing in Hillbrow, a section of Johannesburg. There was tremendous reaction against that integration, and people sought out and reported the "offenders." The police were forced to act [to evict the blacks].

An attorney agreed to take the black residents' cases *Pro Deo [pro bono]*, but the government would not co-operate or allow it. That forced a crisis. With the co-operation of the South African Institute of Race Relations, we obtained the court records — in order to find the people who were being accused, get them to court, and find them attorneys. The most famous case, the Gladys Gavender case, resulted in the government being told [by the judge] that it could not evict "illegal" tenants until it had found them alternative accommodation: The government could not just simply put people out on the street.

ACTSTOP was formed by a group of concerned men and women. It wasn't for pure ideology; it wasn't designed to *wreck* anything. It was simply designed to keep people from becoming homeless. Obviously we are against the Group Areas Act, which now might just disappear rather than be rescinded. But we were surprised to discover that people really preferred to live among their own. Most who lived in mixed areas did so because it was the only available housing.

The government thought the ANC and the Communists were behind the "mixing," that ACTSTOP was being used. But that is unlikely. There was long documentation of attempts by these people to find housing in their own areas. Most of them were gainfully employed in good jobs. Accusing ACTSTOP of being Communist-inspired frightens people away from us; it is an example of the power of government. It is also similar to the campaign they wage against the Progressive Federal Party.

But I am more optimistic for South Africa than ever before. More people want change, and more are prepared to help effect that change. The Conservative Party and sanctions both have been good as a shock to our system. I think they both have served to get us moving.

Visit to Soweto

Most of the world knows Soweto only as the scene of the bloody riots of 1976. It has become the symbol of South African black anger, unrest, and hostility. It is also assumed to be one giant slum on the outskirts of Johannesburg, where black South Africans lead lives of not-so-quiet desperation.

I spent several hours riding and walking around Soweto. As in any other city of two million people, there are are good areas and bad ones. (I confess I was taken aback, on seeing "Millionaires' Row" — with houses that might be seen in the better neighborhoods of any international city.) Again I was impressed, even in the poorest areas, by the lack of outward hostility. People smiled and waved and often wanted to get into the photos I was taking. Groups of school children ran over to talk to me; the contrast to American inner-cities is remarkable.

Shanties and squatter camps still exist in some areas, though it is interesting to note that many of them exist behind "regular" houses and serve as rental income for black "slum landlords." I found the black sections better kept than the coloured, though trash collection seems to be a problem in most areas. There is water and electricity — and no open sewage.

The greatest need is housing for sub-economic groups, houses that will sell for R10,000 ($5000). "Transit housing" — to get rid of the squatter camps — is currently being provided by the government, at a rent of R10 ($5) per week.

Soweto is divided into municipalities, each with its own Council. All nine black language groups are represented, intermingled except in the bachelor men's hostel — where the members of individual tribes apparently prefer to keep to themselves. The Oppenheimer Gardens Home for the Aged is open to all residents.

Over three hundred churches dot the landscape, as do a proliferation of schools, shops, supermarkets, bars, and restaurants. There is a large hospital complex, in addition to privately-run clinics, and the most modern eye hospital in Johannesburg is located here. There are five community swimming pools, clubhouses for Girl and Boy Scouts, a stadium, sportsgrounds, and an amphitheatre. Fourteen railway stations serve Soweto; I saw no graffiti.

I stopped in at the Funda Art and Culture Centre and spoke with Essy Letsoalo, the Director. The Funda Centre offers non-formal educational programs. Different themes — dealing with African life, history, and culture — are discussed on Saturday mornings throughout the year, with the aim of broadening black South Africans' knowledge. University graduates and professors attend these programs alongside high school students, with an average of sixty people attending each week. The Centre is funded by donations — mostly from the white community — and also features a reference library and research agency in addition to the Fine Arts Centre. In the Adult Education and Training Resource Centre, I visited a drawing class. Here students work for a year, then have their portfolios evaluated — prior to the Cultural Day Exhibit where the work may be sold.

Letsoalo is pleased by the attendance and by the progress being made at the Centre, but she finds it discouraging that the South African government still has not made the change to a completely free and open society. Though the majority of people are still keen on peaceful change, she says, she sees that hope disappearing.

The students, who receive assistance from white South Africans, are more optimistic: They see an increasing number of whites willing to get involved and are more confident that the government will be forced to make the necessary changes.

Otto Krause (white)
Political Journalist

There is a cultural rift in South Africa, making it imperative to read both the English and the Afrikaans newspapers — to get a balanced view. Most foreign journalists are English-speaking, so they are influenced by the anti-government English press. At least most of the embassies now finally subscribe to translation services, so they can read the Afrikaans press as well. The English-language press in South Africa is anti-government, but they don't bring in the vote. The government says to them, "You have the circulation, but *we* have the vote." Our press in this country is immensely partisan. People buy the newspaper whose views suit them, and there are dozens from which to choose.

The South African Broadcasting Corporation is a State corporation with a board appointed by the government, exactly like the BBC. But the BBC is anti-government. The English press is more powerful than the South African press.

English vs Afrikaans is not always a question of Liberal vs Conservative. Group interest always comes first, then the breakdown into political philosophy. The less apartheid is in effect, the more "group conscious" people become. Black Nationalists are liberal but White Nationalists are conservative. In the United States you have an assimilating society; everyone speaks English. The British tried that in South Africa but it didn't work. Nor do we have a common culture, as you do. In the United States you all even eat the same food. English in South Africa is the *lingua franca*, but still it is the second language of most who speak it. Afrikaans is seen as the language of the lower classes.

Nationalism in Europe, since the French Revolution, has meant that those with the same culture formed their own nation. The map of Europe was redrawn at Versailles. The National Party, here, wants a Europe-style South Africa, with each culture controlling its own area. The Progressive Party wants something closer to America, with total assimilation. But neither will work in this country.

A Bill of Rights makes no sense in a Third World country. The right to vote must be part of those rights, but first you must have stability and discipline. Britain was a Third World country and came out into the First World with a "qualified" vote. The danger of federation is that we might turn out like Argentina, with a bankrupt state. Taiwan and South Korea are only limited democracies and serve as good examples of what we might try. In Japan only one percent of the people voted, originally. They all started with dictatorships. We must first work to foster economic growth. As we get richer we will more easily talk to each other. As the blacks get richer, the blacks get "whiter."

English South Africans have the values of the British Empire and Western values of leadership. Afrikaners are more committed to South Africa. The English, here, are protected by the Afrikaners' commitment. English South Africans are really quite conservative; they are some of the richest people in the world. They talk liberal; some of them even vote liberal, knowing the liberals won't win. The English still dream of Empire. The upper class controls the press and talks liberalism, but underneath they're saying, "We vote PFP, but thank God the Nats will win."

In the panic of the mid-80s many English-speaking South Africans emigrated, out of fright. As a result, there is less and less of the English creative input into all areas of South African life. There is a lack of commitment among the upper classes, now. [At the same time, the upper middle class English remain fiercely anti-government.] Black Sash says the English should boycott Afrikaner products; they are still basically anti-Afrikaner.

"Separate Development" wasn't working, so the [Afrikaner] government decided to try the tricameral legislature: Get the love of the coloureds a n d Indians, to ensure that those two groups don't side with the [Opposition party] English. That's alliance politics. But the government made a mistake. They set up the tricameral without making a deal with the blacks. The tricameral elections allowed the [ANC-affiliated] UDF to operate fully, to intimidate people and to create unrest. The government didn't expand the police force enough, so we couldn't protect the people during those elections. We have fewer policemen, nationwide, than you have on the force of the City of New York.

Then the government started playing up to the West and allowed worldwide television free run. That shows our post-colonial hang-up, our inferiority complex: We thought the Great White West would protect us, but it didn't. Now we have a love-hate relationship with the West. We made a mistake trying to play up to them. The West will sink us before Russia does. The United States has destabilised us.

Economics will change everything, even the Group Areas Act — just like the American South. The industrialisation of South Africa changed the circumstances for everyone. Now there can be jobs for all. Apartheid was designed for an agricultural society; it is no longer relevant. We may have to make a grand public statement to the world announcing the end of apartheid, but even that might not be enough. You keep shifting the goalposts. As [Boer leader] Paul Kruger said to Lord Milner [in the days leading up to the Anglo-Boer War], "What you want is not reform, it is my country." [1] Foreign diplomats rail against South Africa and her policies, but they have great staffs and live like kings. Many of them even remain here to retire. They love the life.

The blacks will get the vote. We must lead them into a better future. It's in our own self interest: The South African blacks are our allies against the rest of black Africa. We must curtail black nationalism until we can live together in civilised peace. We will uplift the blacks here sooner and better than you will in the United States — because it's in our self interest, and it isn't in yours.

There is a big difference between South African blacks and American blacks. Yours could learn from ours. American blacks who come here are amazed and impressed by what ours are accomplishing.

Labour unions are an unnecessary evil. Developing countries don't need unions. Developed countries are better off with the Japanese system, where they have company unions. Company unions are by definition multi-racial. Why take the inferior model from the West? South African labour unions have devastated productivity: Wages are up 130% over ten years ago, but productivity has increased Nil. Our government's trying to copy the West will be our downfall. The Japanese understand reality; they work together. And they know that the enemy is not your boss, it's the competition.

Our great racist sin is copying white countries that are totally out of kilter with our stage of development. The rich Western societies of the world are simply not like South Africa. It's not just the *world* seeing us as European rather than African; we foster this as well, by copying the United States.

---

1   The story of Afrikaner fear and British frustration is compellingly told
     by Robert Crisp, in *The Outlanders: The Men Who Made Johannesburg*
     (London: Peter Davies, 1964) and in the Stuart Cloete biography of
     Paul Kruger to which I referred in the Introduction.

Johan Liebenberg (white)
Labour Negotiator

Labour unions in South Africa are divided politically. We have no equivalent of your AFL-CIO. Each of our unions is supported by a different political party, from the far left to the far right. And they don't talk to each other. There is fighting at the shop floor level, not just for membership but physical violence because of differing politics. Black-on-black violence is due to radicals attacking moderates and vice-versa. There are no innocents.

The black union movement from 1979 through 1981 brought South African labour legislation into the twentieth century, dictating non-discrimination and dealing with unfair trade practices. But there was no parallel in constitutional reform. This meant that black workers had no channel for expressing their political aspirations, so they use the trade unions and the churches for their platforms. We keep urging the government to open channels for expression and negotiation. The government complains that the unions are too political, but the unions have no other choice. It appears that PW Botha wants to institute reform, but he must move cautiously, as he also wants to remain in power.

There are three political alternatives for South Africa: one man/one vote, which might be a once-only event; keep the *status quo* and make gradual reforms; or go back to the days of strict apartheid, with the Conservative Party. One of our problems is that we have no moderates who offer real, concrete alternatives to the Nationalists. No one has stepped forward with a clear-cut programme. It's not enough to preach tearing down; you must have a programme for rebuilding.

One man/one vote or a black government would be OK if the system is democratic – as understood not in Africa but in the United States and Europe. And we must have an economy based on free enterprise, not socialism. The percentage of black radicals is low. There is basic goodwill in this country and amazingly little antagonism. The capitalists have unwittingly created a link between capitalism and apartheid.

We can't use Japan or the Japanese unions as a model, because we don't have the Japanese culture. Our business heritage is British.

South Africa: Land of Hope?

Unfortunately, the British unions also are our model. My preference would be for multi-racial unions; some already exist. There is no more "job reservation," of course, but we are finding that blacks don't want blue collar jobs even at a higher rate of pay. We must work for a meritocracy, not Affirmative Action.

We must also increase productivity in order to foster black advancement. Twenty percent of the miners now produce eighty percent of the product. We have thousands of blacks who could handle these jobs, but the Mine Workers Union [ultra-right wing] is all white. We are going to have to force this issue, which may cause a walk-out. But we will make them go to arbitration. There are six hundred vacancies for qualified miners and more than that number of qualified blacks. The MWU will fight this tooth and nail but we will break them eventually. It may take several months.

Most of the old tribal clashes have disappeared among the workers with whom I deal. The only exception is between the Xhosas of the ANC and the Zulus who support Buthelezi. But if black trade unions are the most democratically-elected bodies in black countries today, and if their concept of democracy is this violence, intimidation, murder, and intolerance of dissent which we have seen, then I can't blame the whites for their unwillingness to relinquish power. The black trade unions in South Africa are making a mistake: They could construct a model and say to the whites, "Don't be scared; our model of democracy is the same as yours." But when we have eighteen deaths in three weeks, blacks fighting other blacks, the whites say, "If that's democracy à la black Africa, let's rather not have democracy."

Black South Africans aren't really Communists in the Marxist-Leninist sense. That brand of Communism hasn't worked anywhere – in or out of Africa. Socialism could work, because that's what the tribal system is: The tribe owns everything, the individual owns nothing, and the chief distributes the wealth. Where whites can have most influence is in the "informal" sector, because South African blacks are the entrepreneurs of Africa. Given the chance – and some outside assistance – we can all prosper.

Five Freedoms Forum

"101 Ways to End Apartheid"

*During my stay in Johannesburg, an item caught my eye in the **Johannesburg Star**, announcing an open-to-the-public meeting of the Five Freedoms Forum. The topic was "101 Ways to End Apartheid." I made it a point to attend.*

*According to an article written for **The Star** by Forum Vice-chairman Barbara Buntman, the Five Freedoms Forum began in March of 1987, with the idea of developing a unified response against government apartheid action. An important part of its aims, however, was that this response was to be **anti-apartheid** in nature, not **anti-South African**. As Buntman points out, this is a distinction that is not often drawn. The FFF manifesto expresses the commitment to restore to all South Africans the following basic freedoms: freedom from want; freedom from fear; freedom from exploitation and discrimination; freedom of conscience; and freedom of speech and association. The Forum believes that educating white South Africans about the lack of these basic freedoms is an important task, and it is committed to addressing the issues of human rights and to raising the level of political awareness among fellow South Africans. People first need to know and understand what is happening around them before they can be expected to take part in doing something about it. As was pointed out to me time after time, the majority of white South Africans have heretofore lived in a state of ignorance, regarding their non-white fellow citizens. It is the recognition of this fact that has allowed so many of the non-whites to adopt an understanding and accepting attitude towards their situation. They feel that as whites become more aware, they set about changing things for the better.*

The groups and individuals making up the Five Freedoms Forum have one thing in common: They are all working within the white community to bring about an open and apartheid-free society. The Forum also enjoys the respect of and is supported by a wide cross-section of the black community. This campaign — "101 Ways to End Apartheid" — aims to create an awareness among whites that it is possible to oppose apartheid without breaking the law, even within the constraints of the present climate.

Several hundred people attended this meeting, from all the population groups. In fact, there was Standing Room Only. Forum representatives announced an essay competition for high school students; a non-racial sports day; a column

South Africa: Land of Hope?

in *The Star* called *"Star Bridge,"* asking for ideas for breaking down racial barriers; plans for a group going out to one of the squatter camps for a community clean-up and to break down racial barriers; a social history tour to Soweto; and an "open day" for all organizations to meet and share information and to let others know how they can become involved.

First to speak was Dr Beyers Naudé, an anti-apartheid activist who has been ostracized by his fellow Afrikaners for his support of the blacks. "Whites must assist other whites to understand the social revolution that is creating a new society," he explained. "We need a substantial number of whites to help other whites overcome their fears. We need to enter a new relationship of equal partnership and equal responsibilities. Equal rights must be accompanied by equal responsibility. It may take ten or fifteen years to achieve, but we must lay the foundations now for a new relationship. What hope is there that we can succeed? The challenge is difficult. But we must each make some commitment, however small. It is not a question of major movement or change in our national government; change will happen by every seemingly small contribution each of us makes. The small contributions are what will bring about change, and in the long run, that is most vitally important."

Following Dr Naudé, all who wanted to offer suggestions on how to end apartheid were invited to step forward and speak. Those who did so were white and non-white, young and not-young. Here are some samples of what was offered:

- "Get involved with the decision-making councils in your children's schools and your university *alma mater*."

- "Once a week read a black-oriented newspaper; understand what blacks are experiencing."

- "Work from the ground level with blacks, not from a white ideological level. Show the blacks that they *can* work with whites."

- "Teach every white child a song in a black language."

- "Make three friends across racial lines."

- "Each time you take your own child somewhere, take another child from a different population group."

- "Stop using the terms 'black South African' and 'white South African'; just say 'South African.' "

- "*Think* post-apartheid and *act* post-apartheid."

- "Make a contribution to an institution that offers an alternative to the black education provided by the government."

As I left the Five Freedoms Forum meeting, a black woman handed me a flyer with the heading, "A Hundred Good Reasons Why South Africa is a Great Country." At the bottom of the list, in large letters, is the statement, "South Africa is the freest, most prosperous, most democratic country on the African continent" and notice that the flyer was "issued by Women for South Africa, a multi-cultural movement, proud of the achievements of our people and our country."

Some of the hundred reasons:

- "There are more cars in Soweto than in the Soviet Union."

- "South Africa has more black professional women than the rest of Africa put together."

- "South Africa's judiciary is totally independent and stands in high regard even among South Africa's critics."

- "South Africa offers the most comprehensive health services on the African continent."

- "The press in South Africa is generally rated as the freest in Africa."

- "In the fourteen years from 1969 to 1983 the number of black women in professions almost trebled."

- "Black female medical and dental practitioners, during those same years, increased by 550 percent."

- "Black female university and college professors increased from 20 to 751."

South Africa: Land of Hope?

- "The Gross National Product in ten homelands is higher than in 33 African countries."

- "In Soweto, house rentals average less than twelve percent of income, where the world average is twenty-five percent and Third World rentals go as high as forty percent."

- "More is spent on education, by South Africa, than on defence."

- "Seventy-two percent of the economically active blacks in South Africa are in wage-earning employment, compared with between five and twenty-five percent in other African countries."

- "Five-hundred-thousand blacks attempt immigration to South Africa annually — and many others enter illegally."

- "South Africa plans to spend one billion rand [five hundred million dollars] during the next five years to improve underdeveloped towns and cities."

- "South Africa has 18 universities, compared with three in Zaire and one each in Angola, Botswana, Tanzania, Zimbabwe, and Zambia."

- "There are 380 schools in Soweto."

- "All discriminatory restrictions in sport have been removed."

- "Wages of blacks in South Africa are three-to-four times higher than those in the rest of Africa."

- "Black South African workers have virtually the same rights as labourers in America."

- "Some 100 discriminatory laws were abolished in recent years."

- "More than 700 newspapers, periodicals and journals are published regularly, more than in the rest of Africa combined."

- "In 1984 and 1985 the State spent R1.14 billion [$570 million] on housing for all population groups."

- "All South Africans are free to join political organisations which do not espouse violence."

- "Leaders of all black communities have been invited to join the Government in a national body to negotiate democratic power-sharing at the highest level."

- "The National Council is designed to give blacks an immediate say in Central Government decisions."

AZAPO, the Azanian Peoples Organization, is considered by many blacks and whites to be the "left lunatic fringe". Its motto is "Black Solidarity for a Socialist Azania." Azania is the chosen name for the new country. As one black woman objected, the name means "Land of Slaves." I met two of AZAPO's top officials in their modest office in downtown Johannesburg.

Nkosi Molala and Lybon Mabasa (black)

We wish to continue the tradition of Black Consciousness but we play according to the rules, because we do not want to be banned. However opposed we might be to the laws of this country, it is important to engage in *overt* political pressure. Otherwise we leave our people to the designs of the advocates of oppression. Our job is to organise black youth into a very clear political structure. What distinguishes AZAPO from other Black Consciousness movements is that we articulate an alternative system structure. The only way people can benefit from any takeover of any nature lies in the social formation implemented. The only credible social formation would have to be socialist.

Three centuries of apartheid has caused irreparable damage to our people. The elimination of apartheid doesn't repair the system because blacks have never had a stake in the country. We believe we need to intervene at the economic level for freedom and liberation to be experienced. Look at the structure of South Africa: The traditional areas inhabited by blacks have deliberately been those the whites would not have chosen. The homeland system is an effort on the part of the white regime to retain power and privilege. The independent states can never be truly independent; their economies are inexorably intertwined with the South African economy.

South Africa: Land of Hope?

There is no socialist economic model on which we would base our new economy; we must develop our own. We have steered away from the question of models because each country has its own peculiarities. South Africa is different from all other countries. In our South Africa every individual would be gauged, in terms of his wealth, as to what he can contribute and what he is capable of doing. The measure of production will be based on socialism, not nationalism. Russia has "nationalised state socialism." We are interested in running the big financial concerns solely for the people, not to line executive pockets. The West's economists are opposed, but we would like everyone to have the opportunity to work. The West says you have to budget for a certain rate of unemployment; we don't accept this as necessary. The essential means of production will be provided by the government, but we will allow some private initiative and business. Big business would have to be run by the government. We do not equate socialism with Communism. South African blacks have great quarrels with the Communists. Tutu condemns Communism but he attacks capitalism; he talks out of both sides of his mouth, as all Church men do.

If I took over tomorrow, I would build walls around our borders to keep the whites from leaving: Look what happened in Mozambique. The whites have a role to play in our new country. They have expertise due to their position of privilege, and now they have the responsibility to plow it back into the development process. We have no intention whatsoever of throwing the whites into the sea. We want to restore the "human beingness" of blacks and whites as well. We see them not as whites but as fellow citizens. We are trying to destroy the idea that blacks, whites, coloureds, and Indians are different. We are all members of the human race.

We believe in non-violence. In spite of the laws, we plan to carry on and exert the necessary pressure on the government to change. We are not allied with the ANC. The liberation movement has many components, of which we are one. We understand why our brothers and sisters have opted for a military solution; apartheid is also a form of violence. But we want to provide a meaningful alternative to the system without violence. Nor do we agree with the Freedom Charter, the ANC blueprint for the future. The Freedom Charter entrenches ethnicity and the protection of the culture of all national groups and races. We believe tribal differences are

120

artificial: We believe the blacks have more commonness than differences. Language is the only difference. If socialism triumphed in Africa all the borders would fall. We believe that emphasising differences plays into the strategies of the white regime.

We see Buthelezi and Mandela as allied. Buthelezi wants to fight from within. We recognise Mandela as a leader in the liberation movement, but he is not the only one. He is a representative of his historical epoch. We are against the idea of the KwaZulu/Natal Indaba because we are against regional solutions. We are for one man/one vote because we think we are more ready for it than any other Africans.

Our opinion is that Americans are good but their government is bad. We were the first to call for sanctions, because we would rather suffer harm now than harm forever. But your sanctions are not working.

Michael Spicer (white)
Anglo American Corporation (One of South Africa's oldest and largest conglomerates)

We have a vested interest in a modern, industrial economy which we see as to everyone's benefit. But the black entrepreneurial class is seen by the radicals of the ANC as diffusing the liberation struggle.

The influence of the business community on government has always been limited: Government and business, in South Africa, are long-time antagonists. Harry Oppenheimer [early Chairman and long-standing Director of Anglo American], whose companies have been responsible for more of this country's wealth than any other, never sat down with a prime minister of South Africa until 1981. Within the National Party, only five of 120 Members of Parliament have any business experience. Afrikaner entry into business is not reflected politically. Those businessmen are regarded with suspicion by their fellow Afrikaners. The world views of politicians and businessmen are totally different: International opinion is important to business, whilst the National Party currently discounts world opinion as coming from "mischief makers". The government is controlled to a large extent by an influential military with no understanding of business — and our military expenditure is now twenty-five percent of our Gross Domestic Product.

South Africa: Land of Hope?

Americans have a quick-fix mentality, but quick-fix solutions are impossible for South Africa. The long-term good of the American presence in this country has been undone by your leaving. Workers' rights needed long years of attention, and now that is lost. American actions on sanctions and disinvestment are short-sighted, counterproductive, and self-serving. Your own domestic politics are really the issue. Since your companies left, we at Anglo American have been swamped with requests and we are trying to take up the slack. Our company and its directors have always had a firm sense of social responsibility: We put R60 million [$30 million] per year into education, new training facilities, and community projects.

Anglo American actually facilitated the forming of unions, but when wages go up with no tie to productivity it does nothing more than satisfy an abstract idea of a fair wage. With the rise in the price of gold, black wages jumped to such an extent that extraction costs are now higher than in Australia or Canada. Things have been demanded of the South African gold industry that are not demanded anywhere else in the world. You are requiring that we make reparations for the past and grant retribution. Luxury housing is just one example. The creation of jobs will not be so great in the future, with new technology and the increased cost of labour benefits. The world assumes that South Africa is a wealthy country, that its wealth is unlimited and can be turned on like electricity. But that is both naive and incorrect. We are not a rich country; we're a Grade B, by World Bank standards: We suffer high development costs. Equality is necessary, but it must be accomplished with reasonable cost or we can't make it. We must increase the creation of wealth so that everyone can benefit. That is why sanctions are counter-productive. You should be helping our economy to *grow*. Zimbabwe is still feeling the effects of war and sanctions. There are fewer people working in their formal economy now than when the country gained independence, yet during this time their population has doubled. South Africa faces a looming crisis of unemployment, with 100,000 + people coming out each year for five thousand jobs. We also have a discrepancy between our population increases and our food production rate, with forty-six percent of our population under the age of sixteen and an economic growth rate of only 2.8% per year. Industrial modernisation is the best form of birth control.

We are attempting to study how societies modernise, to look at a South Africa beyond apartheid. But there is no model on which to base a future for South Africa, politically. We pay lip service to privatisation, but in truth both the Nats and the ANC want State Government control. Business faces intimidation by both blacks and whites; we dance a complicated minuet with the government.

Illiteracy is a major problem in bringing along black managers and the reason for our high expenditure on training and education — R150-200 million [$75-100 million] per year.

I am not more optimistic now than I was two years ago because of the rise of the extreme right wing. That should serve as an impetus for the Nats to broaden their base of support, but will they understand? I believe PW Botha is saying goodbye to the right and is seeking new alliances, but he may pay the price for his courage. It is true that negotiations have not progressed because both sides [the Nats and the ANC] still think they can have it all.

Anglo American is a major property owner in the "grey" areas, through intermediaries. Three years ago, we announced we would rent directly to anyone who choses to live in these areas and we were threatened by the government, but so far they have not acted against us. We have lobbied extensively for open housing and our black managers live in white areas. All our new properties are being marketed as "mixed" areas, and now other companies are following our lead. With the exit of the Americans and the end of Sullivan the "mixed" residential areas that had been established by the American companies went by the board, so it has been a slow process. But we accept the premise of incremental progress. It should be a lesson for the United States that sudden change is unacceptable to all sides, in South Africa.

Mondli Kunene (black)
South African Institute of Race Relations

Our job is to bring about racial harmony, understanding, and conciliation. The races in South Africa have been kept apart by legislation. There is no way we can have peace if people don't know each other. The blacks have new aspirations and they don't trust the whites. The whites, on the other hand, fear the blacks. We must build a bridge between the two. The Institute holds grassroots meetings where all groups of people attend and meet each other.

There have been great changes in this country in the past few years — and much improvement due to reforms. They are not all readily visible because the silent majority is reluctant to stand on a platform: The current political climate is still too hostile, and they risk attack by both the Left and the Right. But we are convinced there is more big change coming; we are quite optimistic. Afrikaner students want to move forward, and if all groups could vote the majority of blacks and coloureds would vote for the National Party.

What we need in this country is a statesman who will think about the next *generation*, not the next election. Even the majority of whites want reform. A Five-Year Plan would be acceptable, as long as there is commitment.

The Group Areas Act and all forms of race classification must go. It is impossible for the government to bring about change overnight because that would result in chaos, but honest intentions are a step in the right direction. The people are impatient because it has been so long — too long — but they are willing for it to be a gradual process. We would like to see the government declare a number of "open" areas and allow developers to build non-racial housing as an experiment. That would answer white fears. Schools in those areas could also be "open" and the government would thus demonstrate its diminishing intransigence.

What is our relationship with the radical black groups? We accommodate each other. They need our research findings. I think they, too, would accept a five-year plan. But imprisoned leaders must be released and the State of Emergency must be lifted. We disagree with the ANC on two counts: first, of course, the violence; second, the total handing over of power. We believe the latter to be short-sighted and narrow-minded. The whites have nowhere else to go and — whatsmore — we need them to help run the country. Any new system must accommodate both blacks and whites. It's a pity that the ANC is banned, because whites no longer have access to their current platform. The ANC admits that it made mistakes before and is prepared to make changes. But they are reluctant to make promises and adjustments until they know what lies ahead. It would be beneficial to all if the ANC ideas could be openly debated. Then fears could be allayed. The government still uses violence, so the ANC cannot be expected to renounce violence unilaterally: They see violence as the only thing that will bring the whites to the bargaining table. In Zimbabwe there were no pre-conditions, yet the talks went on. During the course of negotiations the stopping of violence may become a point of agreement, but the talks must begin first. Perhaps there could even be a temporary truce, during negotiations. On the other hand, Nelson Mandela would lose his credibility with the ANC if he renounced violence before being released.

The longer we delay the more the black position hardens. Most Afrikaners see change as inevitable. The most effective way to fight Communism is to bring blacks into a growing economy. That way, they have a stake in the capitalist system. As blacks prosper they will reject Communism; they will refuse the nationalisation of their businesses. The Black Management Forum, run by blacks for blacks, is one of our great success stories. Our Black Chamber of Commerce has thousands of members who are pro-capitalism and pro-free enterprise whilst being anti-apartheid.

We see attitudes changing and perceptions as well. Black children go to spend the weekend with their white school friends, then the parents meet, and pretty soon another bridge has been crossed. We're getting there.

Dr Ntatho Motlana is, by profession, a medical doctor. As one of the leaders of the 1976 Soweto uprisings and the Chairman of the Soweto Committee of Ten, he now travels the world as one of South Africa's "resident experts" and was part of the mixed group of South Africans who went to West Germany in late 1988, to meet with representatives of the ANC and the Soviet Union.

We met in Johannesburg, following his office hours.

125

South Africa: Land of Hope?

Dr Ntatho Motlana (black)

It is hard for me to be optimistic because of a conversation I had in 1986 with the late Dr Connie Mulder of the Conservative Party [father of Cornie Mulder, interviewed in Cape Town as a representative of the CP]. He told me at that time that in 1987 the CP would overtake the Progressive Federal Party and become the official Opposition, and that the CP will become the ruling party in 1992. The first part of his prediction came true; I fear for the second part. Every South African government that has ever lost power has lost it to the right, never to the middle or the left. We hear about all the people who want change in this country, but the Afrikaner farmer doesn't attend those meetings; he just votes. And he doesn't vote for change. The CP is appealing to the basest of human emotions.

Where [Jan] Smuts encouraged the immigration of liberal white English-speakers, the Nats — when they came to power in 1948 — cut that off. As skilled workers were needed, the Nats invited selected immigration from among the right-wing workers of Europe. When I read Letters to the Editor in the Afrikaans press, written by some of those immigrants, I have nightmares. I don't believe PW Botha has the courage, the will, or the desire to move more to the middle. He is not a reformer; he is a pragmatist, an Afrikaner rationalist through-and-through.

But even as I say this I realise that the blacks in South Africa live with great hope. They realise that the current political arrangement cannot last forever, and it can only change for the better — though it may appear to be worse for a while, when change first takes place and there is a non-racial government. Blacks know that the majority of the people in this country want change. They're just not sure everyone wants the *same* change. I'm not at all sure that peaceful change is possible, but it will be possible if white South Africans can be made to appreciate the horrors of the alternative.

The ANC has said the violence will stop when negotiations begin. I don't believe the ANC is controlled by Russia. South Africa's struggle is a national struggle, not a class struggle. The ANC are nationalists; they will use Russian support for their own purposes. Most black South Africans couldn't accept Marxism; they're too religious, and they are not sufficiently sophisticated to understand Marxism. And black capitalists would never accept the nationalisation of business. There are radical Marxists in the ANC, but that's because only Russia would give them an education.

Although most blacks in South Africa support the ANC's *goals*, only a small percentage of them support its violent methods. To call a black a "moderate" is to insult him, according to the ANC. But both radicals and moderates seek the same thing — a universal franchise. Only a psychotic would choose violence, if there were an option.

I was originally totally against the concept of the independent countries and the homelands, but we must admit that it has spread the wealth. There can be no compromise on the question of one man/one vote; we will offer protection of people and rights [as opposed to the protection of minorities]. We may be willing to compromise on the idea of a unitary state; Lesotho, Swaziland, Botswana, and Namibia may want to re-join if we set up a federation. We would have a high degree of autonomy and states would be based on common interests and language. But the question is, is there enough of a thread on which to build trust? There is actually boundless goodwill in this country. The black South Africans are basically sweet, wonderful people, which is the reason it has taken us so long to seek real change. South African blacks are not anti-white; that's why "Spear of the Nation" [the radical militant wing of the ANC, known by its African name, *Umkhonto we Sizwe*] isn't as strong as it could be. That bodes well for a peaceful, reasonable future — if it happens soon.

Blacks' burning of their schools is a horror. It is important that we teach our children to aspire to *trades*, as in Israel. When I ask children what they want to be they all say they want to be doctors, but I tell them that I pay the plumber more than my patients pay me! We have a proud tradition as tradesmen; we are great businessmen. Foreign influence has been good for the conscience of South Africa, but sanctions have hit and hurt the blacks. In many cases Afrikaners took over the businesses left by Americans and then sacked the black managers. I wish the Americans would pour money into this country for housing and education. But I am wary of a Marshall Plan: If you are not specific I fear the Afrikaners will find a way to take advantage of it.

We should encourage joint ventures between blacks and whites, so there will be a sharing of knowledge. The young black activists think I am selling out to capitalism, but I always try to tell them that power is two-sided – economic and political – and we must have both. We must continue to encourage those who work with their hands and those who can run their own business. The Small Business Development Corporation plans came from our own "Get Ahead" program. We're delighted to see it working.

There is no way you can convince the poor to stop having babies until their economic standards have been raised. Amongst the more affluent urban blacks the birth rate is dropping. We are in great need of leadership training for our women. The United States could perform a great service by helping us in that area. There is much you can do that would be productive: That is where you should be focusing your efforts.

Dr Louise Tager (white)
Dean of Law, University of the Witwatersrand (Wits)

For the past two years I have been on sabbatical, working on de-regulation legislation for a new constitution. This is socio-economic legislation, not political legislation. We are interested in guaranteeing all South Africans opportunities for economic development. The deregulation of the black community is linked to all of South Africa's racial legislation: The government is in the process of dismantling separate laws and institutions for blacks. We are trying to establish *equivalence*, not equality. Equivalence means equal opportunity.

Most press reports about South Africa that appear in the United States have nothing to do with reality. Sanctions have done nothing positive; they will only achieve the total destruction of South Africa, while lessening the positive influence your country had here for so many years. Unfortunately, the disinvestment groups are too well organised – with the result that those who support positive change in South Africa cannot even get a hearing in America.

In the encouraging of black business, more is being done in this country than is done in the United States. Welfare has been the ruination of the blacks in America. In South Africa, not having welfare forces everyone to do something. We have over 900,000 "hawkers" who are mini-entrepreneurs. The blacks are less interested in the vote than they are in being able to make a good living. They say, "We don't want handouts; just stop harassing us." Democracy is not necessarily one man/one vote. Representation is what is important. There is much greater goodwill in our country, between blacks and whites, than in America. We don't have thirty million seething blacks, here. [Tager has spent considerable time in the United States.]

The old liberals have always been anti-government and pessimistic. But a new group of humanitarians has surfaced in South Africa and human rights are being restored.

I believe the Nats are serious about negotiating with the blacks. They have now accepted the black leaders and the dignity of man. But there is an impasse, as each side remains firm. The government won't say what its plan will be, and the blacks won't come forward until the political prisoners are released and certain commitments are made. But the past is no longer prologue in South Africa. The Nationalist Party is not the same as it was twenty years ago. Who ever believed the South African government would hold talks with Cuba? South Africa is not the same place it was three, even two, years ago. *I'm* not the same person I was two years ago. Every month there are new changes, new businesses and new progress. Come back in another year, and you will be amazed. There has also been a great change in the black position in the past few years: In 1985 they said a bloody revolution was imminent; today they say, "We can wait ten or twenty years, if negotiations are taking place."

A coalition government is not unthinkable, if the CP gains a majority. The strength of the CP is not based on arrogance or contempt for the United States; it is based on economic and social fear. There never has been a sufficient mixing of people on similar levels in this country, because of our laws. Now we are learning that people of different colours can have much in common. The white-black relationship here always has been one of master-slave. Therefore, labourers, mineworkers, and household help were seen as inferior, uneducated, rural, and lacking in hygiene. Now there are opportunities for equality and a chance for blacks to elevate themselves. As the process happens, equality accompanies it, and power-sharing becomes more palatable, reasonable, and likely. It's easier to relate to and have serious discussions with someone you think is your equal and who has similar education and understandings. That's why time is necessary—we must develop this new relationship.

The only way to overcome the population explosion is to uplift the blacks economically. In the 1970s there was a concerted effort among blacks to increase the population if they couldn't gain politically; they said they would "breed out" the whites. If they continue at their present rate, there will be eighty million blacks in South Africa by the year 2000.

The ANC is made up of militant Communists, but I want to see them unbanned: It is a political party. Blacks have no other political channel, so they use the trade unions. But don't forget Inkatha. There is great support for Buthelezi's Inkatha among blacks, even though the ANC gets the headlines. Because of radicals' intimidation schemes the moderates are afraid to come forward, but they are there in great numbers. Our trade union movement has become totally politicised. We did in two years what the United States and Great Britain took fifty years to do, but a Marxist orientation is not good for a free-market system. Even Costa Rica and Guatemala are going the Japanese route.

I cannot understand the reasoning of those who are leaving the country. What future do they have elsewhere? This is an exciting time to be part of South Africa; one *can* make a difference. I am often asked, "But what about the CP?" I believe the wave will overtake the CP and they'll be left standing still. As long as laws permit development, there will be development. My own son has a business in Soweto, with a black partner: He came back from abroad to be a part of the new South Africa. He and his partner represent the future of South Africa and he's very excited about it. The key is people getting to know one another, and that's where the young people are taking the lead.

We are creating a new country and a new constitution, and this is going to be a wonderful place for all its citizens. I'm delighted to be a part of it.

*   *   *

Miscellaneous Comments

In the course of my travels throughout South Africa, I heard many comments worth repeating. Some came out in interviews not presented here, others in casual conversation. I offer these under the broad title of Miscellaneous Comments.

Zach de Beer (white)
Newly-elected leader of the Progressive Federal Party :

"I do not credit sanctions with any of the positive changes that have taken place in South Africa since 1984."

AJ Gumede (black)
United Democratic Front:

"The Freedom Charter expresses for me best how relations can be maintained equitably in a situation of unavoidable co-existence and interdependence in the agricultural, mining, manufacturing and commercial industries on which the economy of the whole country rests. I do not foresee the total expulsion of the governing minority as an option, nor do I foresee the total or significant liquidation of the indigenous population as an option."

Professor Philip Blignaut van der Watt (white)
Vice Chairman and Moderator, Dutch Reformed Church:

"The Bible as a handbook for political issues is no longer acceptable to the Dutch Reformed Church. We do not accept the diversity among people as an excuse for apartheid."

Dr Beryl Unterhalter, Professor of Sociology, Wits University (white):

"One of my students could be the country's first black Prime Minister! That causes me no fear whatsoever. Let the Afrikaners of the CP have their partition. Let them go to a separate place and leave the rest of us alone."

South Africa: Land of Hope?

Indian man:

"I've suffered enough under white minority rule; I'm willing to give the black man a try!"

White man:

"As a Liberal, I'm pessimistic, but I must admit I am now seeing more good than bad. When businessmen offer profit-sharing to their black employees and say, 'By working together we can become the Japan of Africa,' then I realise we can begin to be positive. And that is what is happening here."

White woman:

"The black South Africans are not natural socialists; they are natural capitalists. It is important to help them share the wealth of this country, as it is important that they know what they have to lose. I think it's wonderful that state schools now require all white children to learn a black language."

White mother of two:

"My children have always gone to multi-racial schools, and when we have a birthday party I always invite the non-white children as well. Three years ago those parents didn't even respond; this year, not only did the children come but the parents came, and we all sat in my living room having perfectly normal conversation. I have seen that happen even in Pretoria, the hotbed of Afrikanerdom. We're very excited about what's happening here."

Black male professional:

"Blacks must learn the importance of helping each other. That is a lesson we can learn from the Indians in this country: They create their own jobs, within their community, so they are less affected by the whites than we are. We blacks feel that you Americans are using us for your own ends. The proof is your sanctions, which may impress the blacks in *your* country but certainly are not helping the blacks in South Africa. The more Tutu and Boesak are on TV, the more popular they become in this country. But then when they disappear

132

from television for a while, the polls show they lose in popularity as well. Naturally they like to use you and your television for their own purposes."

White female Afrikaner professional:

"South Africa is fighting a war of perceptions. The outside world thinks nothing has changed here; yet – though admittedly we have a long way to go – the changes have been tremendous. In working with blacks we realise that concepts such as community development, democracy, and self-esteem are new to them. But there has been a poll-measured ten percent increase in feelings of security among blacks in the townships since the imposition of the State of Emergency. Interestingly, the blacks also have positive feelings about the Security Police: Because of the presence of the police, violence has lessened from radical groups. Most blacks and whites recognise the cultural differences among tribes, especially in the workplace and in politics, but we are trying to bridge those differences."

White, English-speaking male, self-described, long-standing Liberal jurist:

"Our system has created a group of "negro-liberals" who, in their pandering to and automatic *embracing* of everything black, are just as suspect as those who mindlessly *reject* everything black. The exoneration of a guilty man is just as much a travesty of justice as the conviction of an innocent one."

White, English-speaking and Afrikaner writers:

"We should go back to the four provinces we originally had and institute a 'qualified franchise' – a franchise based on education and applicable to all population groups."

"Most people in commerce don't stick their necks out politically; they are trying to protect their businesses."

"Abolishing our political system entirely would result in chaos. Quick moves are not relevant to South Africa. Don't anticipate one man/one vote; South Africa is not America. Build from ethnic groups into federal states. Everyone will have a local vote. We will establish a meritocracy, and the media will be the great levelers."

"Offer a local option on rescinding the Group Areas Act. You wouldn't see great changes, but everyone could live where he or she wants. There would be very few objections."

Richard Rive, coloured writer:

"Books such as *Kaffir Boy* and *Move Your Shadow* are so full of exaggerations and half-truths that they don't help our cause. We have no respect for those writers. The same goes for movies like *Cry Freedom*: The truth is bad enough; we don't need the embellishment of lies.... White do-gooders are as dangerous to us as those who are uncritical.... Violence doesn't always mean planting bombs; there is constitutional violence as well, and that is what has been thrown at the non-whites in this country.... The coloured and Indian parties sold out to the white government, which used the tactic of Divide and Rule — like the Roman Empire.... At least non-white academics are now returning to this country. They bring something of value."

White male journalist, writing for a newspaper read mostly by blacks and coloureds:

"The struggle is a non-racial one.... There is great humanity in the [non-white] townships...and it will be that humanity that will ultimately be the bedrock of a non-racial future here.... In general, I am extremely optimistic about the long-term future of South Africa.... I believe that eventually the government will negotiate with the ANC.... The United States is making little positive contribution to ending apartheid at present."

White male Afrikaner, working to improve education for South African blacks, commenting on the movie, *A World Apart*:

"It is actually an accurate portrayal of what went on in 1963. The problem is that people see the movie *now* and think that's the way things are *today* in South Africa, which is *not* accurate."

REFLECTIONS AND OBSERVATIONS

There are few certainties in South Africa—fewer, undoubtedly, than in most countries of the world. But one of them, without a doubt, is change. Not cosmetic but substantive change. That this change has already begun remains unknown to much of the world. Much of that world does not want to know; it prefers the road of high indignation.

But even the Afrikaner Nationalists see change as inevitable. World opinion may not matter to them, but their economic well-being does, and the South African economy incontestably relies on black labor. Apartheid may have "worked" (a highly-debatable premise) for three hundred years, but its death knell sounded with South Africa's entry onto the world stage.

The majority of South Africans are in favor of change and are working towards that goal. There are those, to be sure, who fear that one man/one vote will mean one man/one vote *one time*—a reference to other African countries where single-party states, rather than true democracy, have followed independence. Others, such as Victims Against Terrorism, fear a Communist takeover, feeling certain that the Russians are, even now, manipulating the ANC and other terrorist organizations.

But one of the problems with banning the ANC and forcing them underground, I was told repeatedly, is that South Africans don't really know for sure what those leaders are saying. If they were brought out in the open, their policies could be freely debated. The National Party has refused open debate without a prior renunciation of violence by the ANC, so citizens like Frederik Van Zyl Slabbert and his Institute for Democratic Alternatives for South Africa (IDASA) have stepped in to fill the breach, facilitating the forming of a new, multi-racial political party made up of those parties already to the left of the Nats and, in the process, joining some former adversaries. What the new Democratic Party will be able to accomplish—and how soon—remains to be seen, but the start has been made and hopes are high.

With a new party leader, following the stroke suffered by PW Botha in January 1989, the Nats now appear to be moving further and faster. On assuming the party's leadership, former Education Minister FW de Klerk impressed friend and foe alike with his statement, "Our goal is a new

South Africa: Land of Hope?

South Africa, a totally changed South Africa, a South Africa which has rid itself of the antagonism of the past, a South Africa free of domination or oppression in whatever form, a South Africa within which the democratic forces – all reasonable people – align themselves behind mutually acceptable goals and against radicalism, irrespective of where it comes from." And later, "Our goals have been clearly stated: A new constitution offering full participation to all South Africans – white, black, coloured, and Indian; non-domination of any one group by another; social and economic upliftment for those communities suffering backlogs."

When pressed for specifics de Klerk pointed out, "We also acknowledge that others who participate in negotiations must be free to put their full viewpoint and counter proposals without inhibition and a long list of prerequisites.... In order to gain acceptance, any ground plan will have to provide authentic and full participation for all those who are engaged in it. Any system aimed at keeping some of its participants in a subordinate position through clever or devious means is doomed to failure. It must be visibly just and equitable towards everybody. I want to state unequivocally that the National Party is against domination of any group by others. White domination, insofar as it still exists, must go."

By the end of May 1989 – in a meeting with American Secretary of State James Baker – South African Foreign Minister Rolef "Pik" Botha had uttered the words the world awaited: "The South African government is committed to the dismantling of apartheid and to the institution of a non-racial, representative government in South Africa."

With representatives of all of South Africa's political parties having finally come together to exchange views, and with agreement by the Nats and the ANC regarding group rights and conditions for negotiation, it appears some new initiatives are indeed on the horizon. Skeptics and pessimists may say there's been movement before, with no solution, but all must acknowledge the new sense of urgency inspired by the 1988 gains by the Conservative Party. Chief Buthelezi has met with government officials – at their request – to help "get things moving" again; Nelson Mandela has met with a variety of Cabinet Ministers and, finally speaking with State President PW Botha, has agreed to contribute to a climate that

REFLECTIONS AND OBSERVATIONS (Cont.)

will foster peaceful negotiations; moderate blacks are speaking out in an attempt to quell the violence; white South African businessmen are playing an ever-more-visible role in creating a new, more broadly-based economy. And in a startling reversal of strategy following their municipal victories, stung by the repudiation of their subsequent behavior by even their own supporters, the Conservatives finally have admitted the heretofore inadmissible: They "accept that the majority of black people and a significant number of whites are part of a non-racial South African nation in the making."[1] In a land whose history is replete with ironies, the CP victories may have signalled the CP defeat.

I believe there is real basis for optimism regarding South Africa's future. It lies in large part in the tremendous amount of goodwill that exists among all the people in that country. There is simply not the seething hostility one finds in New York, Los Angeles, Miami, or Detroit. This goodwill, expressed to me over and over again — by blacks, coloureds, and Indians, as well as whites — came as a great surprise. When it was first mentioned by an Afrikaner maintaining his Conservative position, I was — admittedly — prepared to dismiss it as wishful thinking. But as I heard the opinion repeated by members of every other group, I realized that *this* is the glue holding that fragmented society together. The fact is, a great reservoir of moderate thinking exists in South Africa, counter-balancing the extremes. That the Cape Town City Council overwhelmingly voted to restore Cape Town to "open city" status — one where its 1.1 million inhabitants, three-quarters of them non-white, may live based on what they can afford, rather than on the color of their skin — is but one prime proof of this fact.

Most of the academics and political leaders with whom I spoke seemed to think that *federation* is the most likely and reasonable solution to South African politics. Leon Louw and Frances Kendall, in their best-selling *South Africa: The Solution*, which I quote widely in Chapter Five, present the case for a Swiss cantonal system, a system which eliminates the need for a strong central government and achieves the devolution of power

---

1   As Reported in the *Weekly Mail*, 7 April 1989.

through cantonal administrations. Such a system is opposed by those blacks who favor majority rule in a unitary state. As Namibian journalist Eugene Nyati points out, this group sees cantons as "a disguised attempt to retain the essentials of the status quo."[1] But Louw and Kendall have the support of Winnie Mandela, Chief Buthelezi, and Sam Motsuenyane (President of NAFCOC, the black Chamber of Commerce) — no mean feat when you consider the hostility existing between Mrs Mandela and Buthelezi in other areas.

The power and influence of the Conservative Party remain to be assessed. Dr Nic Rhoodie of the Human Sciences Research Council feels their support is overrated: "Just as a few hundred well-organised students can dominate a campus of 60,000, so a small group of fanatical extremists can upset things — for a while."[2] But the Nationalists, complacent after forty years in power, must begin to "sell" their plan — in specific terms — to a citizenry desperate for true leaders who will guide them peacefully but surely into what certainly will be a new South Africa.

Those such as Law Dean Louise Tager, working on a new constitution, are modern-day Founding Fathers: They are creating an entirely new country. And they urge other countries of the world to work with them. If Ronald Reagan, after his last summit meeting with Mikhail Gorbachev, can urge human rights activists to "encourage the trend [in Russia] by openly acknowledging positive change and crediting it,"[3] then why, ask South Africans, can *they* not be accorded the same acknowledgment?

I am convinced that South Africa is on the verge of making positive, substantive changes — changes that will not only impress the world but improve it. I believe the outside world can help speed those changes by *providing* support rather than withdrawing it. I am not alone in that theory: All but a handful of radical South Africans have expressed as much to me.

---

1   Eugene Nyati, "Groundswell: Threat to the Struggle?," *Tribute Magazine*, (April 1988), pp. 118-119.

2   In-person interview. Pretoria, May 1988.

3   As quoted in *The Miami Herald*, 3 June 1988.

REFLECTIONS AND OBSERVATIONS (Cont.)

Let me hasten to add that support does not mean aid with no strings attached. I think we have every right to dictate where our money will go and how it will be used. My own preference would be for America to go back to the humanitarian aid that was provided, as through the Sullivan Code, by American companies in South Africa before sanctions and restrictions forced them to leave – namely, put large sums of money into integrated housing, education, skills training, and creation of jobs.

It may long be debated whether sanctions alone pushed South Africa forward, but that debate is immaterial to those who sincerely wish to help black South Africans now. If sanctions once served a purpose, there is nothing further to be gained from their extension. Women for Peace and a host of other organizations are working with South Africans on the *social* side of the turmoil; it remains for the Western democracies to offer tangible assistance to the economy. As Alan Keyes, then Assistant Secretary of State for International Organization Affairs, said in 1986, "the question for Americans and others in the international community is not with what well-intentioned gestures can we show our hatred of apartheid and our sympathy with the suffering of its black victims but rather how, with concrete acts, we can support the expansion and use of their positive power."[1]

An important fact, again unknown to most of the world, is that the majority of black South Africans oppose sanctions. John Kane-Berman, Executive Director of the South African Institute of Race Relations, addressing British members of the Institute at the Reform Club in London, stated emphatically, "There seems to be a wide view abroad that most black South Africans favour sanctions and disinvestment. The weight of opinion survey evidence suggests otherwise, however." Of fourteen most recently published opinion polls on the issue, in only one was there majority support for disinvestment – and that, among urban

---

1   As quoted by Michael Clough, "Southern Africa: Challenges and Choices," *Foreign Affairs*, (Summer 1988), p. 1081.

blacks in 1985, at the height of the unrest.[1] As recently as 16 May 1989, the South African newspaper, *Business Day*, reported that "in what has been billed as the most comprehensive opinion survey of its kind ever taken, more than eighty percent of Black South Africans say sanctions and disinvestment are a 'bad idea.' "

Also worth noting are comments by some of our European allies, as expressed in a report for the Council on Foreign Relations in New York. First, the Right Honourable Lord Francis Pym, who served as a member of the British Parliament from 1961 to 1987:

> Economic growth has been a direct stimulus to the forces of change in South Africa. It has led to increasing black economic power, the emergence of black trade unions, and improved facilities for black education and training.... The evidence suggests that industrialisation has served to weaken racial barriers and to promote reform as the needs of a modern industrial society override political dogma. The dynamic of events place an increasing strain on apartheid itself, which is precisely the development we wish to encourage....
>
> It can be argued that the South African government is proceeding as far and as fast as it knows to be possible, and that for want of anything better we should encourage it and be patient.... Frustration may impel the blacks to pursue an increasingly extreme policy with which the West will feel progressively more uncomfortable. But violence and extremism must be rejected.... The moderate blacks are more likely to prevail if the West has espoused the black cause in general, which does not mean supporting blacks in every particular; on the contrary, we must feel able to criticise, even to condemn, what we see as undesirable in black policies, pronouncements or actions. Such a

---

1   As quoted in "Blacks Turn Their Backs on Disinvestment," *Race Relations News*, (December 1987), p. 8.

policy would fit with the requirements imposed by two
important premises: the need for the outside world to
bear upon South Africa in the most effective way to
bring about peaceful change as soon as possible; and
the acceptance of the fact that results cannot be quick.
The first requirement is the need for concerted action.
The second is political: bringing the public's hopes into
harmony with what it will be possible to achieve in
practice.[1]

Claude Cheysson, Commissioner of the European Communities
responsible for Mediterranean policy and North-South relations:

We must support the policies of responsible moderate
leaders in their constructive approaches. As one says in
French, 'il ne faut pas insulter l'avenir' (we must not
insult the future). A constant relationship with such
leaders is therefore essential, not only to be well
informed of the actual situation, but also to confirm
their authority.[2]

Herman W Nickel, US Ambassador to the Republic of South Africa from
1982 to 1986 and a former correspondent for Time-Life News Service,
reporting from Johannesburg, adds these comments:

It would be far better if the outside world lent support
and encouragement to those elements working for
peaceful solutions.... The Western allies should
co-operate in efforts to help the disadvantaged majority
develop the skills and the leadership it will need to play
its rightful role in a post-apartheid South Africa....
Programs to advance black entrepreneurship and
executive skills not only strengthen black bargaining
power but also the odds for survival of the free
enterprise system, which is so vital to the economic

1   Francis Pym, "Strains Among Friends: Co-ordinating Western Policy
     Toward South Africa," *Europe, America, and South Africa*, ed. Gregory
     Treverton (New York: Council on Foreign Relations, 1988), pp. 40-42.

2   Claude Cheysson, "Let Information Flow: A Western Approach to
     South Africa Beyond Sanctions." Ibid., p. 80.

L.O.H.—F

future of post-apartheid South Africa. So, too, maintaining links with South African universities ... is absolutely essential. The idea of an academic boycott is an affront to Western principles of the free exchange of ideas....

These are modest proposals, geared to the reduced circumstances of Western influence. No doubt they will find no favor with those who still delude themselves and others that the West could 'end apartheid now' if only it mustered the will. So long as these people continue to believe that the West is the determining factor in the South African drama, they will be disappointed by any policy the United States and its allies adopt. But as they notice that their activist prescriptions to isolate South Africa are producing perverse results, perhaps they will finally realize that there is no quick fix.[1]

Throughout the world, it seems, a new outlook towards South Africa is taking hold. That a new outlook is taking hold *within* the country is borne out by several facts highlighted in the *Weekly Mail* in late June 1989:

- "Anti-apartheid forces consider the possibility of negotiations with the government as more realistic than ever before....

- "FW de Klerk announced on the eve of his visit to [Prime Minister Margaret] Thatcher that he had 'committed himself to negotiations and to expedite the process'....

- "Foreign Affairs Director-General Neil van Heerden said, 'People in South Africa have a heightened belief in achieving solutions by constructive negotiation.... The mind boggles at what can be achieved inside South Africa in the next 18 months'....

---

1   Herman W Nickel, "Forging a Western Consensus on South Africa," ed. Gregory Treverton, op. cit., pp. 93, 117-118.

REFLECTIONS AND OBSERVATIONS (Cont.)

- "Zambian president and Frontline States chairman Kenneth Kaunda intimated he would be prepared to meet de Klerk without preconditions...."

- "After a meeting with ANC president Oliver Tambo, Archbishop of Canterbury Robert Runcie confirmed he had discussed prospects for negotiation 'after the September election' "[1]...."

- "An alliance of unions, representing up to two million black workers, has asked that government representatives attend the labour convention — opening the way for the first-ever forum for collective bargaining between labour, big business, and the government.... The summit comes at a time when evidence is mounting that government and anti-apartheid circles are preparing for possible negotiations later in the year to devise alternatives to apartheid rule...."

- "Helen Suzman and several other prominent Democratic Party members are among the 115 white South Africans leaving ... for a three-day conference with the African National Congress ... co-ordinated by the Five Freedoms Forum ... FFF chairperson Mike Olivier [described] the conference ... on the theme *Whites in a Changing South Africa*...: 'The purpose of the conference is to find out first hand what the ANC believes on a number of contentious issues, and to give them a sense of the fears and aspirations of an important cross-section of the white community'.... Some of the sessions would deal with issues of debate, including sanctions, violence, negotiations, nationalisation, and models for the country's constitutional future. Another series focuses on strategic questions, such as the role of parliament and of extra-parliamentary groups, the position of women in South Africa's future and the role of business in the process of change...."

- "[A recent] working paper is a response to a government request to the Law Commission to investigate a Bill of Rights [and was] hailed as a sharp departure from Nat thinking, because its draft Bill

---

1   *Weekly Mail*, 15 June 1989.

guaranteed basic liberal freedoms .... Besides guaranteeing civil
liberties such as freedom of speech, assembly, and association (as
well as disassociation) and protection from arbitrary police powers,
the Bill also appears to demand a non-racial constitution: it
recommends that all citizens have the right to vote and to elect
representatives to bodies which will have an equal say in the
law-making process."[1]

The National Party's Five Year Plan of Action, also presented at the end
of June 1989, offers proposals which cannot fail to impress both fellow
South Africans and the international community, so strict a departure do
they indicate from what has existed in South Africa since 1948, when the
Nats took power. This Five Year Plan "gives constitutional expression to
the protection of human rights – both individual rights and group values."
Further, it foresees "a new democratic dispensation with full political
rights for all South Africans" and "a secure future...built on a broad
consensus between representative leaders of our total population." The
plan "provides for the elimination of discrimination, the establishment of
adequate housing and facilities as well as the prevention of over-crowding
and unsatisfactory living conditions" and offers South Africans "the
opportunity to live according to their own choice," specifically in
integrated "free settlement areas." It also emphasizes "a strong,
independent judiciary [as] an essential guarantee for the protection of
individual rights and group values and to ensure a stable democracy and
justice for all."

The National Party is not alone in proposing such lofty goals in this
election year, but it is significant that even *they* see this path as the only
way out of the dark. In a country by its own admission untouched by the
Enlightenment or the Age of Reason so influential in Western Europe
and America in the eighteenth century, the light – though belatedly – is
beginning to shine on the descendants of those early, unyielding settlers.

---

1   *Weekly Mail*, 23 June, 1989.

REFLECTIONS AND OBSERVATIONS (Cont.)

Political consensus within South Africa exists to no greater and no lesser degree than in any other country in the world. What does exist is a burning desire for a peaceful solution to the country's problems and a broad body of people ready to effect a change. There is determination and great goodwill among the people of South Africa. With help, and properly harnessed, that goodwill can justify the optimism of those prepared to work for the world's newest democracy.

Let men and women of goodwill, everywhere, wish them Godspeed and aid them in their quest.

TG McC
August 1989

The remainder of this book is designed to fill out the South Africa story, as gleaned from a variety of sources.

Chapters Two and Three contain excerpts of contemporary South African newspaper columns and citations from pertinent articles found in an assortment of recent publications. These are divided into five sections: "Interpersonal Relationships," "Government Action," "Political Parties," "Opinion," and "Business." Chapter Four presents a collection of South Africans' comments on sanctions, published in early 1989.

Finally, Chapter Five will provide some perspective and background information on the history and character of South Africa and its people, distilled from a dozen books written mostly by South Africans and recommended to me both while I was there and following my return. I have arranged the authors' comments in twenty-four broad categories.

Many of those quoted in the pages which follow are among the most influential and committed citizens to be found in South Africa today. Taken together, their statements help to frame a picture of a nation moving forward with determination, confidence, and a sense of destiny.

Chapter 2

SOUTH AFRICAN
NEWSPAPER ITEMS
April - May 1988

Apathy, in South Africa, is not a problem. In few countries of the world are so many citizens so vocal about what is going on around them. As noted previously, the proliferation of newspapers also is great and South Africans can, if they choose, read only the paper that suits their political philosophy.

During the month I was there I read as many papers as possible, in each of the areas I visited, hoping to get a broader picture of what the people were reading, writing, thinking and saying. There is no lack of Letters to the Editor.

It would be disingenuous to pretend that all the news was good or that all the people have a positive outlook on what is happening. The world is acutely aware of the problems facing South Africa, less aware of what is being done to solve those problems. The reader will find, in this chapter, excerpts from a sampling of newspaper items that reinforced my hope for this troubled land.

I have organized the articles chronologically, within five general categories: Interpersonal Relationships, Government Action, Political Parties, Opinion, and Business.

INTERPERSONAL RELATIONSHIPS

"In what will be seen as a major breakthrough for the dismantling of apartheid in South African sport, Soweto Country Club was last night accepted as an affiliated club of the previously white-dominated Transvaal Golf Union....Soweto Country Club boasts about 600 members...[and] there are already a good number of white and coloured members...."
(*The Star*, 15 April 1988)

"Children of all races, given the chance of meeting each other, are 'totally uninhibited' when it comes to making friends, and as a result are ideal bridge builders....Their attitude towards each other has influenced parents of all races and they now accept each other without difficulty."
(*The Star*, 15 April 1988)

"The Promat Colleges [secondary schools]...are representative of a new style of education increasingly being funded by the private sector to overcome the inequities of the black education system....It was assumed, when the colleges were established, that black students would 'do as well as whites if they were taught by teachers demanding the same standards as white schools.' The assumption has proved correct." (*The Star*, 20 April 1988)

"Black and white pupils at desegregated schools are racially more tolerant and more positive about the future of South Africa than their counterparts at segregated State schools, a study has shown....[The study] investigated the influence of desegregated education on the self-esteem, identification, attitudes and adjustment of...pupils." (*The Star*, 20 April 1988)

"The Somerset West Town Council has decided it has no objection to a coloured businessman living in an elite white suburb." (*The Argus*, 27 April 1988)

"While classrooms in some white suburbs are standing empty, Belgravia Convent in Johannesburg is full....The growth of the school has been stimulated by the admission of more black children....A few white parents withdrew their children when more black pupils were accepted, as they were afraid standards would drop. 'But our African parents are as anxious as any to ensure that their children receive the best possible education.' One mother was afraid her child would speak with an 'African accent,' but Belgravia Convent pupils in fact won their sections in speech and drama at the Springs and Johannesburg speech and music festivals....The children are growing up with one added advantage: with the races mixing with each other, colour is no longer an issue. The convent's hostel [dormitory] is non-racial...." (*The Star*, 4 May 1988)

"A Platteland town [Pacaltsdorp, Cape Province] with an enviable reputation for racial harmony has issued a challenge to the rest of South Africa: Try it our way!....They have a white town clerk and a coloured mayor, a Malay shopkeeper, black and white residents — all living in perfect harmony....Race will never play a part in their lives, vow the townspeople, and anyone who owns property in the town will be entitled to vote and stand for office...." (*Sunday Times*, 8 May 1988)

"Jewish children...and [black] children from neighbouring Alexandra met at Temple David in Morningside where they had a bonfire, sing-along and eats to commemorate [a] Jewish festival....The picnic had been planned so the children from the different communities could get to know one another. 'If they can communicate by talking, singing, and spending time together they can find some common ground [said the rabbi]. They can find the positive things they have in common instead of looking at their differences.' " (*The Star*, 10 May 1988)

GOVERNMENT ACTION

"Nearly R800 million [$400 million] is to be pumped into housing for lower income groups through projects run by two major organisations that will yield at least 50,000 serviced sites and more than 35,000 houses in the next three years...."(*The Argus*, 22 April 1988)

"The Government would go ahead with negotiation with those who wanted to take part, and those who wanted to remain outside could stay there, the Minister of Constitutional Development and Planning, Mr Chris Heunis, said today....He said the time for rhetoric was past...and those leaders committed to peaceful development should now begin to talk seriously with each other. The President...had made it clear...that it was a 'Utopian dream' to believe that a final constitution could suddenly be implemented....Impatience among blacks [is] natural but the need among whites for reassurance on the maintenance of their values [is] also natural....White rights [must] be protected, but they could not be protected in the long run without an acknowledgment of black rights...." (*The Argus*, 22 April 1988)

"Britain was 'totally committed' to the fight against apartheid and intended helping provide 'the weapons' to fight it, the British ambassador, Mr Robin Renwick, said....However those weapons would not be bombs but education and economic advancement...." (*Daily Dispatch*, 27 April 1988)

"The proportion of black students at major 'white' universities has rapidly increased in the past few years, according to statistics obtained from the universities. At the same time an increasing number of English-speaking students has been admitted to Afrikaans universities....Approached for comment on the trends reflected by the statistics, university spokesmen emphasised commitment to admission on merit and do not foresee problems arising from the demographic changes...." (*Daily Dispatch*, 27 April 1988)

South Africa: Land of Hope?

"In Transkei, the TDC [Transkei Development Corporation] is to launch a Public Investment Company to enable Transkeians to buy shares in 'some of the most successful large business ventures' in the country....In Ciskei the CPDB [Ciskei Peoples Development Bank]...intends to offer its prestige ventures for sale by public tender [as] part of a new drive to spread ownership of business assets across a wide spectrum of people....[It] would give the man in the street the opportunity to obtain a stake in various successful businesses...." (*Daily Dispatch*, 27 April 1988)

"[Port Elizabeth] city is on the march. So says the mayor, Mr Solly Rubin, who can quote twenty good reasons for saying so....The demand for labour is improving and in some sectors jobs are now chasing people; there has been an average twenty-five percent increase in the wages of black workers; there has been a notable surge in local tourist trade; the number of black buyers applying to buy houses is on the increase; the price of local white housing has risen due to strong demand...." (*Daily Dispatch*, 27 April 1988)

"A significant reduction in the number of unqualified teachers in black schools over the last five years has been revealed in the 1987 report of the Department of Education and Training....The department said it had 'committed itself to employ every means at its disposal to upgrade all facets of teacher education'...." (*Daily Dispatch*, 27 April 1988)

"No action would be taken against 'non-white' students living in hostels [dormitories] at Stellenbosch University as they have been given permission to do so by the government...." (*Daily Dispatch*, 27 April 1988)

"The inclusion of blacks in the election of the State President would be a 'drastic step' which would have to be tested with the public...but...would also require consultation with blacks...through the proposed National Council....It would appear...that this could mean elections for blacks next year." (*Daily Dispatch*, 27 April 1988)

"The House of Assembly [the white House of Parliament]...approved the new Parliamentary Standing Rules and Orders, opening the way for joint sittings of all three Houses. The House of Delegates [Indian] and House of Representatives [coloured] passed them earlier...." (*The Natal Mercury*, 28 April 1988)

156

"Chances of success for the proposed National Council, or 'Great Indaba' as it might be known, [are] far better than they [were] two years ago, a top Government source said yesterday. One reason for this [is] that the perception that South Africa [is] 'on the verge of disintegration' [has] died out to a significant degree...." (*The Natal Mercury*, 29 April 1988)

"Government spending on black education outside the homelands has increased almost tenfold over the past eight financial years...." (*The Natal Mercury*, 29 April 1988)

POLITICAL PARTIES

"Dr Denis Worrall, leader of the Independent Party, said the Independent Party's objective was the establishment of a creative coalition of parties across the colour line....This [is] possible by concentrating on issues which divide both parliamentary and extra-parliamentary politics." (*The Star*, 20 April 1988)

"Behind the façade of opposition disarray, a lot is happening. There is some serious thinking, ideas are in ferment, and signs are emerging of a new approach to South African politics. Divided opposition groups to the left of the Government are finding common ground. They are looking again at Western values that could bind them together....They are certainly not short of ideas and plans. And they are active in the ferment of thought across the colour lines – inside and outside Parliament....A 'creative opposition' across colour lines could include elements from the Labour Party, the PFP, the Independent Party, the National Democratic Movement, Inkatha, Solidarity and other Indian parties, and the United Democratic Front (UDF). Mr Albert Nothnagel and other like-minded Nationalists would have a place in such a grouping...." (*Weekend Argus*, 23 April 1988)

"Two once-prominent Natal Nationalists, Mr Theo Gerdener and Dr Jan Marais, have emerged from political 'retirement' to plead the 'centrist' cause and call for drastic speeding up of reform....Although neither is considered a 'source,' their arguments are believed to mirror in many respects the new Nationalist thinking....In a recent letter in the Afrikaans Sunday newspaper, *Rapport*, Mr Gerdener argued that it was imperative to build up a strong 'middle force' to replace the alarming mistrust and fear among South Africans. This would be coupled with tangible evidence that the reform process was the primary goal in South African politics. He said this could be done in several ways: New and consistent negotiations with all moderates and black leaders...open agendas to establish mutual trust...a fresh look at constitutional structures....establishing a power base across colour lines...Mr Gerdener said he believed that an alliance of moderates as the guiding force behind the reform movement would have these implications: an establishment of the concept of negotiation rather than revolution; an acceptance that solving race problems was more desirable than partition; a constant search for consensus between people rather than emphasis on differences; a strengthening of community interests rather than fostering political party gains." (*The Daily News*, 29 April 1988)

"The ANC has made public the main provisions of a constitution for a free, non-racial South Africa — which will be open for discussion. The draft envisages the establishment of a democratic state system and guarantees rights and freedoms to all population groups, including the freedom of speech and access to information, the right to education, the establishment of independent trade unions and the staging of strikes....All parties and organisations set up according to racial characteristics and professing racism should be banned....The draft constitution...provides for a united centralised power and elected local bodies called upon to safeguard the rights of ethnic minorities. The draft is aimed at avoiding premature and unprepared nationalisation and the mass departure of white specialists." (*Business Day*, 6 May 1988)

"Mr Wynand Malan's National Democratic Movement battled to find a political parking place in an overcrowded liberal arena....The congress unanimously supported suggestions that the ANC should be included in the NDM's efforts to engage extra-parliamentary groups in political discussion. Referring to the Government's refusal to talk to the ANC until it disavowed violence, Mr Malan said he also rejected violence. 'But if there's violence, that is all the more reason to talk. You don't stop violence through counter-violence'....The NDM's aim [is] 'one South Africa with effective political rights for all in one nation moulded from different political communities'....The NDM believes in the politics of inclusion, because its emphasis [is] on value systems rather than political systems...." (*Sunday Times*, 8 May 1988)

OPINION

Albert Nothnagel (NP): "The future of South Africa as a whole, with all its various communities, [is] more important than any one part of it, and this includes the Afrikaner. As an Afrikaner nationalist, and as much as I love the Afrikaner and other groups in the country, the Afrikaner's sociopolitical aspirations and all he claims are not more important in the South Africa of tomorrow than the interests of all in South Africa together. The Afrikaner and the whites alone can not have the total say....Everyone must feel he is free to take part in political and economic activity and... discrimination is not part of our policy...." (*The Citizen*, 21 April 1988)

André van der Walt (NP): "Left and right-wing radicals [are] political bedfellows because they both believe in imposing a solution on the country....The most important question facing South Africa [is] whether a political solution [is] going to be negotiated or whether it [is] going to be arbitrarily imposed....The ability of all moderates and those who reject violence to negotiate a solution [will] determine whether there [will] be peace or violence." (*Business Day*, 21 April 1988)

Gerald Shaw, political columnist: "...The one consolation is that both the ANC and the Botha government seem to grasp that escalation of violence beyond a certain point on either side will kill the goose that lays the golden eggs for all concerned – the South African economy...." (*Cape Times*, 22 April 1988)

Editorial: "The proposals revealed this week for the inclusion of blacks in constitutional structures, make no mistake, herald a continuation rather than departure from current Government philosophy...[but] only those who would naively expect whites to summarily negotiate themselves into impotence would outrightly dismiss these moves. Those like this newspaper, who believe that politics is truly the art of the possible, will see precious toeholes for further incremental reform. The system will create new platforms around which black South Africans can rally....All it needs now are the people with the imagination, creativity and integrity to come forward and seize those platforms....The inclusion of black South Africans, even in the Cabinet, has high symbolic importance....President

Botha, flawed as his proposals may be, has clearly turned his back on any hope of feeding the far right crocodile...and that can only be good news for South Africa." (*Sunday Times*, 24 April 1988)

Letter to the Editor: "Whether your readers love the state president or hate him, the fact remains that he has done more in a few years for reform than all his predecessors together over more than 300 years...." (*The Natal Mercury*, 29 April 1988)

Ismail Omar [President's Council]: "...the National Party is no longer the representative of the extreme right wing in South African politics...." (*Sunday Times*, 8 May 1988)

BUSINESS

"Economic activity was bringing about more political changes in South Africa than was generally recognised, the management board chairman of BMW South Africa, Dr Walter Hasselkus, said yesterday. He said...that economic factors such as economic growth, skilled labour shortages, in-company training and urbanisation had contributed more to sociopolitical progress than 'the actions of politicians or sanctions talk abroad.' " (*Daily Dispatch*, 27 April 1988)

Chapter 3

MISCELLANEOUS ARTICLES
1987 - 1989

Since my return from South Africa, I have continued to read a variety of publications on the subject — most, but not all, written by South Africans for world consumption.

Dividing the articles into the same broad categories as those found in Chapter Two, I continue with the goal of showing the side of the South Africa story which gives reason for hope.

INTERPERSONAL RELATIONSHIPS

Quoting an Afrikaner passenger on the day commuter trains were desegregated: "I am very happy because now we can begin to know each other.... I always watch children playing in the park. They are not conscious of race, and each child waits his turn on the slide. My personal view is that as adults we can learn from the children. There must be respect between us, black and white, and then we will get things right." (*Sunday Star*, 17 July 1988)

Editorial by Ken Owen: "...In a situation where the political ideologies are deadlocked and reform from above is as unlikely as revolution from below, liberal prescriptions come spontaneously into play. The free economy, sucking labour into skilled occupations, created the black trades unions that began to emerge — in defiance of the law — in the early 70s. Urbanisation, an inescapable consequence of a growing market economy, smashed the policy of influx control and destroyed the pass laws. The integration of the work force, creating a commonality of interests for all races, destroyed the feudal practices of apartheid more quickly and thoroughly than any liberal argument. The integrated economy demanded a stable work force close by: the Group Areas Act buckled under the strain. Modern industrial activity demanded educated workers and the education of blacks expanded explosively. Black entrepreneurs, led by taxi drivers, tore great holes in the net of regulation by which a national-socialist government tried to control the social consequences of industrial development. Despite political deadlock, liberation gathers pace by the day...." (*Cape Times*, 18 July 1988)

On the occasion of the pope's visit to Southern Africa: "...he rejected Zimbabwe-style armed struggle as a means for changing South Africa. He urged all 'who bear responsibility for the destiny of the peoples of this region, of whatever racial extraction or ideological inspiration, to renounce the use of violence as a method for achieving their ends'.... His insistence on non-violence matches the dominant view among South Africa's anti-apartheid bishops. Only a few would echo Allan Boesak or Desmond Tutu, who couple appeals for peaceful change with warnings that the unjustness of apartheid makes violent resistance understandable and virtually inevitable.... South Africa should not be singled out for criticism, some bishops from Mozambique and Angola argued, because the Marxism under which they lived was worse than apartheid." (*Weekly Mail*, 16 September 1988)

"...There are private schools in South Africa today which not only scorn the inherited reputation thrust upon them, but rate among the most modern and progressive schools in the world. This kind of private school has no time for the preservation of the elite rituals of class and capital. This kind of private school is too busy preparing its youth for life in post-apartheid South Africa.... It is the establishment of a society beyond apartheid to which many of South Africa's independent schools have committed themselves. To this end in 1987 a new affiliation of schools was added to the arena of representative bodies. Called the Southern Africa Association of Independent Schools (SAAIS), its major objectives [are] to promote non-racial education throughout Southern Africa and 'to provide educational opportunities for the poor and oppressed in both independent and public schools.' " (*Weekly Mail*, 23 September 1988)

Denys Webb, describing his new play: "*Idlozi*, the spirit, knows no colour.... In the end people must realise our gods are the same, our mothers are one and we are all born of the same soil – Africa. White people have their guilt and black people their anger. It's the new generation who have to put things right. History tells us anger and rage isn't going to do it – the solution lies in spiritual bonding. So we are going to have to not only share our cultures but forge new rituals, create new myths which will be shared by all." (*Weekly Mail*, 30 September 1988)

"The history of South African newspapers is about to change forever...[with publication of] the first fully Afrikaans newspaper committed to a 'non-racial, democratic, united South Africa'.... [They] believe the time is ripe for a national newspaper which 'shakes off old taboos' and provides a home for the swelling numbers of Afrikaners committed to a new South Africa; a South Africa they will not necessarily run. The market is 'already there', they believe, and just needs to be stimulated. They are undeterred by the knowledge that white Afrikaners may be on the brink of their greatest electoral lurch to the right.... *Vrye Weekblad* (Independent Weekly), say its founders, sets out to recognise the 'tremendous changes' in Afrikaner attitudes.... 'I am not detribalised and don't see any reason to be' [says one founder], 'but at the same time, I see no conflict between being an ethnic Afrikaner, writing Afrikaans, loving Afrikaans, being Afrikaans in my environment – and not being a Nat, a racist, or in favor of white leadership.' The new newspaper, he says, will have the side-effect of changing the image of Afrikaans as the 'language of the oppressor.' " (*Weekly Mail*, 14 October 1988)

"As South Africa's rugby bosses and the African National Congress met, a newly-formed non-racial sports body gathered in Durban – and gave the...talks its warm backing. The National Sports Congress, formed in May this year by, among others, the South African Rugby Union (SARU) and leading members of the United Democratic Front, met to formulate its 'statement of intent.' In a separate statement the NSC said it was 'encouraged that organisations such as the white South African Rugby Board have taken the bold step for a post-apartheid society.' " (*Weekly Mail*, 21 October 1988)

"The New Africa Movement (NAM) motto: 'Black achievement, Black advancement and Black entrepreneurial success.' If you are not achieving, advancing, or succeeding, then you are part of Africa's problem rather than a participant in its prosperous future.... The usual motto for blacks is 'do as little as possible, take on limited responsibility and blame the white man or the system when things go wrong.' This negative and damaging behaviour is practised in black communities in America, Africa, Europe, the Caribbean and here at home in South Africa. Black people all over the world are in a crisis because the world has lost confidence in them. With the word 'black,' images of poverty, no education, lower class and non-achiever spring to mind. The word rarely inspires confidence, trust, and dependability. In order for the image to change, black people must change their motto in life. In America, where the apartheid laws were scrapped over twenty years ago, black Americans as a whole have achieved little progress. Most black Americans continue to blame whites for their own misfortunes....

South Africa: Land of Hope?

"NAM's goal is to encourage blacks to improve themselves and to create wealth, jobs and a better life for their people.... The feeling of inferiority suffered by blacks all over the world comes from messages given to black children by their own parents. It is time to stop this negative programming and to start telling our black children that 'the sky is the limit'.... To believe is not anything; to do is everything. We blacks must save ourselves. NAM has taken on the challenge of helping blacks to become the achievers they can be....

"In Chinese, 'catastrophe' and 'opportunity' are the same word. One's role, therefore, should be to work miracles by turning problems into opportunities by using one's creative genius. Black South Africans have proved this can be done by becoming successful despite an apartheid system. Blacks must take on more leadership roles in order for South Africa to develop more jobs for black people. Black South Africans are the most dynamic and most intelligent of all the African countries; therefore black South Africans can be role models for the rest of Africa.

"NAM's goals are 1) to improve South Africa's image abroad by presenting the country's future to the world from a black perspective; 2) to change the world's agenda from sanctions, disinvestment and isolation to black achievement and advancement; 3) to encourage investment in the black community and to develop black economic success; 4) to expand Southern Africa's economy so that black income is increased on a regional basis and the quality of life enhanced; 5) to revitalise Africa's economic advancement by encouraging African countries to adjust their policies to attract foreign investment; 6) to build better working relationships between African countries by shifting the agenda from politics to economic co-operation; 7) to assist the world powers in formulating a new African policy promoting economic prosperity, self sufficiency and self reliance; 8) to help black South African businesses penetrate the American market.... NAM's goal is to show the world that *black* means achievement, success and financial prosperity." (*Black Enterprise*, Vol. 14, 1988)

"An informal group of concerned businessmen and women have gathered [to bring] people together in a networking environment and to make things happen by creating opportunities with and for other entrepreneurs and innovators. *Black Enterprise* has played a pioneering role in this movement and hosted the first meeting of BEN (*Black Enterprise* Networkers) at the Johannesburg Country Club recently.... [*Quoting American Bill William Reed, business editor of the black newspaper,* **Capital Spotlight,** *and the group's first speaker*]: 'Much has been accomplished to bring about an equitable situation for all the peoples in this country [South Africa], but there is still so very much more to do. The average American's concept of South and Southern Africa [is] very far from being accurate and correct, and the people of all groups have had a much better working relationship with each other than we in America realize.... The fact that black South Africans have the highest per capita income on the whole continent of Africa has escaped most Americans, including black activists, business people and organizational leadership'.... Reed is formulating a proposal with *Black Enterprise* with the idea of networking among black Americans and South African people of goodwill who are involved in business and economic development." (*Black Enterprise*, Vol. 14, 1988)

"Gainsworth Ewell Mendellssohn Betshanger believes in using unconventional business tactics to get to the top...and now aims to try the same techniques on American congressmen...to appeal [to them] to review their strategy regarding disinvestment.... 'We do not want financial handouts, we want an opportunity to show the world what we can do. There are several banks in the Republic [of South Africa] that are willing to lend the finance.... Disinvestment is only working for the big companies in South Africa. Blacks are not gaining anything from disinvestment.... I personally believe that the majority of blacks in South Africa have no hatred. We are bridging the gap daily.... We get together with whites and talk, share ideas. We do not want them to hate us or to be scared. All we want is a fair chance for survival.... We need to utilise the funds we get to create harmony among a mass of people. The problem is that the masses believe that a lack of money is keeping them from opportunities. However, if we can get money and pledge it to the upliftment of blacks in this country, we believe we will be making a headway towards that harmony we talk about so much.... These large monopolies are buying out companies which feel morally bound to disinvest in South Africa, but they are not helping the moral or the overall economic situation.... We aim to reduce this situation by trying to get the American government to give us a chance to prove ourselves.' " (*Black Enterprise*, Vol. 14, 1988)

"A newly-released poll from South Africa indicates that seventy-five percent of whites want the end of apartheid, with fifty percent wanting it within five years." ("South Africa — A Fact-Finding Mission, 1987", report to the Canadian Junior Chamber/ Jaycees and the Canada JCI Senate)

Quoting English-speaking native South African Jenny Macdonald: "I think the comrades and the university students have brows unsullied by experience, so they all have these violent idealistic ideas. But most people my age want to be able to share this country.... There must be a change. Apartheid is a scourge, it's indefensible, we all want it removed. But we don't know how." (*Sanctions*, 1989)

GOVERNMENT ACTION

Discussing the "National Council Bill", renamed the "Promotion of Constitutional Development Bill": "The most significant change of all in the constitution of the Council concerns the provision for nine elected black representatives of those blacks living permanently outside the homelands [i.e. in "white" South Africa].... The revised bill clearly incorporates some black criticisms of the original proposal. Its reintroduction before Parliament reflects the renewed commitment of the government to political and constitutional reform after a long hiatus: a commitment echoed in the state president's recent announcement that black deputy ministers may be appointed. The government thus reiterates its desire to press ahead with the reforms designated to give blacks a say at all levels of government. And it shows that the government is prepared to resist the demands of the white right wing for a reversal of the reform process." (*South Africa Foundation Review*, August 1988)

Jan Steyn, Chairman of the Urban Foundation: "Let us consider what has changed over the past ten years. Whilst a vast gap still has to be closed, inequality in expenditure on education between black and white, in *per capita* terms, has been reduced by a factor of three. Universities, technikons and private schools are open to all races. Blacks now have full property rights outside the homelands and building societies are lending millions a month to blacks.... Instead of being merely residential 'camps' for temporary black workers, the new Regional Services Councils are now by law required to upgrade the infrastructure and service in the black urban areas. All job reservation has been abolished...."

"The direction in which our society has moved over the past ten years has almost without exception been away from entrenched racial discrimination. It is true that for many of us the pace has been too slow, but the general direction has been more compatible with the values inherent in the concepts of human dignity and justice.

"The President's Council has in many respects played an important low-key part in imparting greater rationality and sensibility in policy areas. Thus, for example on issues such as urbanisation and deregulation, its work has contributed to making our society more equitable and humane. Against the background I have outlined, this constitutional instrument faces its most awesome challenge yet. I believe it would be the fervent plea of all of us that its deliberations produce well-reasoned recommendations that will steer our country towards greater racial harmony and tolerance. Such recommendations will certainly be interpreted both inside and outside our country as indicating a commitment to an ongoing process of change towards a society that is more just and in which the enhancement of human dignity is indeed a fundamental value." (*South Africa Foundation Review*, December 1988)

"It is not often that all the major actors in the South African political conflict speak at one conference. It is even less often that the two main members of the cast – the National Party and the African National Congress – take comparable positions [but] the conference of South Africans and Americans in Bermuda last week saw these two parties concur – at least in broad terms – on two key issues: They both said the renunciation of violence should not be a precondition for negotiations, and they both expressed faith in the recent Law Commission report on group rights as a basis for a new constitution. Organised by the Washington-based Aspen Institute, the conference can probably claim to be the first meeting where every single major political actor was represented....

"In the past, when questioned, the Conservative Party has simply insisted that it stands for old-style...apartheid, or geographical partition. The most intelligent, ideologically pure nationalists in its ranks have questioned the practicality of this policy and proposed in its place a separate *Boerestaat* (Boer state). In Bermuda, the CP announced that this 'strategy for secession' as opposed to 'partition' was official party policy.

This is of extreme significance because, unlike the National Party, the CP said it is prepared to accept that the majority of black people and a significant number of whites are part of a non-racial South African nation in the making.... A separate *Boerestaat* could link to the South African state through some sort of confederation." (*Weekly Mail*, 7 April 1989)

OPINION

Len Abrahamse, President of the South Africa Foundation: "Sanctions...might have an impact on our GNP and there may be a reduced flow of investment to South Africa. But they certainly will not bring about a collapse of the South African economy or the government. Quite the contrary. There are elements in this country which favour an isolationist policy. Sanctions are playing into the hands of the isolationists — both at home and abroad. They encourage a siege mentality.... Sanctions...are not achieving — and will not achieve — the avowed purpose of the exercise.... I do believe that there is a commitment to reform in South Africa (though that process might be slower than many would like) simply because it all boils down to a question of intelligent survival." (*SAF News*, December 1987)

Paul Johnson, "The Future of South Africa": "African social engineering is perhaps inevitably, given the lack of homogeneity, conducted on a racial-cultural basis. Here again South Africa is typical. All African states tend to be racist. Almost without exception, and with varying degrees of animosity, they discriminate against racial/religious groups: Jews, or whites, or Asians, or non-Moslems, or minority tribes or even majority tribes. There is no such thing as a genuine multiracial society in the whole of Africa. There seems to be no African country where tribal or racial origins, skin colour or religious affiliation are not of prime importance in whether people are accorded or denied elementary rights.... When I look at the prospects for South Africa over the next twenty years, I am inclined to be optimistic. Twice in my lifetime, once in the early 1960s and again in 1985-86, doomsday predictions for South Africa, foreseeing a crescendo of violence culminating in a destructive change of regime, have been invalidated by actual events. I no longer have the smallest belief in a catastrophic solution for this country. Too many people, of all races, have too much to lose; and too much to gain from the rational alternatives. Moreover, reason — and the gifts of reason — are the rewards of the open-minded. And by a curious paradox, South Africa – supposedly obscurantist, inward-and-backward looking South Africa, the South Africa of the *laager* – has in recent years, quite suddenly become extraordinarily open-minded about its future.... South Africa is beginning to concentrate its mind; and this process must, in my judgment, propel it along the path where the underlying forces of capitalism are already taking it: towards a society based not on class or caste or race, but on merit. So the next twenty years will see radical reform from above or reform by negotiation, I am not able to say; a bit of both I suspect." (*South Africa International*, January 1988.)

Stoffel van der Merwe, "Reform, Revolution, and Negotiation": "Too much too soon is as fatal as too little too late.... But hardly anyone can compare the South Africa of 1988 with the South Africa of 1978 and come to the conclusion that nothing has changed. No one can describe the power of the trade unions as cosmetic or the equal wages in the pockets of black workers as of no value. No one can describe the freedom of movement of black people since the abolition of influx control and the 'pass laws' as window dressing or the great strides in black education as imaginary. And no one can deny that a right-wing backlash against (imaginary?) reform has developed or that the National Party has paid a huge price in the form of the loss of Afrikaner unity. Yet the world (and the revolutionary) is clamouring for 'real reform' right now." (*South Africa International*, January 1988.)

*From "The State of the Nation," **Style Magazine**, June 1988*:

– "Today the mood has changed. Cautious optimism.... It is the consensus that we have a breathing space in which to try to rectify wrongs and build a new nation.... South Africa has loaded apartheid on the garbage truck and it is now on the way to the dump. The vehicle is slow and the driver not particularly skilled. He doesn't have a road map and may not get there before the load stinks even more than it does now, but the journey has begun. Although right-wing whites deplore this state of affairs, I suspect that they will not be able to do much about it because the majority of whites welcome it.... I am also encouraged by the common sense of many ordinary people who long ago realised that, no matter who runs this place or under what system, black and white have to co-operate if we don't want the wheels to fall off.... You see blacks and whites and coloureds all working together...black and white kids have been going to the same schools.... Then there is the example of Hillbrow. It used to be said that the only people who don't mind integration were rich whites who could insulate themselves from it. Hillbrow is not a rich area, yet in Hillbrow *de facto* integration has taken place with the minimum of fuss. Blacks, browns, and all the rest share apartment blocks, cafes and street corners. Multi-racial families parade along the streets, tenants of all colours lean over balconies to watch the passing show. It works.... There is a kind of peace in the land and a large reservoir of goodwill between blacks and whites." (David Barritt, journalist)

— "There is a lot of goodwill in this country. We must mobilise that goodwill." (Professor Johan Heyns, moderator of the Dutch Reformed Church)

— "There is an awareness that things are not going to change overnight. There's a mood that it's going to be a long haul, that we are not going to change things in a revolutionary way, but in an evolutionary way.... There is a lot of goodwill in this country and that probably is our greatest hope. There is also a lot of ill-will, a lot of extremism on the left and the right, but there is a reservoir of goodwill between black and white. Because of this, I believe we will find a solution." (Raymond Ackerman, Chairman of Pick 'n Pay)

— "I am optimistic about the country's prospects. In many ways we are doing remarkably well. We have a phenomenal infrastructure which is highly sophisticated and under-utilised .... We have an unfortunate predilection for comparing ourselves with the best in the world. We have a clear-cut lead over our peers but we do not compare ourselves with the Turkeys of this world. I can assure you that if we stood absolutely still for ten years, we would still be a long way ahead of countries like Turkey or our fellow African and South American countries. At the moment the economic state of play is roughly thus: Urban whites — their previously high standard of living has deteriorated by about fifteen percent.... Rural whites — a low standard of living and worsening. Urban blacks — a fairly high standard of living by Third World standards and showing very big improvements. Rural blacks — low, but high by Third World standards and improving. Indians — many would slot right in the top end with whites, but [those] in rural areas, much further down the scale. Coloureds – generally on a par with rural whites." (Nico Czpionka, Standard Bank's chief economist)

Letter to the Editor: "In a unitary system of government, whoever rules is free to exploit and dominate all others. Present day South Africa is a case in point – because we have a unitary state, and because the Afrikaner controls the state, we have Afrikaner domination and exploitation of all other South Africans. The problem is not the Afrikaner but the highly centralised (unitary) system. If some other group controlled the state – a majority of all South Africans as determined by one person/one vote, say – the result would be more or less the same. Instead of Afrikaners using state power to tax and repress everyone else for Afrikaners' advantage, the numerical majority would use state power to tax and repress the numerical minority. Majority tyranny would simply have replaced minority tyranny and we would be no closer to democracy or government by consent of the governed.... The most effective protection against abuse of government is decentralisation of power, where local communities have the power to order their own lives as they see fit, and the central government is strictly controlled and limited."(*Weekly Mail*, 2 September 1988)

ST Boya, President, UMSA: "The United Municipalities of South Africa (UMSA), officially launched on 28 February 1988, today has a membership of sixty councils in South Africa.... UMSA believes very strongly that the problems of South Africa have been created by the present and the past governments of this country, and that only South Africans can solve them through negotiation. UMSA believes in negotiation and sees local authorities as the suitable platform for voicing the black man's wishes and rendering much needed services at the local level...UMSA is totally opposed to violence and therefore cannot support it no matter from which source it comes. We believe in democracy and constitutional power sharing. Because of this conviction we have chosen the path of peaceful negotiation to reach our goal.... It is also the conviction of UMSA that, whilst economic sanctions are regarded by some people as the best weapon to bring about change in this country, we have reason to believe that they are counterproductive and will not achieve the envisaged goal. Since these measures were decided upon by some countries, more than 100,000 blacks have lost their jobs and now have no source of income for their families.... It is about time that the outside world considers what will happen if fifty percent of the productive blacks are unemployed." (*South Africa Foundation Review*, September 1988)

André Brink, "The Afrikaners": "The Afrikaner is bursting out of his definitions of himself as well as those of others.... Stereotypes persist, and a caricature of the Afrikaner has been perpetuated in the mind of the world: The rough-edged frontiersman, gun in one hand and Bible in the other, inspired by the conviction of his covenant with God, his divine mission to tame the wilderness and subject the black heathen; his life determined by an obsession with racial purity and an atavistic brand of Calvinism based on an Old Testament view of the world; suspicious of sophistication and most things modern; and ever ready, when confronted by dangers real or imaginary, to retreat into the *laager*, that ring of ox wagons symbolic of 19th-century clashes with black enemies. If indeed there used to be a stereotype of the Afrikaner, it is no longer applicable.... [*Then, quoting Jan "Boland" Coetzee, legendary South African rugby player*]: 'For many years we farmers thought of nothing but capital and land. Now we're beginning to think of people again, and the result is a change in mentality difficult to explain – one has to experience it...I have enough faith in my countrymen, black, white, and coloured, to believe we can find a solution together.' " (*National Geographic*, October 1988)

Dr Robert Shrire, Professor of Political Studies, University of Cape Town, "Hackles Rising: Foreign Pressures and Change in South Africa": "The impact of external pressures on the white electorate is difficult to assess. It seems probable that moderates and liberals, represented in party terms by the Progressive Federal Party and the independent movements, have been the biggest losers. Growing international pressures and the threat and reality of sanctions have contributed to racial and intragroup polarisation and made whites both angry and apprehensive. Moderates [and even more so, Liberals] have found it difficult to communicate their policies in this context and have been effectively branded as anti-South African and pro-sanctions.... Paradoxically, perhaps, it is the National Party that may have been the greatest electoral beneficiary of the sanctions pressures....the NP has been able to convince a large part of the electorate that did not formerly support it to rally round the flag.... The Conservative Party...has since made slow but steady progress.... Whites who perceive themselves to be relatively deprived, such as economically hard-hit farmers, low-level civil servants, blue collar workers and the lower-middle class in general have been particularly susceptible to the appeals of the right....

"One of the significant developments in recent South African politics has been the emergence of organised business as an activist force for change. The 1976 unrest and the subsequent immobility of government led to a growing recognition among business leaders that politics and public policy were simply too important to be left exclusively in the hands of politicians.... [But] in terms of the growing perception of a challenge to the security of the state itself, members of the business community are, both formally and informally, increasingly co-operating with the state to ensure the very survival of the socio-economic order. Both share a common interest in ensuring law and order, in finding ways of neutralising sanctions, and of limiting the damage caused by disinvestment.... The sanctions/disinvestment campaign thus has not contributed to an expansion in the progressive role that capital could play in unfolding developments. By creating a mood of anger and insecurity, it has made it more difficult and costly for business leaders to play a critical role in building reform coalitions....

"The reality of government policy and white politics in general is its relative independence and autonomy from external forces. Foreign pressures are inherently blunt instruments for bringing about changes in domestic affairs and they have succeeded only in uniting whites against foreign pressures.... To the extent that external forces have had an impact on white politics, it has been to strengthen the reactionary elements and to harden white attitudes.... Foreign pressures are only important at the margin. If constructive engagement has therefore failed to bring about major reform, the alternative of destructive disengagement threatens to make reform less likely. This is the dilemma and the challenge." (*South Africa Foundation Review*, November 1988)

Professor Lawrence Schlemmer, Director of the Centre for Policy Studies, University of the Witwatersrand: " The sanctions campaign has been promoted abroad by groups and parties with fairly radical goals for South Africa (the anti-apartheid movements, the black caucus in the US Congress, organisations like Transafrica, etc.).... Sanctions are seen by many in the exiled opposition movements as a necessary accompaniment of the armed struggle. The approach of armed struggle and violent pressure obviously requires the diplomatic and economic isolation of South Africa, and this goal is facilitated by the sanctions campaign. In this context sanctions are merely an adjunct of a much wider, more serious and morally problematic campaign.... By now dozens of analyses have appeared that, on balance, suggest that a successful violent overthrow of the system, or even a serious danger of this occurring, is a fanciful notion.

"An ultimate solution to South Africa's conflict will have to include the development of mutual respect and trust between establishment groupings and popular majority-based movements. If a 'solution' is arrived at as a consequence of a naked capitulation to pressure by one 'side' and what will be seen as illegitimate external assistance for the other 'side' the quality of any settlement will be seriously weakened. Quick-fix solutions, or strategies that depend unduly on seeking international allies in directly damaging white interests, will be a dismal basis for future peace and prosperity....

"A 'liberation movement' that etablishes sound organisation, coherence, discipline and an effective internal democracy has a better chance of being an effective government (or effective participant in government) after 'liberation.' Majority-based opposition movements in South Africa must, as a part of their struggle for success, anticipate and understand the problems of governing a complex country, and develop the talents and institutions to do so. Quite obviously, if these movements demonstrate these capacities, there will also be less resistance to their eventual participation in government....

"If leadership appears to be self-appointed, unrepresentative or drawn from the ranks of people whose claims to leadership are professional or clerical rather than being constituency based, then the chances of government recognition or acceptance are severely reduced." (*South Africa International*, January 1989, pp. 132, 135-138)

Steven Friedman, South African Institute of Race Relations: "Boksburg may prove to be the place where black consumers not only halted the white Right but made the trend towards non-racial cities almost unstoppable.... Opinion surveys show that many Boksburg Conservative Party voters are having second thoughts about the party they opted for on 26 October....

Boksburg may be showing many whites that apartheid in our cities cannot work any longer. And, if resegregation fails because it simply is not feasible any more, far fewer whites are likely to be interested in trying it.... Resegregation may be in trouble there primarily because black people will not accept it — and now have the consumer muscle to stop it. Black consumers in Boksburg might yet do something the Nats have failed to do — stop the CP tide.... Boksburg may begin to show that, as white cities become more dependent on black spending, the idea of a city run on apartheid lines is becoming unworkable." (*South Africa Foundation Review*, January 1989, p. 5)

"United States pro-sanctions legislators who are trying to provide for 'black economic empowerment' have adopted a narrow definition of this which could do serious damage to black self-help groups in South Africa, observers contend.... The self-help projects set up by Operation Hunger in black rural areas are one example of the schemes which would be casualties if the Bill became law.... The tougher provision governing US imports from black-owned businesses was an attempt by the legislators to empower blacks but prevent sanctions-busters — black shareholders fronting for white South African corporations, for example. But it's a shotgun Bill and everyone gets hurt." (*Weekly Mail*, 3 March 1989)

"At the recent African National Congress Conference in Oslo, attended by some ninety leading members, the guerrilla organisation vowed to step up its massive political offensive and its armed actions.... There seems to be a general feeling in international and regional circles that this is the time to forswear violence and engage in constructive dialogue. However, the continuance of the campaign of terror shows that the ANC is mindless of the death and injury it inflicts on innocent South Africans and is ignoring the advice it has received from Western governments." (*The Sowetan*, 7 April 1989)

An extract from Shell South Africa's "Chairman's Review, 1988 Business Report" by John G Kilroe, Executive Chairman: "The fact that there is still hope in this country, that there is still expectation, belief in our future, is one of the greatest miracles yet.... Today, that hope seems almost able to become reality....

South Africa: Land of Hope?

"In the four months I have been back [after four years in the Netherlands], I have witnessed dramatic changes, until again I believe, as I know do many others, that we are on the threshold of one of the most significant periods in our history. [*Then, describing the successful black boycott of white businesses in Boksburg, following the Conservative Party's re-establishment of strict apartheid]:* "People who previously would not be seen in the presence of those with whom they disagreed now joined together to talk. Their political and other differences were not buried, but they understood too well the need for unity and collective action. It was the beginning of a trend....

"There is a growing accent on self-improvement with a view to hastening and preparing [for political liberation]. Despite incidents of repression of the right of free expression in black education, children are again at school, seeking learning. 'Black economic empowerment' has almost become a catch-phrase and black integration into the mainstream, traditionally white economy, is an irreversible fact. There is a great accent on self-dignity, self-worth, and self-esteem...a resurgence of pride and accountability. Some have labelled it 'nation-building'; whatever one calls it, there is a strong tide of blacks regaining control of their lives and their destiny.

"Changed attitudes reflecting the recognition that the new order would not be in place overnight have manifested themselves in other important ways. Shell South Africa puts great emphasis on dialogue with black leaders, on talking with people who are in a position to give our company insight into the thoughts, feelings and aspirations of the black majority....

"This dialogue has enabled us to shape our company's policy and social mission in such a way that it is responsive to the needs and expectations of the community. It has always been our belief, and that of our shareholders, that the withdrawal of Shell from South Africa could serve no meaningful purpose. We have never pretended that our stance was based on pure altruism or emotion. On the contrary, it is a sound business decision. We are here to do business in the long-term, we want to remain a part of this country and its future. We do not, though, do business at any price. We recognise that our responsibility extends into the broad society, that we must contribute to that society beyond our contribution to its economy....

"In this ongoing dialogue with the [black] community and its leaders, we have detected change also. Only a year ago, while still happy to talk to us, there were some who did so on the basis that their belief was nonetheless that multinationals should disinvest. In the last few months, the signals have been different. Demands for disinvestment have all but ceased. Of course, there are still those who receive international exposure who will tell you that this is what black people want. Respectfully, I differ. The messages which we are getting are too consistent.

"Admittedly, there is a caveat, stipulation that if companies do stay, then there are certain things they must do, that their deeds must match their words. That is entirely acceptable....

[*Referring to the anti-apartheid movements*]: "There was a time when ideological and philosophical differences precluded people from speaking together and working together. We live in a divided society. We see the fruitless and sad results all around us. The primary objective of these movements may be the same – the end of apartheid and a free and just society for all. But they have different approaches to achieving that end, different ideas on what the nature of the post-apartheid order should be. Latterly, dialogue has begun. People are now meeting, talking together, working together towards a single ideal. We are seeing the emergence of what I have heard called the 'tactical alliance.' As in Boksburg, a common goal serves to unite.

"It goes further than mere talk among themselves. There is a preparedness to talk with opposing groups also, and to negotiate....

"The need for negotiation has been seen by Shell and others as paramount for a long time, but as polarisation increased, as positions were adopted and held, it began to appear more and more improbable. It is hopeful and exciting that today talk of negotiation is everywhere, and we are beginning to witness it, if only on a small scale as yet...." (*Weekly Mail*, 19 May 1989)

BUSINESS

As an introduction to this section of articles, I present here the "Statement of Principles" of the South Africa Foundation and excerpts from the President's Address to the 28th convention of members in Johannesburg, 16 March 1988. They are taken from the April 1988 edition of **South Africa International**, *(pp. i, 229-234)*

Statement of Principles

The South Africa Foundation, founded in 1959, is an independent organisation of influential businessmen financed entirely by private subscription from corporate and individual members to promote the best long-term interests of South Africa and its peoples. In this regard it has an increasingly important internal role, in addition to its traditional external role.

The South Africa Foundation stands for the orderly establishment of a more just society which is an essential prerequisite for long-term stability.

The South Africa Foundation believes that this is more readily attainable within a strong economy and that only a free enterprise-based system within our mixed economy can ensure the required economic growth. It believes that all South Africans should be free to participate without restriction in that system and enjoy the benefits of their participation. This requires that the remaining statutory, social, economic and educational impediments which prevent this should be removed, as speedily as possible. Further impetus to the growth of the economy requires that the process of privatisation and deregulation should be vigorously pursued.

This Foundation is convinced that South Africa cannot function effectively in isolation and is determined to do everything possible to counter the efforts, both within and outside the country, to isolate the Republic.

The South Africa Foundation therefore fosters economic relations between South Africa and the rest of the world, in the belief that these relationships do and will help to maximise the economic opportunity of South Africa and also the entire southern African region. With development, the region will better be able to resolve its problems and South Africa itself will be better able to fulfill its pivotal role in the promotion of future prosperity in the region. This requires the preservation of links with overseas investors, sources of capital and technology.

President's Address

"...The pressures from many quarters overseas to isolate this country and to prescribe solutions – often patently facile – to our complex problems continue apace even though the pro-sanctions and disinvestment lobbyists now realise that attempts to coerce are bound to fail though such pressures continue; further, there are many abroad who use the anti-South African climate merely to promote their own domestic political objectives; this is especially true in the United States....

"No action in South Africa will satisfy our extreme critics overseas and we should waste no time or effort on countering attacks from such sources. We need to win the support of reasonable moderate opinion so that we may be reaccepted as a member of the Western group of nations; in short that we may break the trend towards isolation. We have to recognise and accept that there is no way that we shall win that support unless we, the whites, are able to bring along with us a responsible cross-section of our fellow black South Africans; again we must not be put off by the manoeuvres and aspirations of those on the extreme left or right. In particular, we must not play into the hands of those abroad and at home who wish to isolate us by forcing us to respond with a siege or *laager* syndrome that would frustrate economic development and domestic reform, thus shoring up even more problems for the future.

"I believe, as I know do many of my colleagues in business generally and the South Africa Foundation specifically, that we still have the time and the opportunity to earn the voluntary co-operation of most South Africans of all races. Of course, we know only too well that there are no easy formulae to achieve what in the final analysis must be a political and constitutional solution....

South Africa: Land of Hope?

"The irony is that, in the minds of many blacks, apartheid is identified with capitalism; apartheid and capitalism are seen as the two sides of the same coin. In fact the opposite is true: apartheid is best cured by economic growth, which in turn is best promoted by the free-enterprise ethic.

"There are few of us here today who would disagree that the most effective means of eroding apartheid and prejudice in this country is to confront it with the stimulus that would accompany higher living standards....

"May I remind you of the story, well-known though it is, of the South African Black Taxi Association. Started in 1979 by twenty-one taxi drivers, it is today an economic dynamo representing 45,000 minibus owners and their 55,000 additional employees who transport some half a million passengers each day. The Association has harnessed its collective economic weight to bargain favourable credit and supply agreements and is today the largest private sector consumer of petrol, lubricants, tyres, and spare parts in the country; it is building a chain of service centres to maintain its fleet and service the general public; it has established education and pension funds for its members and their families. Of course there are problems and at times, shall we say, aggressive marketing, but by any measurement this is a notable achievement, warts and all, and a pointer to the latent entrepreneurial and creative energy within the black community. Think only of the number of jobs created over the past eight years – a time of relative stagnation elsewhere in the economy.

"It is in everyone's interest that this latent energy and creativity be unleashed. The significant entry of blacks into our economic life as owners, entrepreneurs, managers and shareholders will be a key element in the future of this country....

"Elsewhere on this continent economic infrastructure has been destroyed through socialist ideology; with political emancipation has come great poverty and deprivation. We need the stimulus to create wealth, not to destroy it.

"If the business community is to play a meaningful role in the achievement of these ideals it will have to voice its views more effectively in its constructive efforts to influence government with regard to the direction, emphasis and pace of reform....

"I believe that the business community has a right and, importantly, a responsibility to participate in the debate on national affairs to an increasing extent; I believe we are all encouraged at the evidence that this is being increasingly recognised by the authorities....

"If this were an after dinner speech I would ask you to raise your glasses to the future economic development and expansion and political evolution of South Africa and all its peoples; to the re-acceptance of this country in the family of the Western nations; to our emergence as the real power-house of the subcontinent – to all this and more, through the removal of all discrimination which frustrates the free-market economy." (Len Abrahamse)

Miscellaneous Articles

From an introduction to articles on "Black Business and Social Change" in the August 1988 issue of **South Africa Foundation Review**: "Since 1976 substantial energy, both human and financial, has been invested in black business development. As white business has absorbed the importance of a black middle class in the recipe for a future South Africa, it has emerged as a facilitator between black business and government, as well as a strategic resource for the capital and skills required by black enterprise. The state, with a view to retooling the economy to meet the manpower needs of the next century, has also abolished or amended many of the statutory instruments and laws keeping black business on the margins of economic existence. As a consequence, black capitalism is now possibly more entrenched, dynamic and organised than at any previous point in history.... There is considerable black business support for improved relations and closer contact with their white counterparts. They expressed hope (and concrete suggestions) for a more dynamic role for the white private sector in the field of black economic empowerment, and an appreciation of the changes that have already taken place in the black business environment."

Raymond Ackerman, president of Pick 'n Pay, in **Black Enterprise: Special Report**, *Vol. 14, 1988*: "My consumers, black and white, want a peaceful society.... We businessmen can change the face of this country.... [At Pick 'n Pay] we are now proud to have forty-five percent of our management black on merit, not through reverse discrimination.... [Business'] voice should be heard clearly, not only to government, but also to black leaders and people overseas who are thinking of disinvestment, we must show that there is another course.... Visibly contact overseas people and talk out against disinvestment and sanctions because that cannot be the right way to build a future South Africa.... Some of the black leaders I have spoken to may appear to want a radical solution. However, they want the same things as all of us: they want peace, they want an economy that is strong, and they do not want a devastated country. They want a civilised government and are not necessarily asking for a black or white government or a one-party state. I have found consensus with many black leaders that I did not think existed because we live poles apart.... It is because of these contacts that I feel I have more confidence and that there is hope.... I have found that every time I attend a government lobbying session with a group of people (and this is a plus for the government) we have emerged with a victory [including black advancement and integrated housing].... Our sports club [is] open to all races.... Everybody said we were mad to attempt it, but ours was one of the first clubs in South Africa to open its doors. Today thirty-to-forty percent of our members are doctors, dentists, and lawyers who happen to be coloured. We swim together, play golf together and its just wonderful to see.... There have been changes and that is a positive sign. The government is not as unyielding as people like to think. I believe that is why business has a role to keep on fighting and lobbying...."

In late 1987, Gavin Relly, Chairman of Anglo American Corporation, delivered an address at The Hague, Netherlands, entitled, "Towards a Non-Racial Democracy in South Africa." I quote here from that address, as reprinted and published by **Southern Africa Forum** *in April, 1988:*

"The central question in South Africa today is how to go forward towards a non-racial democratic future, building on those fragile institutions which have survived the apartheid years whilst getting rid of the distortions and injustices wrought by apartheid laws.

"Yet there is no clearer indication of how apartheid has made fools of us all than by the loss of rational faculties which so many South Africans and foreigners display when approaching this question.

"...South Africa is often presented as having unique problems wrought by a uniquely evil governmental and social system. The conclusion seems to be that solutions must be sought and applied immediately which, in ignoring a host of realities about South Africa and the developing global context, will not only fail to remove the manifest injustices – political, economic and social – under which so many South Africans labour, but will almost assuredly remove any chance of the average South African, black or white, improving his lot for generations to come.

"It would be silly to pretend that the problems which flow in South Africa from our heterogeneous cultural and ethnic structure are unique: It is only that compared with anywhere else they are infinitely more complex.

"...South Africa has five major languages and about seven major 'tribes'.... Diverse language groups which often cannot understand one another make communication exceedingly difficult, inhibiting progress in much political, social or economic endeavour. Amongst the black population, more than half are still not urbanised. There are enormous developmental and attitudinal differences between urban and rural black people – in fact a vast cultural divide exists. The diversity is reflected in the huge variety of political movements which exists in South Africa.... Pigmentation of one's skin does not, as is often presumed, always denote which side of the political spectrum one falls.

"South Africa currently has a population of over thirty-three million, which is expected to increase to about forty-five million by the year 2000.... In 1985, forty-five percent of the black population of 23.5 million was under the age of sixteen; ...almost 20 percent of the population is estimated to be unemployed. There is a shortage of between 250,000 and 850,000 housing units for black South Africans [exact population numbers have proven difficult to determine], with demand likely to grow to three million units by the year 2000 unless the problem is tackled now. It has been estimated that the proportion of GNP required to provide equal education to all South Africans, to which the government is dedicated, will have to rise from the present level of 4.5 percent to 18 percent by the year 2000 (given three percent growth).

"If we are to improve living standards for all South Africans and by doing so hope to contribute positively to the lives of the other Southern African countries which depend so much on South Africa, South Africa must be a growing economy.

"...I have much understanding with the dilemma which government leaders and international businesses have faced and continue to face in making a choice about South Africa.... However, sanctions are a counsel of despair by those who, maddened by apartheid, have lost the ability to think deliberately about the consequences of their words and actions.

"The argument about whether sanctions hurt black or white South Africans more, and by how much, and over what timespan, is fatuous in the face of the obvious interdependence of black and white South Africans in a modern economy. The reality is that the life chances of future generations are being recklessly squandered through a policy whose historical track record of producing desired ends is abysmal.... There is no way to artificially stimulate the rest of Southern Africa when the economy of its hub is in decline. Sanctions against South Africa are sanctions against Southern Africa and no amount of aid in the foreseeable future will adequately redress the natural growth and prosperity sacrificed.

"...Apartheid in the form of statutory discrimination, unfair access to resources and distorted development carries an awesome responsibility for the magnitude of the problems facing South Africa today. *But it is not the sole cause*, and recognition of this fact is essential if those problems are to be successfully addressed. Many of the problems facing South Africa are common to all societies which are modernising.

"...So if the dismantling of apartheid is a necessary condition in the move towards a democratic non-racial South Africa, it is not a sufficient one. An associated myth fostered by the lack of rational thinking on South Africa, which encourages the view that simply abolishing apartheid will bring Utopia, is the conventional wisdom that South Africa is a rich country. But behind the façade of obvious mineral wealth there lies

another reality: South Africa has a per capita Gross Domestic Product of
$2010.

"If the country's developmental needs are to be met and a more equitable
share of resources amongst the entire population achieved, policies aimed
a t redistributing wealth without ensuring the generation of new and
growing wealth through policies attuned to the international competitive
economy will simply lead to increasing poverty.

"...Most of Africa is beginning to give up its twenty-five-year-old
experiment of socialist-oriented centralised planning.

"...In 1987, after three years of dramatic developments, the following
general propositions can be made:

— Neither revolution nor resolution is at hand.

— The *status quo* cannot be maintained. The changing base of the
economy has shifted significant economic, social, and — not
least — buying power into black hands.... Amongst Afrikaners
apartheid is increasingly a dead ideology: The Human Sciences
Research Council (HSRC) report on Intergroup Relations, the
Stellenbosch academics' rejection of the National Party election
manifesto, the Dutch Reformed Church's rejection of racism, and the
emergence politically of the 'New Nats' and the Independents all
underline the reality.

— The time for negotiation has not passed, but has not yet even
arrived. This because both the governing group and those in
opposition are in a state of flux and have not yet gained their
definitive character.... In this context and since central political
negotiations are unlikely in the short term, regional negotiations take
on an additional importance. Here the KwaZulu/Natal Indaba should
be an inspiration.

—Conflict in South Africa is not a simple clash between monolithic white versus black interests.... Interracial alliances exist both on the side of the State and of its opposition.... Conflict in South Africa has at least as much to do with competing concepts of democracy and economic justice as it does with race. Here too institutions and countries overseas can play a role by sharing their experience.

—Conflict in South Africa is capable of non-racial democratic resolution. Significant agreement exists between almost all actors as to the desired future, though the understanding of what the terms 'non-racial' and 'democracy' entail differ.... Inevitably over the next few years sanctions will, by weakening the economy, weaken the power base of unions and help destroy what, treated correctly, is a beach-head for the future non-racial democratic South Africa.

—Western policies towards South Africa have been short range, based on false analogies and strategically self-contradictory.... South Africa is often understood in the West in the context of decolonisation (as in Algeria) or desegregation. Both analogies are fundamentally flawed.

—Significant untried avenues exist for constructive Western interaction with South Africa. The West needs to become *more* involved with *all* South Africans, seeking to influence all in the direction of a non-racial and democratic future. At the institutional level, Western agencies (governmental and private) can do much to assist in the creation and strengthening of the institutions without which effective non-racial democracy will be impossible. However, this can only be done if it is accepted that time and effort will be required for results.

"In South Africa there is as yet no broad consensus about the nature of an equitable political system. The radical left wants a populist revolution, after which its leaders will determine the nature of the socio-economic system, apparently on Marxist lines. The radical right wants an absolute geographic separation between the races, with overtones of national socialism. The businessman can hardly be attracted to either wing — neither can the ruling party, if it is true to its stated policy of getting rid of apartheid and negotiating a new deal within the principles of a free-enterprise, equal-opportunity society guided by the rule of law.

"Only South Africans can make those decisions, but the international community can help by supporting an inevitably gradual process...."

Chapter 4

SANCTIONS

The 1989 edition of the Leadership publication, **Sanctions,** *featured articles by and about a number of prominent South Africans under a variety of headings. Though many come to similar conclusions, it is interesting to note the widely-divergent perspectives from which these conclusions are drawn. Some of their comments follow.*

IMPERATIVES

Dr Ronald Bethlehem, economics consultant and author of **Economics in a Revolutionary Society:** "It is only continued industrial growth, and the widening of black empowerment that such growth involves, which will make the desired and needed political change possible at all."

PERSPECTIVE

Dr Christopher Coker, lecturer in international relations, London School of Economics: "Most commentators believe that there is no direct linkage between economic deprivation and political change. Where sanctions have been applied, as in the case of Rhodesia (1966-79), they showed all too clearly that while it is possible to have punishment without compliance, or compliance without punishment, punishment on its own rarely guarantees that a country will comply with the demands made of it by another State."

SURVEYS

Patrick Laurence, South African correspondent for **The Economist** *[London]:* "As the Washington-based Investor Responsibility Research Centre (IRRC) has concluded in its assessment of the main survey data, the overall thrust of the surveys points toward one central conclusion: The majority of blacks do not support total disinvestment or comprehensive sanctions."

UNIONS

Riaan de Villiers, free-lance journalist formerly labour correspondent on the ***Rand Daily Mail****:* "A number of surveys have found that most black workers are opposed to sanctions and disinvestment – and that the minority of workers which has supported sanctions has further diminished over the past two years."

Martin Schneider, staff reporter: "Franz Steinkuehler, president of the International Metalworkers' Federation (IMF) [takes a] stand, and the support he receives from aggressive and restless South African unions bears examination. For example, he rejects the persistent argument by pro-sanctioneers that the majority of blacks not only want sanctions, but that they are prepared to suffer the consequences of unemployment and impoverishment in order to enter the political kingdom. 'I am absolutely convinced,' retorts Steinkuehler, '...that there will eventually be the type of change that we all desire. But I know there are many ways of achieving that change. I am a trade unionist and a social democrat. Therefore I cannot favour violence. I understand that my colleagues in South Africa are impatient; I understand that only too well. But our colleagues are realistic people. They have their feet on the ground. They have clearly analysed what the effect of disinvestment and sanctions will be. So it will be more profitable to take the evolutionary path. Unionism can only flourish if you have a strong industrial base. The only movement of relevance to me is the trade union movement. My colleagues in South Africa tell me that we should all try to ensure that trade unions can work more effectively.'

"BMW South Africa's Walter Hasselkus believes BMW has the right to comment on political developments, particularly when they affect business. 'For example, we did not hesitate to express our reservations about the Labour Relations Amendment Bill,' he says. 'But at the end of the day, we firmly believe that business' most important political contribution must be made in the economic field. Economic activity, and lots of it, is what will save South Africa. The intelligent alternative to sanctions is economic growth. We will continue to play a role in many ways. One of the means at our disposal is a comprehensive social responsibility programme aimed, primarily, at upliftment through education and small business development.' "

INVESTMENT

John Kane-Berman, executive director of the South African Institute of Race Relations: "Calling for sanctions satisfies a need to inflict punishment on the South African government. So powerful is this need that questions about the usefulness of sanctions are brushed aside....Punishing the government and eradicating apartheid are not the same thing. The need to do the first should not be allowed to undermine the chances of doing the second....Paradoxical as it may seem, limited sanctions with carrots attached are more effective than punitive sanctions designed not to persuade government to perform but to punish it....American (and other) politicians, because their priority now is to punish and express revulsion, rather than to change South Africa, have caused sanctions to lose whatever utility as a change instrument they might have had....

"One of the consequences of the sanctions that have been threatened or imposed so far is high food prices, which arise in part from costly import substitution industries supplying the agricultural sector. High food prices cause no suffering in the corridors of power. In township and homelands [however] they can make the difference between life and death....

"Blacks have no access to real political power, and no prospect of it in the short term. But, by virtue of their numbers, they are steadily empowering themselves economically. The accumulation of economic leverage by black South Africans has already compelled government to repeal a number of important apartheid laws in the social and economic sphere....

"Whereas black political emancipation in the United States has failed to bring about commensurate economic advancement, political emancipation for black South Africans will not only have been brought about by economic power but will also be underpinned by it....

"It is from this perspective that sanctions must be evaluated. Will they help or hinder the accumulation of power by black people? For most black people, the net effect of sanctions will be higher unemployment and greater poverty — in other words what Americans in their own country call a growing black underclass. Just as the economy's dependence on black collaboration is the Achilles' heel of apartheid, the black underclass is the Achilles' heel of black political and economic action. It undermines the bargaining power of trade unions because it creates a large pool of alternative labour. By lowering the rate of economic growth, sanctions will also slow down the pace of black penetration of skilled jobs and weaken black consumer leverage. Sanctions thus run the risk of destroying the black power base that is necessary to underpin black liberation....

"How and when will blacks translate growing economic power into political power? Nobody can answer this question yet. There are high risks involved and only the people who will have to take them can decide when to take them. The least that others can do is to refrain from action that might weaken black economic muscle by turning the gainfully employed into the jobless, and the poor into the destitute – especially when the great weight of evidence shows that an overwhelming majority of blacks oppose action that threatens their jobs.

"The erosion of the Group Areas Act could prove to be the back door through which blacks get on to the voters' role. As certain residential areas become officially desegregated, apartheid in local government will run into new problems. A situation where only whites can vote for the Johannesburg City Council, even though most people who live and/or shop in the central business district are black, is no more sustainable over the longer term than was the situation where employers could maintain stability in their factories by talking only to white unions and shutting out the black ones.

"One appropriate strategy to start tackling the most strongly defended aspect of apartheid, which is political apartheid, might thus be to tackle it first at local level. Once local government has been effectively desegregated, the maintenance of apartheid in Parliament itself will become less and less sustainable. Blacks who are richer, better educated, more strategically situated in the economy, and living in open areas, will be in a stronger position to organise themselves to press political demands at national level. Experience shows that concessions made by government increase rather than reduce the rate at which black demands escalate.

"The disintegration of socio-economic apartheid is indeed already spilling over into the national political field. The restoration of South African citizenship rights to some of the blacks who have been denationalised, and the granting of freehold in the white-designated areas symbolise the beginning of the retreat from classical political apartheid. Even the half-baked national council now being set up, devoid of legitimacy as it is, is a recognition that there can be no going back.

"Perhaps the best evidence of this is the most recent development among right-wing whites...articulated by Professor Carel Boshoff [son-in-law of the late Prime Minister, Hendrik Verwoerd, architect of Apartheid]...who has recently said that the Conservative Party's promise of a return to orthodox apartheid cannot be fulfilled. Professor Boshoff is now proposing an Afrikaner homeland as the only way for Afrikaners, given his realisation that the process of socio-economic integration under President PW Botha has become irreversible. Professor Boshoff is one of the few people not sleeping through the revolution....

"Whether the job of eliminating [apartheid] backlogs will be done by the private sector or by the State, or by both, makes no difference to the fact that it cannot be done with a moribund economy. If sanctions cause foreign capital to dry up, deprive South Africa of technical know-how, and compel us to close down all the mines or stockpile minerals that we cannot sell, we face a wasteland. Any black government that comes to power will face powerful expectations, but will not be able even to begin meeting them."

STRATEGY

Raymond Parsons, executive director of the Association of Chambers of Commerce: "Can external economic pressure help to facilitate the constitutional debate and peaceful change in South Africa? Is there a strong link between economic deprivation and willingness to change? Or is it more likely to be a source of divisiveness rather than of consensus? Will it smooth the way to a post-apartheid society? Or will it undermine the economic viability of future political models in South Africa? Do we wish to minimise or maximise the human costs of change in South Africa?...

South Africa: Land of Hope?

"Once we plunge into the abyss of full scale economic sanctions, there is no assurance whatsoever that equality, justice or democracy will be found on the other side. Both Archbishop Tutu and the Conservative Party in South Africa want international economic isolation – can they both be right?

"What is the relationship between economic development and the political process? Whatever political model is ultimately decided upon in South Africa, the need for economic growth remains. The challenge of economic performance is still there. This may seem obvious but it is not necessarily fully accepted nor understood, certainly not by those, both inside and outside South Africa, who espouse sanctions and disinvestment. Current experience in the rest of Africa reflects the folly of ignoring this reality....

"Economic growth, in fact, is the great softener of social improvement. In a static economy, change requires severe social friction, since the losers cannot be compensated if no rise in output is being attained. Whatever a nation's goals – more help for regional development, more jobs, a larger share of output for the underprivileged – they can most easily be achieved by producing more resources through the growth of available output per head....

"External political perceptions, sanctions, and a lack of foreign capital have placed a ceiling on economic growth. External threats – whether economic or otherwise – have also diverted resources from socially useful areas to stockpiling and defence spending.

"Economic growth also facilitates equality. International experience has shown that the richer and faster growing an economy, the more successful in promoting equality are market forces which enable people to move from poorer to richer regions and occupations....

" It is *long-term* growth that converts *short-term* growth from an *unequalising* to an *equalising* process. 'A rising tide,' said the late John Kennedy, 'floats all ships'....

"One clear lesson is that black economic progress is a vital key to political progress....Even protest actions need an economic base. It is only possible

198

to have a 'stayaway' if there are jobs to stay away from; there can only be a consumer boycott if there is spending power to withhold.....

"Sanctions and disinvestment may divide opinion, but they will certainly harden it. They will delay a political settlement, not facilitate it. It is therefore very necessary that the economic aspects of the political road ahead should receive a bigger share of attention and support from the international community than they have hitherto, in which sanctions and disinvestment can play no constructive part. Sanctions are a dead end – they lead nowhere. This means that foreign participation in the South African economy should increase, not decrease. Whatever compensatory policies South Africa is able to follow to neutralise external economic pressure, the fact remains that at its present stage of development the country should not be a capital-exporting nation if it is to address its social priorities.

"To sum up: given the broad scope of what needs to be done in the political arena in South Africa, a lack of adequate economic progress could even cause the political process to fail. External pressures which jeopardise South Africa's economic performance can only undermine the constitutional debate which needs to take place about its future. There is little point in pursuing a constitutional debate about a future South Africa if the legacy is to be an economic wasteland."

SOCIAL ACTION

Sheryl Raine, assistant editor of **The Sunday Star** *[Sunday edition of the* **Johannesburg Star***]:* "Whilst all foreign companies have come under pressure to withdraw from South Africa, it has been the American multi-nationals which have dominated the departure list. Because of their association with the Sullivan Codes, now known as the Statement of Principles, the impact of their leaving is more readily measured...

"Few withdrawals were as brutal as Kodak's. The company disappeared, dumping 480 local staff, a third of them black. All corporate social responsibility (CSR) programmes ceased....

South Africa: Land of Hope?

"When General Motors South Africa had a golden pipeline to Detroit, R3 million [$1.5 million] was spent annually on a broad range of CSR programmes despite the company's poor performance. The company achieved top scores on the Sullivan Code rating system. GMSA's last general manager, Bob White, was aggressive in his stand against apartheid. He came close to urging civil disobedience by publicly offering legal and financial support to any black GM employee charged with swimming on Port Elizabeth's then whites-only beaches....

"Of all the one-time Sullivan signatories which have turned their companies over to non-US owners, only one has decided to continue as a signatory....American companies in South Africa are obliged to allocate between ten and fifteen percent of their local payroll every year to CSR....Despite a twenty-five percent drop in the number of signatories reporting in 1987, the amount of money spent on CSR by those who stayed, soared. Expenditure in the year to June 1987 on education for black, coloured and Asian non-employees rose to R31 million [$15.5 million] — an eleven percent increase over the previous year. In the community development sphere more than R36 million [$18 million] — an increase of sixteen percent — was spent on housing, health and welfare, civic activities and recreation. Signatories spent R9.6 million [$4.8 million] on development of black, coloured and Asian enterprise, and a total of R25.8 million [$12.9 million] was devoted to efforts aimed at the complete elimination of apartheid including lobbying, anti-apartheid advertising and anti-apartheid negotiation and legal assistance.

" 'Just think how much more we could be doing if those companies which have pulled out were still here and contributing on this ever-increasing scale,' says Adriaan Botha, executive director of the American Chamber of Commerce....

"The departure of US firms has already resulted in a reduction in support for community development and social change organisations. Total disinvestment would have a disastrous impact on many organisations which depend on American firms for nearly their entire budgets...[in addition to which] wage structures at US firms have been higher than local companies."

OPINION

KwaZulu Chief Minister Mangosuthu Buthelezi: "Those who campaign for sanctions and disinvestment as a weapon against apartheid do so not only against the wishes of the black majority but also in harmony with those revolutionary and political forces which are most committed to the use of violence to bring about radical change. The ANC calls loudest for disinvestment; it also calls loudest for the armed struggle. The UDF, which cannot call inside South Africa for the armed struggle, calls loudest to make the country ungovernable; it also calls loudest for disinvestment....

"After decades of oppression, the pendulum must begin to sway in favour of black bargaining power. It is economic progress and the introduction of blacks to the cash of the economy which have done most to advance that, and more economic advancement, more economic growth, will produce more black bargaining power....

"In view of the legislation now before the US Congress, I address myself particularly to Americans, who must, I believe, stop to think very carefully about what some might call the numbers game. More than half of black South Africans are now fifteen years old and younger; this huge population bulge is bearing down on the market place where there are already terribly high levels of unemployment. That bulge is moving towards an age where people get married and have children – and that means the vast backlogs in black housing, in education, in facilities for health and welfare, will be heightened. Already, many millions of blacks are living in desperate squalor in informal settlements. As the population bulge moves forward in time, these millions will be added to by many more millions.

"Throughout the Third World it has been shown that if political change is not followed by an improvement in the quality of the life of the people, it turns sour in the mouths of the poorest of the poor. Real, spiralling mass poverty is the enemy of democracy. The application of sanctions will first have to be destructive of the South African economy if they are to be effective, and then sanctions will be effective in spreading mass poverty, and in threatening the development of democracy."

THE HISTORY AND CHARACTER OF SOUTH AFRICA AND ITS PEOPLE

Chapter 5   History and Character of South Africa and its People

*T*he information in this chapter is designed to give the reader further insight into South Africa, her politics and people. The twenty-four categories were chosen based on topics treated in and facts and opinions gathered from the twelve books quoted.

The books from which the information is taken are the following:

- Adam and Moodley, *South Africa Without Apartheid: Dismantling Racial Domination*

- Berger and Godsell, editors, *A Future South Africa*

- Butler, Elphick, and Welsh, editors, *Democratic Liberalism in South Africa*

- Wessel de Kock, *Usuthu! Cry Peace!*

- Marq de Villiers, *White Tribe Dreaming*

- David Harrison, *The White Tribe of Africa*

- Louw and Kendall, *South Africa: The Solution*

- Maré and Hamilton, *An Appetite for Power: Buthelezi's Inkatha and the Politics of "Loyal Resistance"*

- Credo Mutwa, *Let Not My Country Die*

- Alan Paton, *Save the Beloved Country*

- Richard Rive, *Writing Black*

- Clem Sunter, *The World and South Africa in the 1990s*

CONTEMPORARY PRESS REPORTS

de Kock

[*Referring to 1820*]: "Then, as now, South Africa was much a moral spa for elder statesmen and up and coming political Elmer Gantrys." (p. 50)

"The Afrikaner is reviled in a way unprecedented since the Third Reich in World War Two. Wrote a Washington columnist: 'In a world hypersensitive to racial slurs, he almost alone may be deemed generally repulsive without causing offense to the arbiter of decency. The phrase 'Boer-bashing' connotes not intolerance but something admirable. Even those within the US administration whose job it is to care genuinely about what happens to South Africa have let their frustrations with Pretoria, not to mention Congress and the sanctions lobby, fester into a loathing of Afrikanerdom as a whole.' " (p. 52)

"South Africa is one of the most ideologically overheated countries in the West and as such the press, local or foreign, has not been inured to the temptation of double-speak and ideological accent. In a country where, as someone put it, theatricality, and not reality, is the yardstick, it is not surprising that Inkatha would attract the odium of some 'freedom now' activists in the press." (p. 121)

"As far as foreign press coverage of South Africa is concerned it does not extend beyond the vogue adjectives." (p. 122)

"When Buthelezi spoke to black Americans in Los Angeles about the press, he complained about a 'tragic lack of realism' and called on the United States mass media 'to put the South Africa struggle for liberation in its true perspective....American commentators write for an audience and are not necessarily conveyors of truth....I have suffered at the hands of Americans, and the liberation of South Africa has suffered at the hands of Americans....' " (pp. 123-124)

"The South African situation has been mythologised to such a degree that what happens inside the country is for all practical purposes no longer relevant to many outsiders." (p. 138)

South Africa: Land of Hope?

de Villiers

"[There are] dimensions to the South African story that have become lost in the clamour of the moment. The image of the Afrikaner flickering across the consciousness of the Outside is shallow, as all media images are, a mix of facts half understood and factoids that have taken on their own life, as they always do when journalists go on crusade." (pp. xxiii-xxiv)

"Some good reporting is being done, but most media coverage is stunningly ignorant. In the national media of the country I long ago adopted [Canada], there is an almost pornographic eagerness for the cataclysm to happen — almost as if they want to whip the Afrikaners." (p. 390)

EARLY AFRIKANERS

de Villiers

"Unlike the Puritans of New England, who expected to look after themselves and who, within a few years, had constructed schools, town halls, and whole communities, the settlers at the Cape found that the Company provided everything." (p. 27)

"The patterns have little in common with the self-assertive awareness of the American Pilgrims, who were already casting and recasting the ideas and the phrases that were to result in their declaration of the notion of inherent rights for all men. The farmers of the Cape, isolated, cut off from the intellectual development of Europe, [were] tucked into their folds in the southern mountains, days from Cape Town....Their way of life was little different from the ways of the Khoikhoi, who had been on the land for millennia: a nascent society already fragmented into clans, small, insular, fierce in defence of their territory, inward-looking and parochial, deeply identified with the land....Only the Bible travelled. Other books were too much excess baggage; they remained in the Cape." (pp. 41-42)

"The Afrikaners' intense involvement and identification with the land was a love less for the land than for the idea of the landscape, with its endless vistas and apparently endless opportunities for withdrawal. Separation has always seemed to the Afrikaners a legitimate option." (p. 52)

"The Boers didn't wish to be totally cut off from the products of civilisation. They just wanted to damp the interference level and filter out the anxiety. It was the *Zeitgeist* of the tribe." (p. 55)

"Free slaves became 'free blacks', not free burghers — the colony maintained the Roman distinction between freemen and freedmen. Freedmen — and free blacks generally — had considerable rights. They could buy and sell property, own businesses, farm, borrow money, initiate court cases, attend church, have their own militia under free black officers. But if the law was officially colour blind, the practice was different. Farmers ran the economy and dominated society, and since blacks never established themselves as farmers, their influence was limited to town: They could do well enough in the Tavern of the Seas but never managed any real impact on the colony as a whole. (This also explains why Cape Town, a racially more freewheeling city than the towns of the stiff-necked interior, resisted apartheid longer than anywhere else.)" (p. 59)

"The Afrikaners were reacting...against a colonial presence, and were in their fibre anti-colonialists. They had come as settlers and turned to conquerors whose presence was, of course, destructive, but they never attempted cultural genocide. That was left to the British they despised and to their wretched missionaries....There was nothing in the Afrikaner heart like the spirit of the Spanish looters who took South America, nothing even of the casual imperial assumptions of the American West, where the Indians were treated like wild ponies to be tamed and shut into paddocks. The Afrikaners wanted only to be left alone....Their desire only to be left alone persisted when they were running the country, and it influenced in some measure the weird edifice they built out of scraps of ideas and called apartheid." (pp. 140-141)

"[The 19th century was called] a Century of Wrong. It had been a century of defeat, retreat, defeat, withdrawal, filled with heroic figures who vanished and heroic victories that turned to ashes; first the Company, then the Xhosa, then the Zulu, then the British — against each the Afrikaner struggled, then withdrew, until the *laager* [the tight circle of wagons, drawn together to withstand enemy attack] became the definitive symbol of his existence." (p. 239)

[*Quoting DW Kruger's history, **The Age of the Generals**]:* "For a century and more Afrikanerdom had managed to preserve its life through heroic action. It now thought to prolong its existence by heroic thought against the whole world. The Age of the Generals was past and done with forever. Afrikanerdom would endeavour to maintain its existence through the age of the politicians." (p. 240)

"Military solutions and the attempt to flee had failed. The Afrikaner would turn to manipulating constitutions." (p. 240)

SOUTH AFRICAN REALITIES

Adam and Moodley

"The civil service forms the main constituency of the National Party, in competition with the extreme right wing, and the government cannot afford to implement a policy of salary freezes and attrition that would alienate the members of its overexpanded bureaucracy." (p. 25)

"The influence of business on government is likely to increase in the severe recession. With a worsening economic crisis, costly ideological projects will become the obvious target for savings." (p. 123)

"That the government would eventually have to negotiate with the ANC...has gained wide currency among technocratic powerholders." (p. 123)

"There are three main arguments for the urgency of fundamental sociopolitical change in South Africa....First, exclusion of the black majority from central governmental institutions...increases the costs of racial domination for the ruling minority....Second, neither side is likely to defeat the other, short of mutual destruction....Third, power-sharing stands as the only alternative to continued instability." (p. 215)

Berger and Godsell

"To many the reforms...cannot be expected to win any praise or sympathy for the government, since the structures so reformed can be regarded as having been an insult to humanity in the first place. Nevertheless, they are slowly transforming South Africa from a society more rigidly segregated than any other in the world to one in which black South Africans can begin to participate in some of the benefits of a modern urban society." (p. 9)

"One senior MP [Member of Parliament] summed up the major interest of white Nationalists as being 'security and standards — there is a great fear (among whites) that a Third World situation will arise in their own areas.' Another senior MP and deputy minister close to the core of National Party thinking gave the central concern a more ethnic flavour but also stressed the composite character of its ideology by listing Western values, Christian values, life views, community cohesion, material security, a

South Africa: Land of Hope?

familiar and recognisable environment, a strong economy, property rights, an objective legal system and the protection of established institutions in general. These everyday or popular interests would be taken for granted in any typical Western society. In South Africa, however, they are clearly much more consciously experienced as constituting a First World sub-society within a Third World continent." (pp. 27-28)

"The State of Emergency seems to be proving successful in suppressing unrest and in reducing the need for security action. One indication of this is the reduction in the number of fatalities from political violence." (p. 35)

"When a handful of progressive South African businessmen meet ANC representatives informally in London or New York, both groups are usually surprised about the ease, or even warmth, with which personal relationships are established on the basis of a common South African background. Notwithstanding different political strategies and ultimate goals, the common aversion to National Party rule and anachronistic apartheid laws provides a backdrop of understanding and even solidarity in some instances. However, these tentative personal alliances quickly fall apart when their mutual expectations are spelled out." (p. 118)

"David Curry, the [Labour, i.e. coloured] party's former chairman, argues that it is a fact of South African politics that the majority of individuals define their political fears and aspirations on a 'race' or 'group' basis (despite popular rhetoric) and that 'all leaders, including politicians, use their particular race or group as bases from which to operate.' " (p. 182)

"The goal of greater black political unity has often been espoused by Inkatha and its leadership. In the context of the deeply divided black community this goal seems important. However, it can only be achieved (if at all) at the cost of avoiding or disguising ideological, analytical and strategic differences of the greatest importance. Equally, the very pursuit of 'black unity' perpetuates an apartheid premise: i.e. that political interests are necessarily defined by race. No actor can ignore race. Yet all actors seeking a nonracial future must seek ways of transcending it....In the past, white liberal opponents of apartheid could see themselves speaking on behalf of, or siding with, some relatively uniform body called the black population. Whatever the validity of that strategy historically, it is no longer appropriate or possible today. The South African black

212

population (now) is an increasingly heterogeneous, economically stratified and ideologically diverse group. There is no black point of view on many of the issues...." (pp. 194-195)

"The hope for some legitimacy in the international community has not been totally abandoned, but far greater stress is now placed on internal stability, self-reliance and co-operation with regimes that are more reliable than the government of the United States, which is accused of constantly shifting its expectations and demanding more and more far-reaching reforms." (p. 204)

Butler et al.

"...since the late sixties, market forces have been inducing a shift of certain labour-intensive industries toward the 'homelands.' We see, therefore, that the record of the reserves [homelands] has not been one of universal and relentless decline, depressing though many of the statistics relating to them have been." (p. 210)

"In the medium term, the best prospects for democratisation lie in a governing coalition between a white party and one or more other parties, either black or nonracial. One is looking in the short-to-medium term at prospects for 'powersharing' rather than at a fully open democratic process. The medium-term future can perhaps be seen as a fairly limited period of transition to a more conventional democracy in the Western mode, offering minorities the reassurance of a power base while the society is developing toward complete democracy....A variety of surveys and polls...have shown that in the metropolitan areas of Johannesburg, Durban-Pietermaritzburg, the Cape Peninsula, and possibly the eastern Cape, majorities or near majorities of white voters are willing to endorse power-sharing with blacks as long as adequate protection of minority interests is provided." (p. 392)

de Villiers

"...Afrikanerdom is never as united as its modern leaders' rhetoric supposes. There was a competing vision of Afrikaner destiny at work in the Cape. This was the inclusive vision of JH Hofmeyr [in the 1880s], which recognised that 'Afrikaners' could be drawn from outside the narrow definition...could include not only those born into the *volk* [people] but also those who shared its love of the land. This competing vision was important then, and it is important still, because those Afrikaners who share Hofmeyr's views cling to the possibility of opening up not only to people of other languages but to people of other colours: the men and women who hold these views could still save the Afrikaner from himself. Hofmeyr's political and intellectual heirs are, in fact, still a part of the Afrikaner body politic, virtually invisible to the outside world, buried as they are in the tidal wave of condemnation faced by the tribe. But [the] inclusive spirit does live on." (p. 180)

"[There is an] ancient tendency for Afrikaners to split into quarrelsome factions, each governed by a hero, a leader of substance....Schism is the continuing nightmare of Afrikaner politicians. The Afrikaners have always been prone to schism – a tribe that follows heroes always is." (pp. 249, 268)

"[To the nationalists] fusion was a material and spiritual threat to Afrikanerdom....Fusion...meant competition with the English. The disinherited could not compete: the fear tapped was the fear of being swamped – first by the English and then by their agents, the black masses. The politics of fear proved decisive in the ethnic mobilisation of the Afrikaners." (pp. 270, 271)

"The ethnic mobilisation to the politics of fear has obscured it, but it's still there to be tapped: a fundamental generosity, an inclusiveness that could be used to turn the Afrikaner from the master to the co-host of his own house. No liberal politician has succeeded in making use of this...factor, this other face of the *volk*. No outside pressure groups seem now to recognise its existence, or, if they do, to see in it a possibility, a chance to make a different future." (pp. 298-299)

Louw and Kendall

"Bureaucratic sabotage is one of the most serious problems facing South Africa." (p. 70)

"South Africa's judiciary has a reputation, even amongst the current government's most bitter enemies, for a reasonable degree of courage and independence." (p. 196)

Mutwa

"Culture forms absolutely no barrier between black and white in this country....Millions of black people in South Africa have adopted nearly every aspect of white culture....In many cases blacks have become more fluent in English and Afrikaans than they are in their native language....Since the birth of South Africa as a nation, *culture* has played a reconciliatory and not a divisive role in this land." (p. 26)

"It is a truth known to all who are black, that deep in our heart of hearts we prefer a one-party state and not a two-party democracy with a governing party and an opposition. We are rabid tribalists at heart." (p. 186)

Paton

"Mr Botha is an Afrikaner who was born in the prison of Afrikaner Nationalism, but he does not want himself or his people to die in prison." (p. 36)

"In South Africa, Parliament is sovereign. Its laws cannot be struck down by the Supreme Court, except in the rare event that they conflict with the entrenched clause of the Constitution." (p. 74)

"The CP will capitalise on undiluted white fear, prejudice, even hatred. It will produce no political philosophy because it is totally irrational. It is led by a man of great intelligence and no sense whatsoever." (p. 193)

"The extreme Right is opposed to fundamental change, now and any other time. The radical Left wants fundamental change, not tomorrow, but now...The radical Left is morally right; the only time for justice is now. But it is pragmatically wrong in supposing that one can have it now. The real political task is to *strive now* for the just re-ordering of society....You cannot radically reconstruct in six months. But you can begin. And you can be seen to begin." (pp. 213-214)

"Any proposal...for a non-racial franchise or a qualified franchise has never received any support from the white electorate, because of the deep-seated white fear of being overwhelmed....But white South Africa might feel less fear of entering a federation or confederation where she might keep some of the things she fears most to lose, where, above all, the Afrikaner could keep his language and culture." (p. 235)

Sunter

"This revealing response to the principle of negotiation came from a well-to-do man...in Pretoria: 'You say negotiation is give-and-take. Tell me, what am I going to take?' My answer was, 'Ask your kids — you give nothing; they will lose everything. You take the future.' " (p. 97)

AFRIKANER NATIONALISM

de Villiers
"What's happening in South Africa now is not colonialism but a post-colonial tribal power struggle....[Afrikaners] have had to withdraw so often, have been dispersed so often, have been attacked so often, that group cohesion has become the highest goal....Accommodation with other groups becomes anathema: integration is the end of...Afrikaner identity. This is true of all nationalisms, but especially true here.

"If you define identity as the Afrikaner nationalists have historically defined it – with the highest allegiance given not to an idea or to a principle or to the individual or to a piece of geography or even to God but to *die nasie, die volk* [the nation, the people], and its mission as an expression of God's will; and if this *volk* is defined in terms of its history and language and Puritan traditions and location and mission and stern Calvinism – if this is the way you look at it, then integration *is* death. And it's no good saying that its identity is doomed anyway – that the management of a modern capitalist state and racist society has already destroyed much of it and will destroy the rest in due course. No good either to point out that the very implementation of the vision perverted its nature. The Afrikaner nationalists are acting as primitives in charge of dangerous machinery always act; they will strip its gears and ruin everything for tribal advantage. The tribe must live. This is the dominant reality." (p. xxv)

"We understood viscerally as children that the monument [raised to the Afrikaner women and children who died in the English concentration camps during the Boer War] was not merely a stone expression of the evil that outsiders do; it is a symbol of how...outsiders, foreign to the fundamental thought patterns of the people, will always try to do you harm. The only solution is a tight solidarity. You must control events if you can, resist if you can't. It is the ultimate internalisation of the *laager*." (p. 237)

Paton
[*Referring to PW Botha*] "Somewhere inside the Nationalist armourplate, a South African is trying to get out...[but] he puts his party before his

country because he suffers from the same psychological impotence that paralysed his predecessor...he thinks the party and the country are one and the same thing....He cannot yet accept that the breaking of the National Party is essential for the salvation of Afrikanerdom." (pp. 37, 44)

"Afrikaner people...call themselves a nation. It is interesting to note that the South African English have never called themselves a nation....South African Indians are not a nation....The coloured people are not a nation....The answer to this riddle lies in history." (pp. 37, 113)

"The powerful Afrikaner Broederbond, which had been formed as a cultural organisation in 1918 with a membership confidential and confined to male Protestant Afrikaners...today hold almost all the prominent public posts in South Africa, including those in the Cabinet. Who rules the country? It is a pointless question, for it is impossible to separate the Broederbond from the Government. The English have none of this nationalistic and commemorative fervour...they just do not have the urge...to find an identity." (p. 119) *[For the complete story "inside the Afrikaner Broederbond," read* **The Super-Afrikaners**, *by Ivor Wilkins and Hans Strydom.]*

"The white English-speaking people of South Africa have only one thing in common and that is their language. They consist of many groups....Though many of them can be as scared of the State as anyone else, [they] do not regard it in the same religious light. The law is there to be obeyed, but if you think it is unjust you may, if you wish, protest against it." (p. 122)

"The English do not have the Afrikaners' extreme regard for law and order. They do not want to rule everything and everybody. In general they are readier to accept the injunction, 'live and let live.' " (p. 122)

"That both Afrikaners and English have a true love of country I do not doubt. But the Afrikaner's love is in general more fierce, more emotional, more aggressive." (p. 123)

"During the last century there was a long series of frontier wars between Afrikaner trekkers going north and African tribes coming south. The memories of those wars lies deep in the Afrikaner mind and some of our white policemen think they are still fighting them." (pp. 151-152)

"[A] tendency to deny the existence of social injustices and to extol the virtues of government is a distinguishing mark of the authoritarian personality and it leads its possessor to the disastrous belief that peace can be maintained by force, that law is the equivalent of justice, and that order is to be preferred above freedom....I could not possibly celebrate a republic which claims to be a democracy and yet has shown such a contempt for the Rule of Law." (pp. 191, 232)

"You must not get the impression that I am anti-Afrikaner. But I am totally opposed to the Afrikaner Nationalism that has ruled us till today." (p. 236)

"This is not a Nazi country, but we...have a grievous sickness, an obsession with racial identity, an exaltation of Order over Liberty, an idolatrous worship of the State....Our rulers are not totalitarians, but they are certainly authoritarians." (p. 241)

"Afrikaner Nationalism had to be lived through (and I hope lived out)." (p. 304)

LIBERALISM

Butler et al.

"One outcome of liberals' identification with the middle ground has been their emphasis on compromise and accommodation, and the adoption of stands that seem conservative from today's perspective....But...there is no support for defining liberalism as anything short of democracy based on a universal franchise." (p. 7)

"Throughout most of South African history, liberals have had to contend against counter-ideologies of the right — nationalist, racist, conservative, even fascist. Now, however, the main theoretical and practical challenge comes from the left...with positions recently advanced by Marxists." (p. 8)

"Many liberals would deny it, but...ethnic rights are compatible with a liberal democracy, provided certain conditions are fulfilled, principal among them the right freely to associate, or not to associate, with an ethnic group...." (p. 10)

"Counterbalancing the weakness of liberals in formal politics...is their disproportionate presence in powerful and prestigious institutions important both to the present government and to any black-dominated successor. This presence...gives them an influential voice in the management of several sectors of society, a voice which might attain political prominence in negotiations for a new South Africa....Four sectors of South African society where liberal values are actually or potentially present: the legal profession and judiciary, the press, education, and business." (p. 11)

"The gradual growth of the middle-class among Afrikaners, Indians, coloureds, and Africans...enlarged the social base that traditionally supports democratic liberal values." (p. 15)

"Liberalism has never been a dominant force in South Africa, or even the core program of a major political party, but it did exist in a limited form in certain institutions and practices of the Cape Colony before 1910....Liberals of the interwar period went far beyond the old liberalism, recognising the necessity of rapid change toward a more equal and more humane order. These aims are still alive today." (pp. 81, 115)

221

"Mainstream liberalism (answers that) 'constitutions and laws cannot abolish prejudice in the human mind, but they can help to create the climate in which the fears that feed on prejudice are more easily dissolved. This is what a federation of Southern Africa, built on strong realistic foundations and constructed on practical lines, could do.' " (p. 155)

"Political liberals...such as Helen Suzman — for many years the lone Progressive Party member of Parliament — argued that apartheid and racial discrimination were not only morally repugnant but economically a pipe dream. The issue that enabled them to appeal to both economic and political liberals was that of black labour: with a great deal of courage and persistence they argued for at least a decade that if blacks were allowed to work where they wished, to acquire skills, and to earn higher wages, the result would be accelerated economic growth and higher incomes for the entire population, without any need for the whites to pay for black advances. An expanding cake, they argued, would result in larger pieces for all...."

"Much of the liberal analysis of the 1950s and 1960s has proved remarkably prescient, and its plea for a radical expansion of South Africa's internal market by upgrading black skills and wages should be seen as a harbinger of today's proposed 'inward industrialisation' policy. The South African government...has now adopted, in many essentials, the liberal position of twenty-five years ago....The proposed new policy of inward industrialisation, for example, would actually encourage permanent urbanisation (starting with a massive campaign to build urban housing for blacks) in the hope of creating a growing internal market as the new generator of economic growth." (p. 265-266).

de Villiers

"[There is] a small but not forgotten band of Afrikaner liberals who reject the weird edifice of apartheid in all its forms. The tribe does not speak with a single voice. These Afrikaner liberals have been holding fast to their vision, which is that the Afrikaners have a place in the larger Africa, not just a refuge in their ethos of singularity — not just a mission to build a Calvinist fortress in the continent's Deep South." (p. xxvi)

"...the Afrikaner liberals...took from defeat the same desire for liberty, but looked for its nourishment to reconciliation. Their vision, they believed, was the true heir to the endless horizons — the grander vision of a larger inclusiveness." (p. 238)

"The liberal vision of accommodation and respect between groups that grew out of the heartland...was overwhelmed. But it is there, yet, latent perhaps, almost invisible, but there." (p. 303)

"The great difference between Afrikaner liberal and Afrikaner nationalist: the liberal is a person who puts his loyalty to his country and all its people above loyalty to his race or his party — it is an inclusive nationalism, broadly based, in contrast to the narrow, exclusive nationalism of the Afrikaner nationalist." (p. 343)

APARTHEID

Berger and Godsell

"It may be absolutely true of its effects, but it is nevertheless oversimplified to regard the South African system as institutionalised racism." (p. 41)

de Kock

"In May, 1986, the head of the powerful Anglo American conglomerate, Gavin Relly, held that 'no one, the ANC included, has done more to halt the ideological thrust of apartheid than Buthelezi.' Relly had earlier been one of the first, and indeed the most influential, South African businessman to make contact with ANC leaders in Lusaka. 'It is easy to forget that he was the only black leader with an authentic power base to have faced the heat, a long time ago, of a government still determined to enforce apartheid,' added Relly, '[but] I think history, if reasonably and objectively written, will endorse the fact that [Buthelezi] was the anvil on which apartheid ultimately faltered.' " (p. 10)

de Villiers

"Fusion demanded a collaboration with the English and the world culture that the Afrikaners feared more than the blacks — they feared being submerged in a culture stronger than their own, one that ridiculed and belittled them in their own country, and one to which they had no response except to hurl accusations of disloyalty. None of what followed, the sad history of apartheid, can be understood unless the deep psychological scars and insecurities of the Afrikaner proletariat can be set against the actions of the nationalist politicians: Malan succeeded in persuading the Afrikaners that Smuts would swamp them in English and that the English would allow all whites to be swamped in turn by the inchoate black masses." (pp. 308-309)

"Hardly anyone believes in apartheid anymore, in the theology of apartheid, in the vision of apartheid as a just social order....No one any longer subscribes to the belief that through apartheid they could manage a just transition to a new order...." (p. 382)

Harrison

[*Quoting ninth-generation Afrikaner Ernie Malherbe, describing 'simmerings of unease' at former Afrikaner strongholds, Stellenbosch and Potchefstroom universities*] : "Young people are essentially pragmatic, especially Afrikaners who have become educated enough to realise what the ultimate consequences of Apartheid will be. They know that Apartheid will not work in the long run and while they have no cut-and-dried solution themselves they are now prepared to seek another solution." (p. 273)

Louw and Kendall

"There is a world-wide assumption that apartheid benefits whites. However, it can be easily shown that laws which interfere with voluntary exchange are bad for all the people involved." (p. 63)

SOUTH AFRICAN BLACKS

Adam and Moodley

"The permanent urban African working class will carry the most weight in any successful attempt to stabilise the government....Seventy-five percent expressed agreement with foreign investment because 'it makes jobs for all people in South Africa' and ninety percent still favor genuine negotiations between government and 'true leaders.' " (p. 151-153)

"Black nationalism, on the whole, aims at capturing capitalism for its own benefit rather than overthrowing it." (p. 198)

Butler et al.

"There is evidence of a rising trend in average real black per capita incomes for most of the twentieth century....From 1970 to 1980 black per capita incomes have grown faster than the average and considerably faster than those of whites. These growth rates mean that average real black incomes more than doubled over the fifty years from 1920 to 1970 and quadrupled by 1980. It is still possible to be skeptical: average gains are always compatible with no gains or even losses among the majority. However, we think there is sufficient evidence to suggest that gains among blacks have been reasonably widespread; the gains were not confined to an urban (or industrial) elite but were shared by people in reserves and on farms....While there is serious poverty at the bottom of the income distribution, eighty-five percent of households showed substantial real income gains and seventy percent experienced 'just over a doubling of their 1960 per capita incomes in the twenty years between 1960 and 1980.' " (pp. 215-216)

"A key problem for everyone is the assessment of realised conditions ('outcomes') in a context where people desire different ends....Equality is relevant not at this level but at the level of opportunity." (pp. 224-225)

de Kock

"As the Afrikaner era in South African politics slides to a close, two men emerge as paramount symbols of impending black liberation. Nelson Mandela is the figurehead of the revolutionary and foreign-based African

South Africa: Land of Hope?

National Congress; the other is Mangosuthu Buthelezi. While the long-imprisoned martyr Mandela has been elevated on to a messianic pedestal by many, Buthelezi is sure and firm-footed on his homeground.

"Inkatha is no less insistent and radical than the ANC in its demands for a democratic South Africa...but a vast divide in strategy, in tactics — confrontation and negotiation — locks the two organisations in a crucial battle for the hearts and minds of black South Africans....And this is the real drama of South Africa — its real crisis." (p. 21)

Louw and Kendall

"Socialism forged the chains which shackle South Africa's blacks....If they are free to participate fully in a market economy, within a few years there will be an explosion of economic growth in South Africa that will astonish the world." (p. 17)

"Whites say there has been change and reform in South Africa which they can see and feel. Blacks are allowed in places where they were prohibited before; there is black advancement in jobs; blacks share restaurants and theatres and play sports with whites. Opinion polls show a dramatic change in white attitudes. To whites, these changes are substantial, and they cannot understand why blacks keep saying there has been no real change and that all reform to this point has been mere tokenism. The reason for these divergent perceptions...is that most of the changes which have occurred affect only the ability of blacks to interact *socially* with whites, which is relatively unimportant...it [is] the violation of their *economic* rights that concern them so deeply." (pp. 62-63) [*italics mine*]

"South African blacks are more sophisticated, better educated and have higher living standards than the vast majority in the rest of Africa....The majority of blacks would support some kind of moderate alliance [of political parties]....None of the four independent homelands have adopted the policies whites most fear. They have all repealed all race laws, but none have espoused Marxism....All four have been more financially responsible than the South African government." (p. 169)

"Even if black leaders could be persuaded to attend a national convention it would be difficult to ascertain who are the 'real' representatives of the people. So many organisations and parties currently claim to represent most blacks that the total of the alleged followings of all these groups is equivalent to several times the present population." (p. 201)

Mutwa

"[Blacks'] forefathers left [them] a vast treasure-trove of knowledge that could place [them] in the forefront of the world's most respected nations....Telepathy, telekinesis and ESP are things that are well known to the black people....[They could] assist those American scientists who are doing research into the paranormal...[and] would make a dramatic contribution to this new and extremely important field of science that would enable the USA to surge far ahead in parapsychological research....There are many great secrets that actually survive in Africa...and one of these secrets is that of hammering and tempering copper in secret hot fluids and so make it even harder than steel, a secret that was known to the ancient Egyptians who used copper chisels tempered in this way to shape the great blocks of stone with which their temples and pyramids were built." (pp. 137-138)

Paton

"I have always believed that a narrowing of the black-white income gap would lead to a lessening of racial tension, and it seems to be possible that under a declining authoritarianism the standard of black living would begin to rise appreciably and...it would be accompanied by the growth of a stable, urban, property-owning, African middle-class, which would be conservative and non-revolutionary." (p. 112)

"Their relations with white people are often good. But they hate the laws that control their lives with a bitter hatred. Their children hate these laws more than their parents. They show their hatred by stoning and burning buses, schools, shops." (p. 151)

SOUTH AFRICAN COLOUREDS

Rive

" 'Non-European' and 'Non-white' are highly insulting labels. They imply that the persons described are negative entities, non-somethings....The term 'coloured' I find as offensive in the South African context because it has hierarchic implications, implying inferior to whites and superior to blacks." (p. 2)

"Liberal writing may be loosely defined as writing mostly by whites about blacks to move whites out of their socio-political complacency....Protest writing on the other hand is writing mostly by blacks articulating their position to a white readership they feel can effect change." (p. 21)

"Ethiopians...just could not understand my nonracial views. They were shocked at my dismissal of their nationalism as chauvinistic." (p. 42)

[*On hearing an Irishman claim he had proof the Afrikaners were bent on genocide and already had concentration camps and gas-chambers outside Cape Town and Johannesburg*]: "He refused to accept our explanation that things were bad enough without any extra embellishment." (p. 74)

[*On seeing anti-apartheid posters in Copenhagen*]: "The intention was good, but the exaggeration and inaccuracy of the drawing theatrical, unnecessary and indefensible....I appreciated and identified with the intention behind the poster, but the distorted depiction was entirely unnecessary and in fact self-defeating. The system itself is so reprehensible that it needs no sensationalism of this type to add to its well-deserved notoriety." (pp. 96-97)

"I remained on in my Claremont flat which was in a declared white area. I stayed there openly and illegally...." (p. 126)

"Blacks in Birmingham [Alabama], as almost all over the South, are still a people living under social, political and economic siege....I could sense little observable difference between the Midfield ghetto in Alabama and the Guguletu Location in South Africa." (p. 185)

231

South Africa: Land of Hope?

"There is a distinct difference between the South African emigrant and the South African exile. The emigrant has left voluntarily, the exile has left under duress. If the exile's position is sad, then the emigrant's, in many ways, is pathetic. He is metaphorically adrift and geographically disoriented....The political exile is in a more favourable position....He is a full-time activist....The emigrant...lacks the sense of dedication of the exile. He is usually a professional or skilled craftsman from the ranks of the 'coloured' middle class. He is seldom a black South African as such....An important reason for his leaving is the thwarting of his upward social mobility aspirations, so that the decision to go abroad is not in order to assert his basic humanity but to entrench his middle-class status, free from the impediments of colour discrimination. He has all the prejudices of that group and seldom identifies with the working class either at home or abroad....He is comparatively safe from the black South Africans he has left behind....He can identify by proxy with their cause without the embarrassment of physical contact....Although, once abroad he voices his disapproval of apartheid, he seldom mixes with his black countrymen....Some forwarded the apology, 'We did it for our children.' Although this was true in many cases, the price they paid was a terrible one: a sense of rootlessness and in some cases a sense of guilt at having opted out of the struggle. Not only does the emigrant not have the singularity of purpose and dedication of the political exile; he has not the strength of his beliefs and faith in future change in South Africa to pull him through. The emigrant knows he can never return with an easy conscience." (pp. 195-197)

GOVERNMENT ACTION

Berger and Godsell

"More than one government department is actually engaged at present in attempts to facilitate talks with the full spectrum of black political groups, including the UDF." (p. 38)

"It appears that a review of constitutional thinking will now take place." (p. 38)

"The broad *idea* of continuing evolutionary reform and change has become part of the popular wisdom and political culture of the National Party government. The following are some typical examples of 'keynote' statements: 'A white power monopoly has become intolerable.' (Minister of Constitutional Development, Chris Heunis)....'Any system aimed at keeping some of its participants in a subordinate position through clever or devious means is doomed to failure. It must be visibly and honestly just and equitable towards everybody.' (Minister of Education, FW de Klerk)" (p. 38)

"The deputy minister who was assigned to the State President's office to give special attention to the constitutional incorporation of black people has firmly committed himself to negotiation with even the most radical movements." (p. 46)

"The most 'progressive' members of the [National Party] caucus and the executive appear to be among the most able intellects in the party, hence recent promotions have favoured the change-oriented wing of the party....Hope of achieving a negotiated solution which would be manifestly legitimate in the eyes of most blacks runs strongly in the party caucus." (p. 47)

"The recent acceptance by government of the principle of open areas, no matter how limited in scope such areas may be, fundamentally contradicts the present implicit political model and racial 'subsocieties.' It opens the way, therefore, for a steady erosion of the presently dominant sphere of white social exclusivity in South Africa." (p. 49)

Butler et al.

"As President Botha expressed it somewhat crudely in his authorised biography: 'I realise that there are today tens of thousands and hundreds of thousands of brown people who are in all respects better than the weakest whites. This is one of the burning questions of our population. We must give these people a say, a greater share in the land — in the administration of the country, as civil servants, and in many other positions which you cannot fill with your weak whites....If we don't do this we will cause our own downfall.'(Translated)" (p. 372)

POLITICAL PARTIES

Berger and Godsell

"Of...alternatives facing South Africa, partition is [to the right wing] the only one which can bring peace to such a deeply divided society. They consider this to be a fact established by international precedent: 'As partition brought relative peace to Europe, Cyprus and the Indian subcontinent, so too will it bring peace to South Africa; partition led to the establishment of Europe as it is today; the partition of Cyprus into a Turkish and a Greek territory has brought peace, and the partitioning of the Indian subcontinent into Bangladesh, Pakistan and India has limited the continual bloodshed and violence. Extended to the Sikhs, peace will return once again to mainland India, at present torn by Sikh/Hindu conflict.' " (pp. 70-71)

"Inkatha, the Labour Party, the Progressive Federal Party, and business...are four very different groups....Nevertheless, they share a number of common values, interpretations and attitudes to change in South Africa....They are all operating within what can be called a common strategic logic, that of incrementalism....

What are the four groups' common values and attitudes? Firstly, they reject the present apartheid policy....Secondly, they reject revolution as the best way of changing the present situation....The third belief...concerns what has been called by Chief Buthelezi the 'multistrategy' approach to change....Fourth...is the recognition of the enormous power of the existing state....Fifth...is a shared recognition that change in South Africa requires economic growth as one of the essential motors for increased deracialisation and the continuing development of the society....Sixth...an explicit recognition that participation in state-created institutions or structures... needs to be assessed for each particular situation....Seventh... these actors do not see apartheid and capitalism as synonymous....Eighth...is a commitment to the rights of the individual, the rule of law and civil rights [and the belief in] a bill of rights....Ninth... a commitment to negotiation [and] a negotiated settlement....Tenth...a common opposition to...'protest politics'....Finally...a common attitude to white people.

South Africa: Land of Hope?

"They accept the responsibility and contribution...of whites in the struggle for a nondiscriminatory society as well as their place and necessary role in that future society....These actors are involved in the process of peaceful change in South Africa, based on a commitment and willingness to negotiate with the relevant authorities, which inevitably involves them in a process of incremental changes to the *status quo*." (pp. 164-167)

BUTHELEZI AND INKATHA

Adam and Moodley

"Buthelezi, with his shrewd analytical capacity, stands head and shoulders
above all other homeland leaders, quite apart from his different policy.
To lump him together with other 'homeland puppets,' as the ANC now
does, is propaganda rather than reality." (p. 87)

"[Buthelezi and] Inkatha perceives itself as 'the modern expression of the
aims and objectives so clearly stated by the ANC's founding fathers.' It
rejects the notion that it is a 'third force' and insists that it represents the
continuity of black opposition. However, unlike the ANC Mission in
Exile, Inkatha proudly claims democratic accountability. Because the
ANC Mission in Exile is prevented from 'consulting with ordinary South
Africans,' Buthelezi argues, it is out of touch with grass-roots feelings and
has no real right to speak on behalf of black South Africa on such issues as
disinvestment." (p. 87)

"While Buthelezi admits that the threat of violence 'plays a positive role in
the process of bringing about change' and while he expresses
understanding of the ANC's military strategy, his organisation rejects
violence more for pragmatic than for moral reasons. Violence or 'the
politics of anger' will be suicidal in the South African situation, exploited
by 'vultures of death' for ulterior motives." (p. 88)

"[Disagreeing with] Tutu...Inkatha asserts that the ANC Mission in Exile
'was never given a mandate to declare the armed struggle'....According to
Buthelezi, blacks do not want to 'starve for Oliver Tambo'....Buthelezi
[asserts] that he 'will not be dictated to by South African exiles who sit
drinking whisky in safe places.' " (p. 88)

"Buthelezi's nonviolence lacks the mystique of Ghandi because he is not
himself seen to have renounced privilege. While the Inkatha leadership
has never been close to the Nationalists, and Buthelezi personally has had
only a few frosty encounters with Botha, he is nevertheless perceived as
being on their payroll." (p. 89)

"Inkatha practices an appealing pragmatism...'ending discrimination' was
most important to more than three-quarters of a sample of Inkatha

respondents...while only eight percent stressed 'one man/one vote.' "
(p. 91)

Berger and Godsell

"KwaZulu gives Buthelezi a base from which to develop the politics of
negotiation, rather than merely engage in 'protest politics'....Buthelezi has
often advocated the politics of mass mobilisation, using the power which
blacks have in South African society through their economic muscle as
workers and consumers....The multiracial Buthelezi Commission and the
KwaZulu both provide nonracial alternatives to the policies of the
present government." (p. 177)

[*Quoting Buthelezi*]: "You cannot create a decent modern society through
violence. Increased violence will result in increased polarisation and will
reach such magnitudes that it will take generations to overcome its
aftermath...." (p. 178)

"...Inkatha's statement of belief endorses 'respect for individuals,'
'individual equality before the law,' 'the rule of law'...and the movement's
support for the KwaNatal Indaba Bill of Rights as a prototypical liberal
Bill of Rights provides for individual liberty and freedom of movement,
thought, conscience, religion, opinion, and expression." (p. 307)

de Kock

"It is an irony of history that a people code-named for ferocity —
Zulu! — should today be in the forefront of a war for peace in South
Africa; that a people who had fought Afrikaner and English settler alike,
bitterly, until forced into submission, should forge a spearhead of
conciliation and compassion between the races.

"This spearhead is Inkatha, the movement of black liberation which is led
by Mangosuthu Buthelezi.

"The New York correspondent for a South African newspaper remarked
in mid-1986 that American preoccupation with black South Africans was
confined to the two Mandelas, Nelson and Winnie, to Archbishop Tutu,
and to 'that Zulu chief.' In fact, in the line-up of black politicians moving

towards a new South Africa, Mangosuthu Buthelezi is among the most controversial and, in terms of experience, certainly the most adept.

"As elected leader of one of the largest ethnic groupings in Southern Africa, that of seven million Zulu people, he is one of the most confident and visible politicians, and the personification of Inkatha. He bridles – with some justification – at the sneer of 'ethnic' leader, for he can claim to be one of the few if not the only black South African leader since Union in 1910 who has not only achieved legitimacy among a large number of fellow blacks but has also carved for himself a white constituency which includes, significantly, thousands of nationalist-thinking Afrikaners. Since its founding in 1975, Inkatha has established itself firmly as a vital political factor in South Africa.

"No journalist can but be intrigued by the stunning consistency with which its president has stuck to his belief in non-violence and the courage with which he has survived personal humiliation as a black man, and survived the calumnies of 'government stooge' and 'sell-out' of his enemies. This in spite of the fact that for nearly a decade the government would not grant him a passport." (p. 9)

[*Quoting a young black South African who joined Inkatha*]: "We are busy with peaceful warfare in this country. The decision to adopt violence was not taken by ANC members inside South Africa but by those outside. Non-violence is a strategy and a moral principle but still warfare against apartheid....I joined Inkatha to reach out to ordinary people, to the poor, to the masses....At last we blacks can achieve unity...." (p. 18)

"Buthelezi has put it succinctly, 'Black South Africans are now historically faced with a choice between armed struggle and the politics of negotiation...a choice which cannot be shelved. South Africans will either be liberated by the forces of violence which will go on to form a one-party state – and which will be faced with the awesome task of reconstructing this country on a foundation of ashes...or it will be liberated by democratic forces which achieve the liberation of this country through the politics of negotiation which will give rise to a government of national unity.' " (p. 22)

South Africa: Land of Hope?

"It is Inkatha, through Buthelezi, that has progressed beyond mere protest politics to take an active part in shaping events and political developments inside South Africa....A moderate only in terms of his strategy, Buthelezi is no milksop pacifist and no less insistent on black rights than any black militant. Espousing free enterprise economy rather than socialist ruin — 'where in Africa has socialism worked?' — he rejects hardline capitalism, envisaging a brand of communalism to assist the poor and those reliant on a subsistence economy." (p. 31)

"The Inkatha leader heads a well-drilled grassroots organisation with a paid-up membership of 1.5 million in more than 2500 branches. These are mostly in Natal but as far afield as the Orange Free State and with a sizeable representation in South Africa's largest black city, Soweto...."

" 'My opponents may be vociferous,' Buthelezi told a reporter, 'they may have access to the press, and to churches and radicals abroad who have their own programmes. But Inkatha [is] the largest political organisation this country has ever seen....I consult my people more than any other leader and tens of thousands of people attend my rallies.' " (p. 35)

"Alan Paton has said of him: 'A stooge he will never be.' " (p. 36)

[*Quoting Buthelezi*]: "Some liberal journalists deliberately try to scale down my leadership as if it's not national. They keep on saying we're Zulu-based. Really, there's no justification whatsoever. No one says to the National Party they are Afrikaner-based. The Progressive Party is predominantly Jewish and English, but no one ever mentions that. And why did Tambo himself in his London evidence claim that he is the one who advised me to found Inkatha? If it were a purely Zulu thing, how would Tambo have been involved? But it suits them to crush me, to say I'm divisive, that I'm ethnic, not a national but just a tribal leader...." (p. 46)

[*Quoting Buthelezi*]: "When I talk of freedom and liberation (I am not) thinking of the Zulus as distinct from my other African brothers in South Africa. In fact, our enemies are deliberately trying to propagate this falsehood...there is no Zulu freedom which is distinct from the black man's freedom in South Africa. Black oppression has no ethnic boundaries." (p. 83)

Chapter 5   History and Character of South Africa and its People

[*Quoting Buthelezi*]: "I have said, and I repeat again, that if asked I will work under any democratically elected black leader and I have mentioned Dr Nelson Mandela by name. My role as an elected and traditional leader in South Africa is directed solely at gaining political rights for black South Africans." (p. 114)

"Professor Lawrence Schlemmer, then of the University of Natal, described the Buthelezi Commission, which had reported in 1982, as 'a very substantial and indeed historic gesture of willingness to struggle with whites, coloured people, and Indians to find a path between all the pitfalls of hostility and antagonism which make the solution to our problems so difficult.' " (p. 138)

"In the upheaval of the eighties and the collapse, through school boycotts and violence, of the black educational system in large parts of the country, KwaZulu zealously guarded its schools....Education for the KwaZulu government and for Inkatha was 'in the forefront of the struggle for full freedom'....Inkatha was determined that the 'liberation now, education later' cry of the Eastern Cape and Transvaal townships would not erode KwaZulu schools....

"It is noteworthy that the Zulu people from the very beginning of their 'banishment' under the Nationalist government did not beg for handouts. Self-sufficiency was Buthelezi's watchword and one of the foundation stones of Inkatha." (p. 144)

"Buthelezi is aware that half the black population of South Africa is fifteen years old and younger. He is also intensely aware of the pressure on youths to skip the borders and fight a glamorous war of liberation and he has tried to channel youthful anger into constructive ideas. His success in keeping these youngsters motivated is probably one of his greatest achievements under the circumstances....

"Buthelezi addressed the problem of anger in most young people: 'There is a feeling amongst some of our young that they must smash, they must burn and they must kill. That feeling is not our feeling....The real battle is the one to make life worthwhile after victory....The impatience of youth, the courage of youth, the determination of youth, and the anger of youth

241

are great assets and the youth must employ these by preparing the groundwork for self-help development in African communities.'

"Inkatha strategy is founded upon a mobilisation offensive involving cross-ethnic black, worker, union, multi-class and consumer power to confront white oppression, and thereby force what concessions may be wrung." (p. 145)

Louw and Kendall

[*Quoting Buthelezi*]: "Apartheid has to go and it has to be replaced with a social and political system which will give both black and white a meaningful stake in the government of their country." (p. 147)

Paton

[*Quoting Buthelezi*]: "Of course we'll defend the country if you give us a country to defend." (p. 28)

"Buthelezi is still one of the most powerful figures on the political stage, fluent, extremely knowledgeable, impossible to buy (whatever some of his more foolish critics assert)." (p. 104)

*Following are excerpts from the book, **An Appetite for Power: Buthelezi's Inkatha and the Politics of "Loyal Resistance."** The book was handed to me by a Liberal contact in South Africa, with the warning, "Here is the **truth** about Buthelezi." Capitalists may not find much, in the book, that disturbs them, but I quote it, here, as representative of the anti-Buthelezi forces:*

"Buthelezi and Inkatha stand today for a multi-racial capitalism untainted by apartheid; for the politics of non-violence towards the central state, and hence for negotiations with the current holders of power....

"They represent 'stability'...away from demands for universal franchise and...the structure of a future South Africa away from a unitary state....Inkatha defends the federal option on the basis that it is practical politics during a transitional phase in which white people would become accustomed to shared power....

"Buthelezi's populism...is the populism of the dominant classes demanding a reordering of the alliances of capitalism rather than a populism directed against capitalism itself....

"For some Inkatha offers the last hope for a peaceful, negotiated settlement....For millions Inkatha is a sellout." (p. 6)

"Inkatha's strategy of pursuing non-violence...is pragmatic. However, a non-violent strategy is only valid with a regime as ruthlessly entrenched as the NP government if there is a simultaneous threat that it could change to violence." (pp. 79-80)...

[*Quoting Buthelezi*]: "We must not destroy the foundations of the post-apartheid society we long for." (p. 81)

"The consistency in Inkatha's approach to the economy lies in its favourable perception of capitalism, or the 'free enterprise system'....[*Quoting Inkatha secretary general, Oscar Dhlomo*]: 'I believe what Inkatha would like to see happening is the overhaul of the free enterprise system aimed at ensuring that black people have equal access and that they derive equal benefit from the system.' " (p. 98)

[*Quoting Buthelezi*]: "If Inkatha were to wield state power I would never allow a situation where whites — or blacks — were deprived of the fruits of the sweat of their brows...though, after 'liberation,' capitalism would probably have to be 'diluted' with African 'communalism.' " (p. 98)

"...what informs Buthelezi's suggestions for economic change is the reasoning that 'people won't burn down buildings in which they have a stake.' " (p. 100)

"Inkatha sees investment in South Africa as a 'strategy for liberation.' " (p. 101)

[*Quoting Buthelezi*]: "There will be no real victory in the struggle for liberation unless it is a victory that blacks and whites achieve together; a victory that workers and management achieve together." (p. 127)

"Inkatha is engaged in campaigns to subvert unions and attack unionists, in what it would define to be the interests of the liberation of black people in South Africa." (p. 127)

"It was clear that Inkatha had assumed the task, performed elsewhere in the country by the police and the government, of forcing children to return to school and punishing those that didn't." (p. 185)

"In effect, the political position of Inkatha's leadership, and the political actions of some of its supporters, can hardly be distinguished from those of the central state." (p. 215)

"Despite the populist rhetoric of unity and common interests, Inkatha displays class political and economic interests that increasingly mesh openly with the forces of conservatism in South Africa, and has in fact never challenged those forces in any fundamental way. What we find in Inkatha confirms previous contentions that populism and populist mobilisation should not be taken at face value, though there can be conservative and progressive, or even revolutionary populism.

"The Inkatha leadership has shown a firm commitment to the principles and ideology of capitalism (the 'free enterprise system') as a motor of development, guarantor of democratic rights, provider of employment, and agent of desirable change for all in the country....Inkatha has, in effect, drawn a distinction between the *apartheid* state and the *capitalist* state, in a manner similar to the Thatcher and Reagan administrations. While clearly antagonistic towards the apartheid system and working towards its abolition, Inkatha has become an integral part of the system of ensuring the survival of capitalism in South Africa.

"Inkatha's political practice clearly serves to maintain capitalist relations of production through disciplining the working class, through the creation, in May 1986 of UWUSA [United Workers Union of South Africa], with its pro-capitalist, anti-strike, anti-boycott, anti-sanctions, and anti-disinvestment line." (p. 221)

On January 20, 1986, Chief Buthelezi met with members of the British Parliament's Foreign Affairs Committee. The following excerpts are taken from his statements to the Committee, as quoted in **Usuthu! Cry Peace!**:

"The vast majority of black South Africans demand the normalisation of South Africa in which there is equality of opportunity in a free enterprise system and a parliamentary democracy which is a heritage the British presence in South Africa bequeathed to us." (p. 162)

"Members of the Foreign Affairs Committee will be aware of opposing black views about South Africa and what needs to be done to eradicate apartheid for the scourge it is. I would appeal to them not to fall into the trap some foreign observers fall into, of tracing differences of opinion amongst blacks to differences between leaders and to conflicts of interest which arise out of personal idiosyncrasies amongst black leaders. An understanding of the South African political process and an awareness of the real issues which the black struggle for liberation has always focused on are lost when media representations of the South African scene are used as guidelines." (p. 163)

African National Congress

"Those now in the ANC mission in exile who reject me, pretending that they do so because I occupy the position of chief minister of KwaZulu, do so as part of their propaganda campaign. They know the truth. My only sin is that I refused to make Inkatha a surrogate organisation of the external mission of the ANC....

"The blunt truth is that those who reject the free enterprise system reject Western forms of democracy and reject the politics of non-violence and the politics of negotiation which Western democratic principles demand of black South Africans now.

"Black South Africa gave me massive support as a tried and trusted leader when I brought Inkatha into being in 1975. By then the ANC mission had been abroad for fifteen years. During this period the harshness of apartheid, and the growth of draconian laws on South African statute books, bore testimony to the ineffectiveness of the leadership in the ANC mission in exile. They became so preoccupied with their own unilateral choice to make the armed struggle the primary means of bringing about change in South Africa that a very debilitating political vacuum emerged in black South Africa.

"Faced with the growth of horrendous legislation and faced with growing social and economic deprivation, black South Africa resented the ANC mission's behaviour. We realised that it is we inside the country who have to do something. The political ferment inside South Africa which was produced by the ANC mission's failure emerged to inspire two different political fronts. One was Inkatha and the other was the Black Consciousness Movement." (pp. 163-164)

"I never accepted the unilateral decision the ANC mission made to commit black South Africa to the armed struggle as the primary means of bringing about change. It never consulted black South Africa about this very fundamental step. It made the decision unilaterally only after it had been in exile for some years....

"I rejected the argument by prominent members of the ANC mission that any involvement they may have in democratic opposition in South Africa would detract from their main purpose which was to pursue the armed struggle. I rejected this because it was patently clear to me that it would be foolish for black South Africans to model their liberation struggle on struggles elsewhere, where circumstances were entirely different." (p. 165)

"Transcripts of ANC mission in exile broadcasts from Radio Freedom obtained from the British Broadcasting Corporation's monitoring service show that the ANC is intent upon:

1. Generalising black violence which has broken out in our townships.

2. Going beyond threatening the South African economy to actually destroying it.

3. Spreading a reign of terror in which targets are civilians. It is particularly intent now on trying to get black violence directed against white suburbia.

4. Ordering the elimination of all blacks who do not agree with the ANC's tactics and strategies. It is particularly bent upon the murder of any black who could play a meaningful role in negotiation and reconciliation.

5. Undermining the evolution of black democratic forces working for change within the institutionalised life of South Africa.

6. Engaging in a battle of minds in which the ANC's point of view is that it is the nature of the free enterprise system and the nature of the Western industrial world's commitment to non-violent change in South Africa which constitutes the real threat to liberation.

"The ANC is now not waging a struggle against apartheid and the South African government. It is pitting itself against South African society." (pp. 165-166)

"Any group in exile which commits itself to the armed struggle resists sharing power....

"The Foreign Affairs Committee should ponder upon the nature of exiled revolutionary groups. If it did it would come to the conclusion that the ANC mission sees itself as a government in exile and wants to return as a revolutionary government to take over South Africa. The ANC mission is not working to establish democratic rights for the people of South Africa to choose whom they will to form a government. It regiments its members ideologically and inculcates in them the view that only the ANC mission can be allowed to direct the affairs of the struggle for liberation. It wants to take over control and it is ruthless with those who do not act as fetch and carry boys." (p. 169)

Violence
"I know of no society in the world where the kind of violence now employed by the ANC mission in exile has produced an open, democratic society....

South Africa: Land of Hope?

"It is a central argument to my whole political position now that forces working for change in South Africa are being detrimentally affected by the levels of violence we are experiencing. There is now in South Africa a yearning for a normalised society amongst all population groups. Whatever the National Party says and does, white South Africa recognises that apartheid has failed and that South Africa must move towards meaningful reform in which black South Africans are integrated into a central political system. The South African government is now floundering around not knowing how to go about normalising South Africa.

"It still contains white right-wing elements, but it is doing so in the face of a recognised inevitability that power-sharing will come. There is widespread recognition that there will be no recovery from the country's dire economic circumstances unless blacks are accommodated politically. When one goes beyond sentiments as determinants of political action in the white group, the harsh driving realities in the economic field must be seen to be producing an escalating impetus towards real change.

"There are no longer illusions left in white South Africa that there can be an economic separation of white and black interests. Big business in South Africa across both white language groups wants meaningful reform, and big business has now declared its intention to participate fully in the process of bringing about real change regardless of government action.

"The National Party is under siege by the forces of economic reality and the prime actors in the economic field now want the very kind of change which the British Parliament wants, which the Western world wants, and which the general black population of South Africa has always struggled for." (pp. 166-167)

Mandela

"I call for the immediate unbanning of the ANC and for the release of Nelson Mandela so that South Africans can judge for themselves. Myths woven around heroes and martyrs created by the South African state could be misleading." (p. 170)

Utopia

"There will be no Utopia overnight in South Africa....

"A new democratic and free South Africa will not be authored by street corner violence. It will be authored by men and women in black and white society who accept that apartheid has to be replaced with a social and political system which gives both black and white a meaningful stake in the government of their country.

"If there is no hope of succeeding, I would not be doing what I am doing. The very substantial constituency support I enjoy could make me a very prominent leader amongst those who have opted for violence. I do what I do because the politics of negotiation are in all reality far more potent as a force of change than the politics of violence. I do what I do because it can succeed." (p. 173)

THE AFRICAN NATIONAL CONGRESS

de Kock

"The ANC is, wrongly, barred from a fair platform inside South Africa. But its message is unequivocal and well-publicised. Its strategy of social polarisation is logical within the communist orientation of its national executive council (NEC). The movement's dedication to revolutionary violence has as its mythical underpinning a social theory which explains the advance of 'democracy' in terms of conflict and the Leninist belief, to use the descriptive phrase of Camus, that 'nothing but bloodshed makes history progress.'

"The ANC's ideological hide-boundedness does not necessarily cancel out the movement as a vehicle for African liberation. Millions of the unfree hold the ANC in love and respect. But the fact that the Marxist tail wags the dog must affect the organisation's future manoeuvrability." (p. 126)

"The comfortable equation that a release of restraints on an organisation pledged to violence will turn the lion into a lamb is spurious." (p. 127)

"When in October 1985 [ANC Chief] Tambo, Thabo Mbeki, director of information, and Aziz Pahad, both members of the NEC [National Executive Committee], gave evidence to the [British Foreign Affairs] committee, Tambo in effect admitted that the ANC's strategy of violence had been an abysmal failure. All the organisation could offer was an intensification of violence....When asked about black against black violence, Tambo replied that he regarded it as 'unavoidable'....Throughout the sixties and seventies, he observed, the ANC had confined itself to attacking economic installations — 'pylons and so on.' Then in June 1985, the organisation decided it had maintained selective sabotage for 'twenty fruitless years' and accepted the inevitability of shedding innocent blood and the possibility of 'more bloodshed than ever...before.' " (p. 128)

"Tambo in his speeches refers to the ANC liberation plan as three-pronged: international pressure, internal mobilisation, and 'the armed struggle.' Indeed, this shows the ANC in exile now regards the armed struggle as an integral part of its liberation strategy. The ANC can thus caress businessmen, journalists and peace-minded sympathisers with one hand and kill with the other." (p. 129)

"The ANC mission in numerous statements regularly broadcast over the air by Radio Freedom urges South Africans to create a situation of civil war." (p. 136)

"In January 1987, at a celebration in Lusaka of the ANC's 75th anniversary...the London-Lusaka men...uncompromisingly confirmed their commitment to violence." (p. 136)

"In a speech to the KwaZulu legislative assembly in 1985, Buthelezi said with a touch of bitterness: 'Mr Oliver Tambo forgets what courage it took to defy apartheid and to act in this way during the years in which he himself was urging me not to rock the boat too much lest I endanger my position and jeopardise what I was doing for the sake of the people. He forgets that it was I more than any other South African who campaigned constantly for the unbanning of the ANC and campaigned ceaselessly for the release of Nelson Mandela, Walter Sisulu and others. Mr Oliver Tambo also forgets that, while vast oceans separated him and I who were brothers in the struggle, on those occasions when we did meet, we grasped each other with hugs of comradeship. He forgets the extent to which I was responsible for the veritable revival of black political sentiment as I led people to sing freedom songs in the open air, whilst others only whispered about things that mattered. I hoisted the colours of freedom — recognised across the length and breadth of Africa — in the name of the people.'

"What Buthelezi was saying was that the ANC leaders had forgotten what it meant to be a black in South Africa." (p. 140)

"Mbeki told [Buthelezi] the ANC wanted him to know that they were embarrassed by his espousal of non-violence — while they had opted for violence. The ANC asked him to avoid mentioning non-violence so often. They also indicated their opposition to Buthelezi's stand [against] disinvestment." (p. 141)

THE ANC FREEDOM CHARTER

Adam and Moodley

"The Freedom Charter's terms resemble the old-fashioned values of liberal democracies...a pluralist document: 'national groups' coexisting in equality, with mutual tolerance." (p. 213)

Berger and Godsell

"To this date, the Freedom Charter is regarded as the spiritual manifesto for a democratic South Africa by the extra-parliamentary organisations [ANC, UDF]." (p. 128)

Louw and Kendall

"The charter is important as it represents the first formal expression of the aspirations of a group possibly representing the majority in South Africa. However, it means different things to different people and contains sweeping generalisations which are highly ambiguous and open to widely varying interpretations. This may prove to be a good thing. The charter includes the following aims: all 'national' [race] groups should have equal rights; land should be shared among those who work it; there will be work and security for all, houses and comfort for all, and peace and friendship. There will be private land ownership and most of commerce and industry will be private. The charter would nationalise mineral wealth, banks, and monopoly industry." (p. 78)

Paton

"They must consider the Freedom Charter anew, for it embodies – in my opinion – two incompatible aims. One aim is the guarantee of what are called human rights, such as are found in the American Bill of Rights; the other is the nationalisation of the banks and the mines and State control of all other industry and trade, such as obtains in the USSR. No country in the world has yet succeeded in reconciling them." (p. 185)

REDISTRIBUTION OF WEALTH

Louw and Kendall

"Redistribution doesn't help the people it's intended to help. The poor are not helped by the destruction of the rich." (p. 93)

"In South Africa, many laws have been passed which interfere with free exchange, especially with black freedom of exchange. It is these laws which have held blacks back, not white advantages....Redistribution of wealth from whites to blacks failed to improve the lot of blacks, whereas a very small measure of black participation in the market achieved remarkable results." (p. 95)

"In the past, attempts to redistribute wealth have invariably resulted in a redistribution of poverty." (p. 100)

"Free markets lift people out of poverty far more rapidly than any other economic system known to man." (p. 102)

"Subsidies actually increase prices; and instead of helping the poor, they benefit suppliers and manufacturers." (p. 180)

VIOLENCE

Adam and Moodley

"The harassment of black state employees by the [ANC] revolutionary forces may in fact drive the threatened dependents closer to their masters than to their opponents. After all, they have more to fear after a black takeover." (p. 144)

Berger and Godsell

"The use of violence to thwart dissent, for example the stoning of buses ferrying [black] commuters during work stayaways, has undoubtedly contributed to some loss of sympathy for the resistance movement....The position of 'victor' and 'victim' becomes blurred when the tactics employed increase anguish and suffering." (p. 161)

"The practice of violence against opponents of the resistance movement does not augur well for democracy." (p. 163)

de Kock

"Buthelezi has called this tendency of the West a 'kind of dangerous romanticism about freedom fighters,' an empathy with the politics of violent protest diminishing those forces which will eventually be called upon to salvage South Africa from the ruins of apartheid." (p. 10)

"Before the British Foreign Affairs Committee, Buthelezi said: 'The ANC attempts to reduce South Africa to chaos...to escalate the use of violence in South Africa and to do so regardless of whether or not civilians are maimed or killed....I know of no society in the world where [this kind of] violence has produced an open, democratic society.' " (p. 26)

[*Quoting Buthelezi*]: "I know that a lot of blood has been shed in this country. I don't see why more blood should be shed. Black or white. We shouldn't be such fools and allow it to happen again." (p. 39)

[*Quoting Buthelezi*]: "I've said in many public speeches that Inkatha is based on the ideals of the [original] ANC as propounded by the founding fathers. The option of violence was not sanctioned by the people of South

Africa. No one gave the ANC mission a mandate to opt for violence."
(p. 44)

[*Quoting Oscar Dhlomo*]: "At the time of the founding of Inkatha, the
young Zulu people were very aware politically and were as angry as all
young people are. The difference lay in the manner in which they
expressed their anger. I can't remember ever considering that the
solution to the country's problems lay in picking up a stone or throwing a
bomb. As young people we were very angry. But, as Chief Buthelezi
would say, we channelled our anger towards constructive pursuits."
(pp. 81-82)

"Buthelezi has right through his political career spoken forcefully about
what he regarded as the duty of the church in the complex society of South
Africa. When he met [British] Archbishop Runcie in 1985, he expressed
dismay that the forces working for violent confrontation in South Africa
'are so often rewarded with Christian acclaim in the Western world....'
Meanwhile, he said, those who struggled to salvage the country from
violence were stigmatised as 'sellouts.' If ever violence in South Africa
was to be judged as 'just and retributive,' such a judgment could only be
made after every stone of non-violent action had been turned over and
after every Christian act of reconciliation had failed. But, Buthelezi said,
there were still a great many stones to be turned over." (pp. 119-120)

[*Quoting Buthelezi*]: "Those who are committed to violence have to preach
hatred....Those who train people to kill cannot make an assessment which
includes recognising that there is a prospect for change." (p. 129)

"One of the most unsettling aspects of the black on black violence has in
fact been the degradation of whole communities of adult blacks who
remained supine in the face of intimidation by militant youths. An adult
forced to quake in front of a frenzied teenager and swallow soap powder
as 'punishment' cannot be expected to exercise a free and independent
vote. The extent of internecine violence is not appreciated by most
outside the black townships." (pp. 129-130)

"The image of pin-stripe suited men in London and Lusaka, who are
guerrillas against their will, forced to employ violence against the evil of

the South African regime...is shattered by the grubby war of chopping and hacking of often helpless black people in the townships." (p. 131)

"Professor Crane Brinton has pointed out that those who take control by violence can eventually not control violence, that there is no 'liberal' phase in a revolution and that to stay in control repressive measures are inevitable." (p. 137)

Louw and Kendall

"In 1969 the ANC confirmed a policy of violence against the South African government." (p. 77)

Mutwa

"My people, I have written this book as a message calling on you to first try and explore the path of peace rather than the way of violence and confrontation...." (p. xi)

"For years now black people have entertained quite bizarre and utterly groundless beliefs about whites, which are all known to, and are exploited by, subversive organisations such as the ANC." (p. 96)

"At all costs, South Africa must avoid making the mistakes that Rhodesia made...the Rhodesians fell easy prey to manipulation by black guerrilla leaders." (p. 124)

"I cannot understand why men who profess to be the children and followers of Jesus Christ — the reverend men and women of the World Council of Churches, the men and women who should be working for peace throughout this troubled world of ours — are the same people supporting terrorism....I feel nothing but cold hatred and contempt for those so-called black leaders who are urging our people along the path of violence and death, and I want to ask these supposed leaders these questions, if I may: Do you want South Africa to become another LEBANON?... Do YOU have the courage to die the death you so smilingly prescribe for others?" (pp. 180-182)

"I wish to throw down my gauntlet at the feet of the Archbishop... Desmond Tutu.... Stand up and lead a mass spiritual reform among the different races in Southern Africa. I say it is wrong and immoral for reform in South Africa to be of only a POLITICAL NATURE." (p. 183)

"I wish most especially to say this to Mr Terre'Blanche, leader of the AWB: Sir, I have warned Oliver Tambo and now I am warning you. Please put away your ridiculous flags and command your *stormvolke* warriors to go back to their father's farms....All this troglodyte thuggery and Neanderthal violence on the part of your followers is doing incalculable harm to the Afrikaner people at an extremely critical time." (p. 187)

"South Africa, no matter how strong and militarily prepared she may be, would never survive a race war." (p. 187)

"South Africa requires moderation and not extremism in these dangerous times, and we have no time for extremism of any sort, whether it comes from the left or from the right." (p. 187)

Paton

"Many blacks believe the white man will listen only if they burn things down. The black churches have not condemned outright the violence of black youth." (p. 146)

VOTING, UNITARY STATE

Berger and Godsell

"It has frequently been argued that the National Party is the handmaiden to agricultural capital. There certainly was a time when farmers were a vital segment of the party's support base....[But], as one MP who was interviewed put it: 'We have been afraid of white farmers far too long — we must be prepared to lose votes.' " (p. 23)

[*Regarding ANC strategies*]: "With every bomb or mine which explodes in white areas, the National Party gains new voters....The white electorate on the whole moved to the left on apartheid laws, but to the right on security issues." (p. 103)

"On 6 May 1987...the governing National Party won the election on a ticket of security and reform." (p. 125)

"Whereas all polls show significant support [among black voters] for the ANC, there is equal evidence of a popular rejection of change through violence, despite the fact that the ANC is committed to the armed struggle." (p. 307)

Louw and Kendall

"Few of the countries which put pressure on South Africa to become a unitary one man/one vote state have such a system themselves. South Africa currently has one of the most centralised government systems in the world. The only other countries which approach our degree of centralisation, such as the Scandinavian countries, are geographically small and have homogeneous populations." (p. 120)

"When blacks are asked in surveys what upsets them most about the current system, the factors which rank highest are red tape, queues, bureaucracy, corruption, harassment and intimidation [rather than the lack of the vote]." (p. 68)

"Many observers ... believe that Mandela has become such a folk hero and the ANC so much a symbol of the 'black liberation struggle' that they would win an overwhelming majority in, at least, a first election...."

However twenty-eight percent of the national population is non-black, which means (assuming that not many non-blacks would vote for them) that the ANC would need to win seventy percent of the black vote in order to gain fifty percent of the national vote, which seems highly unlikely by any analysis. It should also be remembered that most blacks, especially rural blacks, have a strong ethnic consciousness. Neither Zulus, Sothos, Xhosas nor any of the other main black groups are likely to vote in substantial numbers for a leader from a group other than their own. This is not a fashionable view, but it is nonetheless true....Add to this the fact that four-to-six million blacks are followers of the Zion Christian Church which has a moderate policy and leader, and we are led inexorably to the conclusion that most blacks would support moderate leaders, and that no single group has a chance of a clear majority." (p. 232)

"All evidence indicates that the vast majority of blacks will support freehold title, free trade and free competition." (p. 232)

Paton

"A unitary State could be achieved only by revolution. And a sad unitary State it would be, of decaying cities, idle ports, broken-down railways and, worst of all, a destroyed agriculture." (p. 91)

"Universal suffrage and a unitary State imposed from without is not — for me — compatible with a liberal ideal." (p. 217)

DEMOCRATIC SOCIALISM

Berger and Godsell

"Many of the supporters of the Freedom Charter — the program for economic transformation which was accepted, *inter alia*, by the ANC and the Congress of Democrats at the historic meeting at Kliptown in 1955 — believe that South Africa could become the first truly democratic-socialist country in the world. For here, in contrast to other countries which have experienced socialist revolutions, the capitalist economy is already fully developed." (pp. 221-222)

"A wide spectrum of people have expressed an interest in a democratic system which leaves the present structure of production largely intact but which redistributes resources, usually from growth and for purposes of social investment. Whereas businessmen often prefer the term 'social market,' stressing the fact that the market rather than government bureaucrats will take the most important decisions, it is clear that they are willing to live with a northern European or Scandinavian type of social democracy." (p. 223)

"Social democracy...provides a middle ground for the coexistence of opposing interest groups." (p. 223)

"The conclusion is that this is the only type of system which could emerge from a negotiated settlement, under the present circumstances." (p. 224)

"The economy needs to grow at more than five percent if there is to be a reduction in the proportion of the labour force unemployed. A growth rate of about six percent is needed for absolute numbers to decline. Only a negotiated settlement could possibly make growth rates of this magnitude attainable." (p. 228)

"In order to improve the chances of success for a social democratic type of settlement, it would make good sense for all South Africans to demand concrete guarantees of international support for the new South Africa as part of the settlement package." (p. 234)

INDABA

de Kock

"In explaining the impetus that has led to the Indaba, Buthelezi has said:
'We in KwaZulu have long argued that the rigid separation of
decision-making in Natal and KwaZulu is a very costly affair, foisted on
the people by segregationists of the last century and apartheid bosses
subsequent to that.' He told the legislative assembly in March 1985 that,
'All reality demands that we break down the apartheid barriers between
KwaZulu and Natal decision-making and that we move in this province
towards the kind of power-sharing at provincial level and at local
government level which is becoming so imperative for the well-being of all
the citizens of Natal of whatever race, colour or creed." (p. 139)

Paton

"KwaZulu/Natal was lucky to have two men of the calibre of Chief
Buthelezi and Brank Martin [of the Natal Provincial Executive], two
sensible idealists, both of whom preferred co-operation to conflict...

"The organisers invited a wide range of organisations and persons to
attend the Indaba [a Zulu word, which in this context can be taken to
mean a gathering at which important matters are to be discussed]....The
UDF refused to accept the invitation. This is hardly surprising, since it is
hostile to Chief Buthelezi and is ideologically committed to a unitary State
with a universal suffrage. Mrs Winnie Mandela, who is strongly
sympathetic to the UDF, had stated in public that the time for gatherings
such as national conventions was past and that the next inevitable step was
for the National Party Government to abdicate and to hand over power to
the black majority, a forthright but quite useless suggestion....

"What and whom did the Indaba represent? It represented the moderate,
peace-loving, conflict-hating, middle-of-the-road people of KwaZulu and
Natal. These people are often called the 'silent majority' and are often
supposed to be starry-eyed and useless, but...they proved themselves to be
neither silent nor useless....

"Indaba was a great success largely because Buthelezi is the Chief
Minister of the KwaZulu Government and because the white people of

265

Natal are not afraid of him. He speaks a language that they can understand. It is this quality that his enemies regard as hypocritical....

"The Indaba was not characterised by any denial of racial differences, or any denial of racial fears, or by any lofty declarations that the concept of race was unimportant, and that all the delegates were brothers and sisters together....The Indaba did not attempt to deny the importance of the concept [of race]. What it did do was to confront it openly and sensibly and to suggest ways and means of preventing it from endangering any further the lives of millions of human beings....

"If a new province of Natal should become...an example of a successful non-racial Government, it might inspire the people of other parts of South Africa to set up Indabas of their own and so open the way to the creation of a Federal Republic of South Africa." (pp. 159-163)

"Of all [the] efforts 'to do the best things in the worst times, and to hope for them in the most calamitous,' I shall give the place of honour to the Natal/KwaZulu Indaba." (p. 299)

[*Alan Paton was born and lived his life in the province of Natal.*]

ECONOMICS AND BUSINESS

Adam and Moodley
"Capital's need for stability and productivity now transcends ethnic boundaries." (p. 24)

"It is greatly in the interests of business to use its clout to ensure fundamental deracialisation. And a precondition for serious deracialisation must be a massive public re-education effort, primarily of whites in the civil service. Their ideological confusion, vested interests, and anxiety about the future block fundamental progress." (p. 209)

Berger and Godsell
"The problem for a post-apartheid society would seem to be...how to attract massive new foreign investment for creating employment in a growing urban population. In order to fulfill the heightened expectations of a liberated constituency, an ANC-controlled government could not afford the mistakes made by Mozambique and Angola by not retaining its skilled human capital. After all, the potential wealth of South Africa lies in its fragile social relations above ground, and not merely in its minerals underground. Nigeria or Zaire are as rich in scarce minerals as South Africa, and yet they count among the less developed states. Even more so than in Zimbabwe after the 1980 ZANU takeover, a nominally socialist Azania would have to safeguard the conditions under which private sector initiatives could flourish." (p. 116)

"Different members of the business community usually agree that South Africa must move towards a nonracial democracy, in which group identity would be based on voluntary association. The concept of democracy – most extensively described in the Federated Chamber of Industry's Charter of Social, Economic and Political Rights – is clearly liberal and pluralist." (p. 170)

"A series of strategies pursued by the business community can be described. Firstly, business has tried to change or influence government policies in a wide range of broadly political areas....[Examples of early success are] the scrapping of the Masters and Servants Act...the repeal of job reservation and the extension of state-recognised union rights to blacks...the repeal of the influx control laws...[and the] campaign to abolish the pass laws.... Secondly, business has itself been part of creating a post-apartheid society through the evolving labour relations process....Thirdly, through the economic resources which it can command, business has been able to participate directly in social change...significantly influenced by the low-cost, self-help housing projects undertaken by the Urban Foundation. Equally important innovation in nonracial education has been significantly promoted by corporate grants and involvement." (pp. 171-172)

"Business has publicly committed itself to a future nonracial society and to a process of negotiation in order to facilitate movement from 'here' to 'there.' " (p. 192)

"There are at least five different groups who believe that the elimination of apartheid calls for the destruction of both the economic and the political systems...the Trotskyites...the Marxist-Leninists...the African socialist nationalists...the 'Pol Pot' types of cadres...and a small but committed fundamentalist Muslim movement." (p. 214)

"The greater the resistance groups' success in destroying the economy, the greater the problems they will face in a post-revolutionary government....It is clear that the price to be paid in terms of human lives and suffering, both during the conflict and in the post-revolutionary years, will be very high indeed. Only the most cold-blooded will demand destruction of the economy if a negotiated settlement is a feasible alternative." (p. 218)

"South Africa has a long tradition of opposition to the apartheid system, based on the contention that it is economically extremely wasteful....Economic rationality calls for the abandonment of apartheid legislation." (p. 219)

"Quoting surveys taken among blacks in Soweto regarding the preferred economic system, the free marketeers argue that although blacks claim to favour socialism, their choices regarding the type of economic activity they would prefer indicate that they in fact favour a free market system. Some free marketeers argue that blacks have lived under a socialist system all these years, as some of the restrictions imposed on blacks are very similar to those implemented in socialist countries." (p. 220)

"It would not be in the interests of anyone to carry on with a long and destructive conflict because of the resistance movement's intention to socialise or nationalise the land and the large companies, when these goals are not tenable in any case." (p. 232)

"Countries develop best when they engage the world economy through trade and investment links...held in private hands....Three decades of independence on the African continent lead to the same conclusions drawn in negative terms: centrally-directed economies whose link with the world lies chiefly in development aid do not grow." (p. 297)

Butler et al.

"All major groups of capitalists have supported attempts to reform [the modern racial order]." (p. 212)

"South African employers, most of them raised in South Africa, have had little experience so far with black unions. They are accustomed to hierarchical relations with Africans and adversarial relationships with unions generally, and do not therefore find the spirit of negotiation easy to achieve. They do, however, share an interest with the black unions in a stable and productive society. Workers and management together represent class interdependency. The bargaining process is one that both sides understand." (p. 326)

de Kock

[*Quoting Buthelezi*]: "We have prepared with confidence for the day when this [apartheid] system will be gone. We don't support strategies like telling children to stay away from schools. That's destructive. That's why we don't support the idea of destroying the economy either, because we know the economy is not like a tap that can be turned off and on. How shall we resuscitate it again? Black people should be the last to cause the economy to disintegrate or be destroyed." (p. 40)

Louw and Kendall

"Black African countries are not impoverished because blacks run them, but because their economic policies are wrong. Most black South Africans are not frustrated simply because whites rule them, but because they suffer under bureaucracy, red tape, over-regulation and officialdom. The real problem is not the colour of the people who control the machine, but the nature of the machine. If people have entrenched property rights, freedom of movement, exchange, and association; if they are equal before the law and not subject to the whims of officialdom, then racial differences will cease to be so crucial." (p. 65)

Sunter

"It would be a delusion not to acknowledge that there is now significant power-sharing in economic terms." (p. 93)

SANCTIONS

Adam and Moodley

"Events in South Africa are little influenced by America, but they increasingly influence United States policy." (p. xviii)

"Sanctions against South Africa are only rhetorically endorsed by front-line states, most of which are secretly participating in ending the economic isolation of the apartheid state." (p. 120)

Berger and Godsell

"Past achievements of pressure lobbies do not offer persuasive proof that the government will respond positively to pressure on issues perceived to be of major significance for its power base....[There is] far less concern about external economic pressures than about internal violence. Not one of the members of Parliament (MPs) interviewed spontaneously mentioned sanctions as a problem, when asked to indicate the major challenges and issues facing the party....Any specially accommodating response to divestment pressure is very unlikely indeed....Furthermore, any accusation that the government is dancing to the tune of the pressure groups abroad carries severe penalties for the government." (pp. 18-19)

"What [was] even more alarming for United States business were the decisions taken by some state and local governments...which made it increasingly difficult or even impossible for companies with operations in South Africa to bid successfully on state and municipal government contracts. In voting for or against such measures, interviews in diverse cities and states suggest that legislators were not responding to voter pressure. They report that their constituents rarely raised questions about South Africa. By assuming a clear anti-apartheid posture, however, legislators took the precaution of protecting themselves from potential attack for being 'soft on racism.' " (p. 246)

"Despite the promissory wording of the Comprehensive Anti-Apartheid Act, a financially pinched Congress...did not significantly increase funding for black South African educational programming. Indeed, with a diminution of support from corporations relishing relief from the difficulties of investor responsibility in South Africa, the number of scholarships available for university study in the United States under the Institute for International Education's South African Education Program (SAEP) decreased in the aftermath of the sanctions enactment." (pp. 253-254)

Butler et al.

"Many union leaders have quietly entertained second thoughts about the political wisdom of the disinvestment campaign." (p. 325)

de Villiers

"Do the political leaders calling for sanctions even understand the questions, or do they act as if South Africa is just one large violation of civil rights, as if it were nothing more than Selma, Alabama, writ large?" (p. 387)

"South Africa is an international pariah, and its people have brought it on themselves. It is also a scapegoat: the Western world's moral indignation can legitimately be viewed with the deepest cynicism." (p. 391)

Mutwa

"The United States of America really ought to do itself justice and play down its often strident criticism of South Africa, because it too is guilty of the very offences of which it so fiercely criticises South Africa. I could write volumes about the cruel racist treatment meted out to Negroes and Red Indians in some parts of the United States. I would not write hearsay but things that I saw....I know that in the USA, the FBI and the CIA keep secret dossiers on tens of thousands of American citizens of all races exactly as South Africa's security police and National Intelligence Service keep dossiers...." (pp. 8-10)

"Isolating an unwanted nation only makes it much stronger and more determined to survive and prosper....Far from weakening under the weight of boycotts and sanctions the country tends to flourish and even tends to end up having acquired atomic weapons....People who want to see the end of violence in South Africa, who want to see men such as Mandela released from prison, and people who want to see reconciliation between black and white...should resist all attempts to isolate my fatherland....Please be careful of how you handle the South African issue because should you make mistakes and bring about a racial upheaval in this country your own countries too would be engulfed by the ripple-effects....As a result of all-out sanctions and trade boycotts our people would die in far larger numbers than the Ethiopians died....The black people would die like flies BUT THE WHITE PEOPLE WOULD SURVIVE." (pp. 167-172)

"American firms must not be forced out of South Africa...because these firms have done much in the last twenty years to make the lot of the black man easy in South Africa....There is not a seriously workseeking black person in our townships who does not dream of one day finding a job with...firms associated with America." (p. 175)

"In the homes of black people that I know, the question of sanctions is a topic of urgent and fearful discussion. Don't people in America realise we are going to starve to death? Why do they not realise that the death of apartheid can be brought about by rapid upliftment of the black people, not actions that threaten to deprive us." (p. 175)

Paton

"There is only one firm statement that I can make on disinvestment – I will have nothing to do with it. I will not, by any written or spoken word, give it any support whatsoever." (p. 7)

"We don't want our problems solved by outsiders." (p. 28)

"We shall do nothing much to please the West, who, in the mistaken belief that a ruined economy will lead by some kind of miracle to an African Utopia, will no doubt tighten the grip of sanctions." (p. 105)

"I have no doubt that the imposition of sanctions will further delay the policy of reform....We won't have money to proceed with it. A great deal of human energy that would have been directed into reform programmes will now be diverted into attempts to minimise the effect of sanctions." (p. 298)

South Africa: Land of Hope?

Sunter

"Once you fully isolate a nation its rulers do not change to suit your wishes; nor do its people become more reasonable to one another – probably they grow less so." (p. 100)

RELIGION

Adam and Moodley

"Even implacable opponents of the government grant its sincere Christianity....Praying together to the same God, be it for rain or the dismantling of apartheid, binds the rulers and the ruled, in a situation unique in the annals of contemporary oppression." (pp. 198, 200)

de Kock

"To [a] meeting of ministers in Natal, Buthelezi stated his belief that, were it not for Christianity in South Africa, the very fabric of the country's society would long since have been torn apart. 'Running through South Africans of all race groups there is a strain of human Christian decency which is beginning to permeate ever deeper into society.' " (p. 120)

Louw and Kendall

"It was the sincere conviction of the Afrikaners that the Bible forbade them to consort with heathens, that the children of Ham [i.e. people of colour] were condemned to perpetual servitude and that it was God's covenant that whites should be the guardians of blacks." (p. 24)

Paton

"White South Africa prides itself on being a moral and Christian nation. That is why moral arguments are so uncomfortable, especially when they are advanced by black people." (p. 60)

"There are many white people in South Africa who will be angry with me for saying they are afraid. They are religious people, and they want to believe that their laws are Christian. God made the races and therefore He wants them kept separate. He wants each race to achieve its own noble destiny. The laws may sometimes be cruel but the end is so noble that a little cruelty can be forgiven. In other words, Apartheid and Christianity are almost the same thing. We suffer from a terrible blindness that will not let us see that apartheid is not a grand and majestic racial plan." (p. 69)

South Africa: Land of Hope?

"The Nationalist Afrikaner philosophers found the perfect solution. Man had two first duties — one to obey God and the other to love and defend his nation. Now luckily these two could be reconciled in that intellectual and moral monstrosity known as Christian Nationalism, which was never taught in the Gospels....The NHK [ultra-right Church] performed the intellectual and moral miracle of identifying its race exclusively with its religion." (p. 202)

BISHOP TUTU

de Kock

"Buthelezi and Inkatha have been particularly critical of the Archbishop of Cape Town, Desmond Tutu, for what they regarded as his open endorsement of the African National Congress to the exclusion of other black movements. Buthelezi was not alone in this judgment. In a statement to the political correspondent of *The Sunday Star* in January 1986, members of the black consciousness organisation, AZAPO, accused Tutu of openly siding with the ANC and destroying his ability to act as a mediator in chronic violence between blacks in the townships.

"According to Buthelezi those who argued for disinvestment were in fact undermining the forces of democratic, non-violent opposition to apartheid. More than one observer has noted that Buthelezi, the politician, held out more hope for a Christian accommodation between the peoples of South Africa than Tutu, the theologian. There is no doubt that Tutu has taken on himself — for reasons which have become hoary in restatement — the role of a key campaigner for the economic isolation of South Africa." (p. 119)

[*Quoting Buthelezi*]: "It is not only in his pronouncements that Bishop Tutu separates himself from positions which the Anglican Church has in fact adopted, but he separates himself from the Anglican Church by some of his actions....He again and again identifies with the ANC mission in exile, and here in this country he became a party politician when he accepted nomination as a patron of the UDF.

"The Anglican Church, as a church, recognises that there is gross injustice in South Africa. It recognises the right of black individuals to struggle for their liberation from this injustice. The Anglican Church recognises the hideousness of apartheid. [But] the Anglican Church has not blessed the ANC as the premier liberation organisation and it has not expressed the view that the UDF represents the church's best interests in this country in this struggle for liberation. Bishop Tutu, however, talks and behaves as though this were the case, not only in South Africa but throughout the world....

277

"It is atrocious that churchmen hum and haw when it comes to condemning atrocities planned and executed by the ANC mission. Churchmen cannot balance their mild protestations about ANC atrocities by vehement attacks on apartheid." (pp. 135-137)

Mutwa

"I cannot understand why men like Archbishop Desmond Tutu, why men like Teddy Kennedy should call for sanctions against my country. I wish to ask these two gentlemen, as well as the others who have contributed towards the sanctions that have been forced onto my country: DO YOU REALISE WHAT YOU ARE DOING? How can you, on the one hand, claim to be Christian God-fearing people and on the other hand be willing to destroy an entire country? Dare you stand one day before the vast audience-chamber of human history, and say to men of the future and women of years to come, that you were people of justice? Do you really think that by punishing South Africa with sanctions you are going to solve our problem for us? If so, you are politically naive, as well as dangerously misguided and stupid." (p. 178)

Paton

[*Addressing Tutu*]: "You are, in fact, the first black man to assume a position of national responsibility since the days of Albert Luthuli, your predecessor....I do not understand how your Christian conscience allows you to advocate disinvestment. I do not understand how you can put a man out of work for a high moral principle....I think your morality is confused just as was the morality of the Church in the Inquisition, or the morality of Dr [Hendrik] Verwoerd [South African Prime Minister, 1958-1966, and architect of Apartheid] in his utopian dreams. You come near to saying the end justifies the means, which is a thing no Christian can do." (p. 180)

NELSON MANDELA

de Kock

"The belief that Mandela, giant as he is to fellow blacks, can neutralise the ANC's strategy of violence at will, a Pope Clement raising his hand against Attila the Hun at the Tiber, is naive." (p. 126)

Mutwa

"Mandela must be released, UNCONDITIONALLY, if only as an act of compassion and as an act of calling the radicals' bluff in South Africa." (p. 159)

"Mandela is regarded by thousands of young black people in South Africa as the spiritual leader of the ANC; but he enjoys little support and respect among the grassroots supporters of the Pan Africanist Congress." (p. 159)

"Mandela's death in prison would be the greatest disaster ever to strike South Africa. It would unite blacks across the broad spectrum of class, tribe and educational standard and unleash a bloody holocaust in this land....Like Chief Buthelezi, Nelson Mandela is also a double-status black leader, with one foot in the modern political world and the other foot in the black traditional world....Should he die in prison thousands of people would take up arms and fight...because according to black tradition, if a prince or chief dies while held captive by an enemy tribe, it is an insult that must be cleansed by both our blood and that of the enemy tribe in whose captivity our prince or chief died." (p. 163)

"By remaining in prison Nelson Mandela poses the greatest single threat to the peace and security of South Africa. He holds a sword to South Africa's throat and he knows it. He is achieving far more behind bars than he would if he were a free man...." (p. 164)

HOPE

Adam and Moodley

"Today racial policies are disintegrating and are decisively challenged on various fronts. Momentum has been building to alter the social face of South Africa....Formerly excluded groups [are] being drawn into the ruling sector....Reform has replaced maintenance of traditional racial discrimination....The expressed ideal is that consensus politics be substituted for racial coercion...compromises instead of intransigent insistence on past policy." (pp. 9-12)

"If free elections were held in South Africa tomorrow, the whites would be astonished by the diversity of black voting. Surveys suggest that a free political contest under universal franchise would still result in one of the more conservative governments in Africa, in which radical socialist demands on the left would compete with black and white conservative groups on the right, with the government determined by a broad centre of social-democratic and liberal voters in shifting coalitions." (p. 211)

"There are reasons to hope for a more peaceful resolution in South Africa than in other divided societies. This realistic hope is founded in four distinct features of the South African conflict: 1) economic interdependence in a resource-rich country gives all groups a stake in accommodation; 2) African nationalism recognises Afrikaner nationalism and vice versa. The terms of coexistence, not the domination of one over the other, are the points of contention; 3) common Christian values and a common Westernised consumerism engender similar aspirations; and 4) an ethnic technocracy has begun to perceive the rising costs of apartheid domination and is engaged in modifying its control through reform." (p. 248)

Berger and Godsell

"...a broad movement towards reform is still occurring, despite popular perceptions of the 1987 election." (p. 39)

"In surveys among whites, a majority felt that the government should negotiate with black leaders immediately, and less than ten percent of respondents were completely opposed to negotiations." (p. 107)

"In the midst of polarisation between the Left and the Right, influential sections within government, big business and the ANC are pinning their hopes on a negotiated settlement. From discussions and interviews it is clear that there is more support for real negotiation than public rhetoric would have us believe. In spite of very different motivations and aspirations, a wide spectrum of individuals would prefer a negotiated settlement to a destructive civil war." (pp. 218-219)

"The degree of political freedom that does exist in South Africa, however circumscribed, holds out the hope of new needs being able to result in new institutions. The emergence of new political parties and coalitions within the presently enfranchised is an example of this." (p. 284)

Butler et al.

"...Dugard traces unmistakable signs of the growth of rule-of-law notions in the Afrikaner legal establishment, most notably in the strong interest in a bill of rights – a development which he attributes to the dogged advocacy of liberal jurists and legal scholars." (p. 12)

"The liberal belief in the rule of law and the recognition of human rights as necessary pillars of a decent society have at last penetrated Afrikaner nationalist thought and begun to influence the legal process and the constitutional debate." (p. 271)

"Afrikaners have played a major role in the establishment of Lawyers for Human Rights, an association of lawyers committed to the promotion of human rights in South Africa....The advocacy of human rights and the criticism of government and judiciary for failing to show sufficient concern for this priority is no longer the preserve of liberal politicians and academics. If not a part of the mainstream of Afrikaner legal opinion, it is at least an important tributary." (p. 279)

"In January, 1986...[the] business charter [of] the Federated Chamber of Industries...committed itself to a wide range of rights and principles, including freedom of thought, equal educational opportunities, freedom of movement, freedom of association, freedom of peaceful assembly, separation of state powers, supremacy of the law, freedom of the press, and free formation of political parties." (p. 380)

"...Positive signs do exist....There is considerable communication between the races through the newspapers, some of which have considerable readership in all groups, and among opinion leaders in the religious, educational, academic, and business spheres. Presumably, harmonious relations persist between the races in public places, in commerce, and, despite episodes of sharp industrial conflict, in normal employment situations. Moreover, large numbers of the [older] unemployed blacks have learnt to generate their own opportunities in a variety of informal sector pursuits and small businesses. An independent black trade union movement, despite the economic difficulties and its occasional radical rhetoric, is establishing norms of negotiation and compromise in industry that serve as a model to the rest of society. Finally, a tradition of social protest and an active commitment to social justice have developed among most mainline churches, the universities, and in several important voluntary organisations." (p. 391)

de Kock

"In the words of Anglo American's Gavin Relly, 'South Africa is not a country for the faint-hearted. It presents immense challenges but also immense opportunities, as well as the excitement of involvement in one of the greatest historical processes of change seen in the twentieth century.' " (p. 147)

"The struggle for liberation has been long and daunting—for Inkatha no less a struggle to motivate its own followers to retain hope in the goodwill between men, even if some of these men were white. And this, possibly, beyond the errors, the hatred and the anger, is Inkatha's legacy to a tortured land." (p. 147)

de Villiers

"The Joint Councils consisted of a dozen or so men and women, black and white, meeting once a month to discuss common problems, such as wages, education, and working conditions. Not much to set against the Calvinist ideologues, perhaps; but their existence, and the existence of the Institute of Race Relations, has kept alive in South Africa a fund of interracial goodwill long after it should have been used up." (p. 300)

"That the Afrikaner regime is now morally bankrupt is, ironically, one of South Africa's best hopes — it means that other Afrikaner ideas might emerge, as they have in the past....The deadness at the centre means the Afrikaners are freer to think as individuals again." (pp. 386, 388)

"What the outside world misses, and what no one's policy has been designed to let surface, is the common ground — the deep reservoir of goodwill still existing, incredibly, in South Africa in spite of the manifold injustices stretching over generations." (p. 388)

Louw and Kendall

"[The government] has already openly accepted the principles of power sharing." (p. xv)

"There is no logical reason why the various political groups should reject a solution which fulfills their requirements simply because it is being implemented by the current government. Most parties are calling for the eradication of statutory discrimination, for universal franchise, the recognition of minority rights, and genuine control of people over their own lives. If the government is openly committed to a plan which meets all these requirements, then it should receive the full support of all the other groups." (p. 202)

Paton

"Mr Botha is the first Nationalist...who has much appeal for non-Nationalists...the first...to have given hope to those South Africans who think that social, political, and economic change is essential and inevitable." (p. 43)

"Mr Hendrickse and his party have a political clout that no 'coloured' party has had before." (p. 46)

"I have lived on the edge of the Valley of a Thousand Hills for more than thirty years and I have been down into the valley, say, 1500 times. In all those years I encountered only on one occasion what one might call racial hostility." (p. 157)

"It is ground for hope that there is a growing realisation on the part of the white South African that the wage gap, which has been rightly been called the gap of shame, must be narrowed for reasons both of justice and her own survival." (p. 233)

"Many Afrikaners today acknowledge that their Government did great damage to the Rule of Law and want to see it restored." (p. 253)

"I would say without hesitation that the people of South Africa are more vocal and less afraid than they were....I would say that people like myself have more confidence in the judiciary than they had...and that our judiciary has more confidence in itself than it had...." (p. 289)

"I get my fits of gloom but I never cease to find encouragement when I look at the efforts of so many people to improve the quality of human life in our society, to help those in need and to uphold and reaffirm those moral ideals and principles on which all democracy is based." (p. 299)

Finally, an observation by author Clem Sunter, which sums up the hopes and aspirations of all who are working to create a new, democratic South Africa:

"Just think that 200 years ago, in the summer of 1787, there was a nation which was in danger of falling apart. Then fifty-five men assembled at a convention and drew up a document which has served as the basis of government for that nation ever since (with 26 amendments). The place was Philadelphia and the nation was America. That event was not predictable – it was made to happen by great men. The same can be made to happen here." (p. 111)

APPENDICES

Appendices

APPENDIX I

COMPLETE LIST OF PERSONS INTERVIEWED

(CHRONOLOGICAL LISTING)

Population Group Code
black (b), white (w), coloured (c), Indian (I)

IN-PERSON INTERVIEWS

Pretoria

Herman Stadler (w), South African Police
Frank Land (w), Director, American Desk, Dept of Foreign Affairs
Ekhart Posselt(w), Deputy Chief, Dept of Education and Training

Pietersburg

Mabel Makgole Chueu (b), "Mama Afrika"
Abram Rabbi Napo (b), Information Officer
Professor Jan Pretorius (w), University of the North
Afrikaner family, students (w)

Tzaneen

Dr and Mrs Lindsey Milne (w), Westfalia Estate
Professor Marthinus Burgers (w), Deptartment of Agriculture,
    University of the North
Evert van Dijk (w), Business Advisory Bureau
Makgothi John Tlhapane (b), Public Relations Officer, University of
    the North

GaZankulu (Homeland)

Professor Dr Hudson William Edison Ntsanwisi (b), Chief Minister
Wallace Blade Matthews (w), Secretary to Department of Finance

South Africa: Land of Hope?

Cape Town — Stellenbosch

Margaret Williamson (w), Editor, Women's Section, *The Argus*
George Stamelatos (w), Crossroads Administration
Patrick McKenzie (c), Labour Party
Sheila Camerer (w), National Party
Helen Suzman (w), Progressive Federal Party
Students, University of Stellenbosch (w)
Reverend Edward Jacannathan Mannikam (I), House of Delegates
Anonymous English and Afrikaner writers (w)
Adrienne Koch (w), President's Council
Shirley Kaplan (w), Delegation for Friendship Among Women
Richard Rive (c), writer
Mary Burton (w), Black Sash
Di Bishop (w), Department of Sociology, Univ. of the Western Cape
Anonymous Afrikaner medical student (w)
Pieter Schoeman (w), National Democratic Movement
Corné Mulder (w), Conservative Party
English South African social worker (w)
Anonymous oil company executive (w)
Professor Sampie Terreblanche (w), University of Stellenbosch
Rural Foundation for Human Resources (w)

Ciskei (Independent Country)

Wonga Fundile Tabata (b), Deputy Director-General, Department of
    Foreign Affairs
Headman Somtunzi(b), Director-General of Information
Radio Ciskei (b)
Joe Rowles (w), Ciskeian Small Business Corporation
Eunice Tunyiswa (b), Ciskeian Small Business Corporation
Neville Williamson (w), Ciskei Peoples Development Bank
Anonymous Afrikaner working in Ciskei (w)
Ben de Kock and Percy Shaw (w), Directors, Montage, Ltd
Rob and Alison Sayers (w), Keiskammahoek Irrigation Scheme
Professor Norman GK Holiday (w), University of Fort Hare

Durban

Adhir Singh (I), Small Business Development Corporation
Jugadhusan Devar (I), Indian Department of Education and Culture
Peter Badcock (w), KwaZulu/Natal Indaba
Khaba Mkhize (b), Editor, *The Echo*
Bishop Mngoma (b), Marianhill
Father Dieter Gahlen (w), St Wendolins Development Centre
Mike Abel (I), banker, "Ombudsman"
Professor Anthony Arkin (w), co-author, *South African Jewry*
Jill Addelson (w), Curator, Durban Art Gallery
Milicent Gcaba (b), Inkatha

Johannesburg

Anonymous volunteer (w), ACTSTOP
Essy Letsoalo (b), Soweto
Otto Krause (w), political journalist
Johan Liebenberg (w), labour negotiator
Five Freedoms Forum, "101 Ways to End Apartheid"
Nkosi Molala and Lybon Mabasa (b), AZAPO
Ismail Ayob (I), attorney to Winnie and Nelson Mandela
Bongi Dhlomo (b), Alexandra Art Centre
Michael Spicer (w), Anglo American Corporation
Professor Carl Nöffke (w), Director, American Studies,
    Rand Afrikaans University
Mondli Kunene (b), South African Institute of Race Relations
Leon Kok (w), South African Institute of International Affairs
Cindy Leontsinis (w), Victims Against Terrorism
Dr Ntatho Motlana (b), Soweto activist
Anonymous Lebanese-South African mother of two (w)
Dr Louise Tager (w), Dean of Law, University of the
    Witwatersrand (Wits)
Iris Lazarus (w), Women for Peace

South Africa: Land of Hope?

Andries Oliphant (b), Editor, Ravan Press
Dr Beryl Unterhalter (w), Deptartment of Sociology,
    University of the Witwatersrand (Wits)

Pretoria

Dr Nic Rhoodie (w), Human Sciences Research Council
Professor Philip Blignaut van der Watt (w), Moderator,
    Dutch Reformed Church

Interviews Through Intermediaries and By Mail

Anonymous editor (w), black/coloured newspaper
Zach de Beer (w), Leader, Progressive Federal Party
AJ Gumede (b), United Democratic Front
Dr Richard Hoar (w), Psychiatrist

APPENDIX II

ORIGINAL INTERVIEW QUESTIONS

Based on reading done prior to my trip, I formulated the following sets of questions, as a starting point for the interviews:

Political Leaders

- Do gains in the Conservative Party represent a white backlash against too-rapid reform? (Is the CP made up of those who stand to lose the most?)

- Do you believe the statistic that shows the Far Right and the Far Left with only 50,000 people each?

- What is the current attitude of South Africans towards America?

- What changes have taken place, in the past three years?

- Have you seen a *rapprochement* between the Afrikaners and the English-speakers?

- Can South Africa exist in a state of "Permanent Transition"?

- Do you view (and would you like the world to view) South Africa as *African* or *European*?

- Do you see birth control and overpopulation as major problems for South Africa?

- What changes do you consider necessary in South Africa's education system?

- What about the Group Areas Act? How do you feel about "grey" areas?

- Do you view the trade union movement as a positive or a negative force in South Africa?

- How do you view South Africa's present business climate?

South Africa: Land of Hope?

- What has been the effect of sanctions on South Africa?

- What do you think are the Government's intentions? What are the prospects for the National Council?

- Do you see the State of Emergency as necessary for the stability of South Africa, at the moment?

- How do you feel about the KwaZulu/Natal Indaba?

- Would you like to see a universal franchise in South Africa?

- What changes have there been as a result of external pressures and/or the Sullivan Code?

- Is there any justification for "Own" and "General" affairs, i.e. categorizing issues as some more reasonably pertaining to specific population groups, individually, ("own") and others to South Africans as a whole ("general")?

- Has the proliferation of political parties caused excessive fragmentation of South African voters?

- Would you like to see the ANC unbanned? How do you feel about the organization and its support of violence and terrorism? Does the fact that they are financed by Moscow disturb you?

- Do you believe the ANC's goal is to destroy the black moderates?

- Would you like to see Nelson Mandela released? Should the renunciation of violence be an issue?

- Is it true that 85% of white South Africans want to dismantle apartheid completely?

- Is there any society *anywhere* that South Africa could use as a model?

- What is your blueprint for change in South Africa?

- What message would you like to send to Americans?

Non-White Leaders

- What further changes would you like to see in education for blacks?

- Is the idea of separate-but-equal acceptable?

- Would you be willing to integrate one grade at a time, i.e. to take twelve years to reach full integration?

- Do you see birth control and overpopulation as issues of prime importance to your people?

- Are you pleased by the progress made by black trade unions? What is being done in the areas of workers' training and literacy?

- Are black entrepreneurs coming into their own and being accepted by other South Africans?

- Do you agree with the statement, "Violence will lead to chaos and increased opportunities for the Communists"?

- How do you feel about the policies and pronouncements of AZAPO?

- Do you consider the ANC and UDF to be "peace-loving" organizations?

- How do you feel about the ANC Freedom Charter?

- Do you believe it is the ANC's design to destroy moderates?

- Are Tutu, Mandela, and Tambo representative or "celebrity leaders"?

- Is the concept of democracy difficult to explain to those who have lived under tribal traditions?

- Is inter-tribal conflict real or a fabrication of the whites?

- Is it true there are 271 African languages, but there is no word for "opposition," only "enemy"?

INTERVIEW QUESTIONS (Cont.)
Non-White Leaders

- The South African government has said, "The upgrading of black socio-economic conditions is a priority of this government." Do you believe it?

- Would you like to see laws to implement black urbanization?

- How do you feel about the KwaZulu/Natal Indaba, and what are the implications for the rest of South Africa?

- Do other tribes fear the Zulus?

- Has the repeal of the Separate Amenities Act satisfied you?

- What changes have taken place as a result of external pressure and/or the Sullivan Code?

- How likely is it the Group Areas Act will be rescinded?

- Are blacks satisfied with "grey" areas, if white and black areas remain?

- Is the Crossroads story a lesson?

- Is there any justification for "Own" and "General" affairs, i.e. categorizing issues as some more reasonably pertaining to specific population groups, individually, ("own") and others to South Africans as a whole ("general")?

- Does the saying, "Give me a fish, I eat for a day; *teach* me to fish, I eat for a lifetime," apply in South Africa? (Is welfare an issue? How do you feel about welfare?)

- What are black attitudes towards voting locally, if not nationally?

- What are black attitudes towards the TBVC (independent) countries?

- Are the TBVC countries actually prospering?

- How do you view the Homelands vs. the Independent Countries?

- Do you agree that "Apartheid cannot be reformed; it must be abolished"?

- Is universal suffrage realistic, for South Africa? If not now, what about in the future?

- What are your top priorities?

- Do you agree with the statement, "The primary opponent of apartheid is capitalism."?

- Is it true that the "conflict is not between tribes but between generations, and rural vs. urban blacks."?

- How do you feel about the South African Council of Churches and "liberation theology"?

- What do you see as the greatest hope for South Africa? Do you think that, if you wait long enough, all the white ultra-conservatives will die out and leave the rest of you in peace, or is there a *new* generation of ultra-conservatives?

- Where are blacks making the greatest gains? fewest?

- Is black-white animosity increasing or decreasing?

- How would you characterize black-coloured-Indian relationships?

- How does crime in the rural areas compare to urban crime?

- Do South African blacks think American blacks understand their problems?

- What message would you like to send to America, and to American blacks?

South Africa: Land of Hope?

Women's Editor

- Is black-white animosity increasing or decreasing?
  Regarding the above, are there differences depending on: age groups? males or females? geographic areas? professional or nonprofessional status?

- What about relationships among blacks-coloureds-Indians?

- What changes have you seen in South African women in the past ten years — at home and in the workplace?

- Have women become more visible in the professions than previously?

- Are certain professions more racially integrated than others? Are blacks and whites seen together on television?

- Have white South Africans existed with an "ostrich mentality," all these years — unaware of the way blacks have lived?

- "It's hard to be an old Afrikaner *woman*." — true? (Is the Afrikaner attitude towards women still one of "kirche, kinder, kuchen"? Is it different among the English-speakers? Among the non-white population groups? Are there generational differences?)

- Does South Africa have anything like Affirmative Action programs for women?

- Are more women assuming positions of leadership? Which population groups?

- Have English-Afrikaner relationships changed?

- Are South Africans concerned about the youth drain and brain drain, with so many people leaving the country?

- Are students more or less political now than in the 1960s?

- What major changes have taken place in South Africa in the past five years? Two Years?

- How has daily life changed for South Africans?

- What changes do you note in Letters to the Editor?

- What are the greatest concerns expressed by your readers?

- Are South African children aware of the country's problems? Do they talk about them?

- What changes have you noticed in radio, television, and literature? How about comments made on Talk Radio?

- What opinion is held of those who choose to leave?

- How are expatriot *writers* viewed?

- What are your expectations, in terms of government-ordered change and South Africans' reactions to it?

Business

- Is South Africa's Gross Domestic Product up again?

- What about foreign investment?

- Opinions on the importance of establishing a strong black middle class?

- Describe the work of the Black Management Forum.

- What has been the effect of sanctions?

- What has been the effect of the trade union movement?

- What changes have you seen in the business climate, since sanctions?

- What is being done to train black workers, entrepreneurs? To what extent is illiteracy a problem?

- Is there a problem of associating apartheid with capitalism?

- Do you see any likelihood of a truce between black radicals and black entrepreneurs?

- How are you compensating for the youth drain and the brain drain?

- How would you describe the business-government relationship?

- Do you see business taking a more active role in changing South Africa? How do you view the role of American business in South Africa?

- Have those who took over from American companies continued any of the Americans' progressive policies?

- What are your ideas for a new South Africa?

Education

- Is it true there has been a 40% increase in black education spending, in the past few years? With what results? Is 40% enough?

- English vs. Afrikaans vs. black education.

- What is the likelihood of complete integration of schools?

- Education as an "own affair," i.e. determined by each population group for itself.

- Why not compulsory education for all population groups?

- What significant changes have taken place, in black education?

- Are black and white teachers paid the same?

- Success rate of black students, at various levels

- Problems

- Curriculum

- Languages

- Private vs. public education

- Future plans

APPENDIX III

SOUTH AFRICA'S POPULATION GROUPS[1]

South Africa's population represents the cultures of three continents — Europe (whites), Africa (blacks), and Asia (Indians) — and a large community of people of mixed origin (coloureds). Not one of the country's eleven major languages is spoken by a majority of the people.

The blacks comprise nine major ethnic groups, descended from four major ancient peoples who migrated south from Central Africa. Nearly eighty percent profess Christianity, primarily as members of the Independent Church, which combines Christian doctrine with traditional beliefs. Thirty-two percent of the blacks live in urban areas.

The whites are divided, basically, into two language groups — the Afrikaners (descendants of the first Dutch settlers; Afrikaans-speaking) and the English-speaking, mostly from Britain. However, there are also communities of Portuguese, Germans, and Greeks, and a close-knit Jewish population originating primarily from Lithuania. While almost all Afrikaners belong to one of the Dutch Reformed Churches (now split over the apartheid issue), the English-speakers are spread over a wide range of protestant denominations. Ninety percent of whites are urbanised.

The coloured community is the product of miscegenation among the original Hottentot tribes encountered by the early settlers, slaves imported by the Dutch East India Company from the East, the early white settlers, and later, the blacks. Within this population group are two distinctive communities — the Griquas, largely of Hottentot-European descent, and the Cape Malays, a mixture of Eastern groups brought together by the Muslim faith.

The vast majority of Asians are Indians descended from indentured labourers imported to Natal to work the sugar plantations. Indian traders

---

1   This Appendix quoted in its entirety from *South Africa Profile (Pretoria: Bureau for Information, July 1987)*.

Page 303

came later, as did a group of Chinese, following the discovery of gold and diamonds in South Africa. Most Indians speak English, but Indian languages are also spoken — Tamil, Telugu, Gujarati, Urdu, and Hindustani. Seventy percent of the Indians are Hindus, twenty percent Muslims, and ten percent Christians or other faiths. Over eighty percent of all South African Indians live in Natal, the majority within a 150 km [90 mile] radius of Durban.

The numerical breakdowns are as follows:

BLACKS   **23,661,000**
    Zulus   (6,700,000)
    Xhosas   (6,240,000)
    North Sothos (2,900,000)
    Tswanas (2,856,000)
    South Sothos (1,900,000)
    Shangaan-Tsongas (1,100,000)
    Swazis (1,005,000)
    Vendas (520,000)
    Ndebeles (440,000)

WHITES   **4,900,000**
    Afrikaners (2,940,000)
    English-speakers (1,960,000)
      Jews (120,000)
      Portuguese (70,000)
      Germans (40,000)
      Greeks (20,000)
      Others (1,710,000)

COLOUREDS   **2,800,000**
    Griquas (100,000)
    Cape Malays (200,000)
    Others (2,500,000)

ASIANS   **880,000**
    Indians (869,000)
    Chinese (11,000)

TOTAL = 32,241,000

APPENDIX IV

POLITICAL PARTIES[1]

The proliferation of political parties in South Africa is both impressive and bewildering—for South Africans as well as foreigners. In some cases the differences are subtle; in others, the divide is vast. Here, in alphabetical order, are the major political parties in existence as of April 1989:

African National Congress (ANC)

Black party formed in 1912, banned in 1960. Leader Nelson Mandela convicted of sabotage and sentenced to life in prison. In 1969 confirmed a policy of violence against the government of South Africa and in the 1980s active in terrorist attacks and "necklacing" of fellow blacks it sees as "collaborators." Oliver Tambo, current leader.

Afrikaner-Weerstandbeweging (AWB)

Ultra-right wing party of Afrikaner nationalists. Leader is Eugene Terre'Blanche, who changed his name to mean "White Land." Seeks strict segregation and a white homeland.

Azanian Peoples Organization (AZAPO)

Black party. Socialist. Seeks one national culture. Anti-capitalist, anti-racist, anti-sexist. Black majority working class would rule and nationalize almost everything.

---

1   The major portion of this information is taken from *South Africa: The Solution*, by Leon Louw and Frances Kendall.

South Africa: Land of Hope?

POLITICAL PARTIES (Cont.)

Conservative Party (CP)

Broke away from National Party in 1982 in opposition to National Party policy of dismantling apartheid. In 1987 overtook the Progressive Federal Party and became the official Opposition party in Parliament. Seeks resumption of apartheid and partition. Party leader is Dr Andries Treurnicht.

Democratic Party (DP)

Formed in early 1989 by the joining of the three major anti-apartheid opposition parties (Independent Party, National Democratic Movement, and Progressive Federal Party) and led by a triumvirate of those parties' leaders.

Independent Party (IP)

Formed in the Spring of 1988 and led by Dr Denis Worrall, seeks a coalition of political parties across colour lines. In early 1989 became part of the Democratic Party.

Inkatha

Black party led by Zulu Chief Mangosuthu Gatsha Buthelezi. Pro-capitalist, moderate. Believes in black unity as a priority, non-violence, the politics of negotiation, and peaceful political co-existence beyond ethnic and racial boundaries.

Labour Party (LP)

Coloured party in the House of Representatives, led by Rev Allan Hendrickse. Anti-Communist, pro-democracy and rule of law. Favors mixed economy combining capitalism and socialism. In 1984 proposed a federal system in which "racist" and "non-racist" states could co-exist.

National Democratic Movement (NDM)

In 1987 broke away from the Progressive Federal Party, feeling a lack of direction and leadership. Met with ANC leaders. Seeks movement and reform now, under the leadership of Wynand Malan. In early 1989 became part of the Democratic Party.

National Indian Council (NIC)

Affiliated with United Democratic Front, subscribes to the ANC Freedom Charter. Opposed to the 1983 constitution and tricameral legislature which are seen as continuing a policy of racism.

National Party (NP)

Formed in 1915, ruling party in South Africa since 1948. Formulated the master plan for "separate development" in 1959 under then-leader, Dr Hendrik Verwoerd, who was later assassinated. Leader and State President PW Botha committed to reform and dismantling of apartheid, campaigned in 1977 on platform of "Adapt or Die." Botha suffered a stroke in January 1989 and was replaced by former Education Minister FW de Klerk.

Progressive Federal Party (PFP)

Founded in 1977, open to all races. Official Opposition party until 1987. Has long advocated total equality for all South African citizens. Best known Member of Parliament, Helen Suzman; party leader, Zach de Beer. Pro-capitalism, but accepts that state must provide some welfare. Seeks release of Nelson Mandela and talks with the ANC. In early 1989 became part of the Democratic Party.

Solidarity Party

Indian party in the House of Delegates, led by Mr JN Reddy. Pro-capitalism and Bill of Rights guaranteeing individual rights.

South Africa: Land of Hope?

United Democratic Front (UDF)

Seen as a front for the banned ANC. Supports the Freedom Charter.
Started by Rev Allan Boesak in 1983.

APPENDIX V

HISTORICAL OUTLINE[1]

1652	Dutch arrive at the Cape
1657	Dutch settle on what had been Spring grazing land of the Khoi-Khoi (Hottentots)
1660	A hedge of bitter almond trees is planted across the Cape Flats to cut off 6000 acres of the Cape Peninsula from the interior. The Khoi-Khoi and the whites were kept separate by this hedge and both were forbidden to cross it. This was the first apartheid measure in South Africa.
1663	First separate schools for blacks established
1678	Inter-racial "concubinage" forbidden
1681	Whites forbidden to attend parties with slave women
1685	Marriage between blacks and whites forbidden
1770s	Border Wars between blacks and whites
1800	White missionary visits Nguni tribe
1806	British Colonial Government takes over
1822	English becomes the sole official language of Cape Colony
1834-1854	The Great Trek, a mass exodus of Dutch away from the Cape and British rule, into the interior
1835	16,000 Mfengu, Natal blacks displaced by the Zulus, settle in Cape Colony at the bidding of the Governor, who uses them as a buffer between whites and Xhosas.
1840s-1890s	Xhosa and Mfengu flourish in Cape Colony, surpassing productivity of whites. Whites move to restrict blacks and to force them to work as labourers rather than working independently.

---

1   Louw and Kendall, *South Africa: The Solution*

South Africa: Land of Hope?

1859   Indians brought into Natal as indentured servants to work in the sugar cane fields.

1878-1879   Zulu Wars

1892   Forced registration of blacks

1899-1902   Boer War between English and Dutch

1902   Treaty of Vereeniging ends the Boer republics of Transvaal and Orange Free State. Article 8 of the Treaty makes enfranchisement of non-whites dependent on the consent of a white majority.

   Lord Alfred Milner, High Commissioner of British South Africa, calling himself "an imperialist out and out" and a "British race patriot" attempts to increase the British population by immigration until the majority of South Africa is English speaking. Milner is against granting political power to blacks.

   Indians outnumber whites in Natal

1905   Colonies granted independence; Milner recalled to England.

1910   Union of South Africa formed from the four colonies (Cape, Natal, Transvaal, and Orange Free State)

1911   Job Reservation[1] implemented

1913   Native Land Act, demarcating part of South Africa as black territory and prohibiting sale of land in remaining (white) area to blacks.

   Immigration Act passed, to stop influx of Indians

1924   Industrial Conciliation Act covers labour disputes by whites, coloureds, and Indians, but not blacks.

---

1 The system of setting aside certain jobs for members of specific population groups.

Appendices

HISTORICAL OUTLINE (Cont.)

1936   Franchise for blacks abolished in Cape Province.

1948   National Party comes to power.

1949   Prohibition of Mixed Marriages Act[1]

1950   Immorality Amendment Act

Population Registration Act[2]

Group Areas Act

1951   Separate Representation of Voters Act removes Cape coloureds from white voters' roll

1953   Reservation of Separate Amenities Act establishes "petty apartheid"

Bantu Education Act enforces segregated education

Native Labour Act enforces segregated unions and forbids blacks to strike

1955   ANC presents Freedom Charter

1960   Sharpeville riot

1961   South Africa declares itself a republic.

1976   Soweto riot

1977   National Party elected on slogan "Adapt or Die"

1978   Dismantling of apartheid begins

1984   Tri-Cameral Parliament established to include coloureds and Indians but not blacks

---

1   Prohibition of sex and marriage across the colour bar.

2   See Introduction, p.3, footnote 2.

Page 311

APPENDIX VI

THE DISMANTLING OF APARTHEID

Those who have not studied or kept abreast of developments in South Africa may be surprised to learn of the extent to which the apartheid system already has been dismantled.

From an updated report by André Thomashausen,[1] first researched and written in 1985 at the request of the U.S. Embassy in Pretoria, the following will help to clarify what legislation has been passed and what reforms have taken place. The period covered is 1978-1988, and reform policies have been implemented on four levels:

Level I.

Apartheid-free enclaves. Four Self-Governing Territories, or "homelands" were released into full independence. Known as the TBVC countries (Transkei, Bophuthatswana, Venda, and Ciskei). Since 1980, governmental efforts have concentrated on improving the economic viability and independence of the new Republics.

Level II.

Equal political status of Indians and coloureds. Under major constitutional reform which took place in 1983, the South African Parliament now consists of three houses: one for whites, one for Indians, and one for coloureds. Each group has its own Ministers Council. (Black South Africans were excluded from representation.)

Level III.

Democratization of the townships. Black local self-government was introduced in 1982-83, starting with the Black Affairs Administration Act and implemented by the Black Local Authorities Act and the Black Communities Development Act.

---

1   Thomashausen, André, "The Dismantling of Apartheid" (Pretoria: Sigma Press, 1987).

DISMANTLING OF APARTHEID (Cont.)

Level IV.

Single Reform Measures. This involved the abolition of over 100 discriminatory laws. Among the most important (in chronological order):

- Labour Relations Amendment Act (1981). Unrestrained freedom of labor organization and association (i.e. freedom regarding trade unionism) and abolition of all racial discrimination in labor relations.

- Group Areas Amendment Act (1982). Complete integration of sport and sporting facilities.

- Income Tax Amendment Act (1984). Uniform income tax laws for all population groups.

- Universities, National Education Policy and Technikon Amendment Act (1984). Admission of non-whites to tertiary educational institutions.

- Group Areas Amendment Act (1986). Mixed business districts in hitherto exclusively white areas.

- Immorality and Prohibition of Mixed Marriages Amendment Act (1985). Repeal of the prohibition of mixed marriages and of sexual intercourse across the color bar.

- Laws on Co-operation and Development Amendment Act (1985). Granting of permanent residential rights to blacks who have been resident in a primarily "white" area since birth or who have either been resident or have occupied/been employed in a "white" area for a period longer than ten years.

- Constitutional Affairs Amendment Act (1985). Repeal of the prohibition against mixed political parties.

- Liquor Amendment Act (1986). Abolition of all race restrictions on the sale of liquor.

DISMANTLING OF APARTHEID (Cont.)

- Matters Concerning Admission to and Residence in the Republic Amendment Act (1986). Granting of residential rights to Indians and coloureds in the Orange Free State and in Northern Natal, and abolition of race restrictions in immigration law.

- Abolition of Influx Control Act (1986). Granting freedom of movement to all population groups.

- Prevention of Illegal Squatting Act (1986). Toleration of "orderly" squatting.

- Identification Act (1986). Abolition of different identity documents for the several population groups.

- Restoration of South African Citizenship Act (1986). Restoration of a uniform South African citizenship to all citizens.

- Black Communities Development Amendment Act (1986). Ending all compulsory resettlements, repeal of the prohibition against the acquiring of immovable property by blacks, and the conversion of all 99-year leasehold rights into absolute ownership. Also, transfer of full ownership of land to black municipal administration and local authorities.

- Regional Services Council Act and Abolition of Development Bodies Act (1986). Creation of multi-racial and integrated provincial administrative bodies and the abolition of special jurisdiction over blacks on a provincial level.

- Removal of Restrictions on Economic Activities Act (1986). Abolition of restrictions on freedom of trade affecting blacks.

South Africa: Land of Hope?

DISMANTLING OF APARTHEID (Cont.)

- Special Courts for Blacks Abolition Act (1986). Reform of the judicial system abolishing special courts for matters arising between blacks.

- Group Areas Act Proclamation (1986). Relaxation of the restrictions on rights of residence in areas reserved for another population group; relaxed procedures for the issuing of special permits, e.g. for the lawful residence of blacks in "white" residential areas and the discontinuation of prosecution in cases of violation of the Group Areas Act.

- Proclamation R17 (1986). Complete elimination of statutory racial barriers in hotels and restaurants and partial accessibility to cinemas and theatres, and accessibility of blacks to most publicly controlled recreational facilities (including the beaches) in various, although not all, white communities.

- National Council Bill (1986). Proposal of an integrated National Council comprising elected black representatives for the black population living outside the Self-Governing Territories, for purposes of deliberating further constitutional reform together with black leaders.

- Provincial Government Act (1987). The establishment of Joint Executive Authorities for "white" provinces and neighboring Self-Governing Territories, as in the case of Natal and KwaZulu.

- National Road Traffic Act (1988). Integration of countrywide transport services.

APPENDIX VII

THE SULLIVAN CODE [1]

Statement of Principles of U.S. Firms with Affiliates
in the
Republic of South Africa

1. Non-segregation of the races in all eating, comfort and work facilities.

2. Equal and fair employment practices for all employees.

3. Equal pay for all employees doing equal or comparable work for the same period of time.

4. Initiation of and development of training programs that will prepare, in substantial numbers, Blacks and other non-whites for supervisory, administrative, clerical and technical jobs.

5. Increasing the number of Blacks and other non-whites in management and supervisory positions.

6. Improving the quality of employees' lives outside the work environment in such areas as housing, transportation, schooling, recreation and health facilities.

---

1 Introduced by Reverend Leon H Sullivan, member of the Board of Directors of General Motors, in 1977. In 1987, Sullivan abandoned the Code and demanded, instead, that American companies pull out of South Africa altogether. This Appendix is reprinted from a publication by the International Council for Equality of Opportunity Principles, Inc., Philadelphia.

South Africa: Land of Hope?

Amplification

PRINCIPLE I
Non-Segregation of the races in all eating, comfort and work facilities

Each signator of the *Statement of Principles* will proceed immediately to:

- Eliminate all vestiges of racial discrimination.

- Remove all race designation signs.

- Desegregate all eating, comfort and work facilities.

PRINCIPLE II
Equal and fair employment practices for employees

Each signator of the *Statement of Principles* will proceed immediately to:

- Implement equal and fair terms and conditions of employment.

- Provide non-discriminatory eligibility for benefit plans.

- Establish an appropriate and comprehensive procedure for handling and resolving individual employee complaints.

- Support the elimination of all industrial racial discriminatory laws which impede the implementation of equal and fair terms and conditions of employment, such as abolition of job reservations, job fragmentation, and apprenticeship restrictions for Blacks and other non-whites.

- Support the elimination of discrimination against the rights of Blacks to form or belong to government registered and unregistered unions and acknowledge generally the rights of Blacks to form their own unions or be represented by trade unions which already exist.

- Secure rights of Black workers to the freedom of association and assure protection against victimization while pursuing and attaining these rights.

- Involve Black workers or their representatives in the development of programs that address their educational and other needs and those of their dependents and the local community.

PRINCIPLE III
Equal pay for all employees doing equal or comparable work for the same period of time

Each signator of the *Statement of Principles* will proceed immediately to:

- Design and implement a wage and salary administration plan which is applied equally to all employees, regardless of race, who are performing equal or comparable work.

- Ensure an equitable system of job classifications, including a review of the distinction between hourly and salaried classifications.

- Determine the extent upgrading of personnel and/or jobs in the upper echelons is needed, and accordingly implement programs to accomplish this objective in representative numbers, insuring the employment of Blacks and other non-whites at all levels of company operations.

- Assign equitable wage and salary ranges, the minimum of these to be well above the appropriate local minimum economic living level.

PRINCIPLE IV
Initiation of and development of training programs that will prepare, in substantial numbers, Blacks and other non-whites for supervisory, administrative, clerical and technical jobs.

Each signator of the *Statement of Principles* will proceed immediately to:

- Determine employee training needs and capabilities, and identify employees with potential for further advancement.

South Africa: Land of Hope?

SULLIVAN CODE (Cont.)

- Take advantage of existing outside training resources and activities, such as exchange programs, technical colleges, and similar institutions or programs.

- Support the development of outside training facilities, individually or collectively—including technical centers, professional training exposure, correspondence and extension courses, as appropriate, for extensive training outreach.

- Initiate and expand inside training programs and facilities.

PRINCIPLE V
Increasing the number of Blacks and other non-whites in management and supervisory positions

Each signator of the *Statement of Principles* will proceed immediately to:

- Identify, actively recruit, train and develop a sufficient and significant number of Blacks and other non-whites to assure that as quickly as possible there will be appropriate representation of Blacks and other non-whites in the management group of each company at all levels of operations.

- Establish management development programs for Blacks and other non-whites, as needed, and improve existing programs and facilities for developing management skills of Blacks and other non-whites.

- Identify and channel high management potential Blacks and other non-white employees into management development programs.

PRINCIPLE VI
Improving the quality of employees' lives outside the work environment in such areas as housing, transportation, schooling, recreation and health facilities

Each signator of the *Statement of Principles* will proceed immediately to:

- Evaluate existing and/or develop programs, as appropriate, to address the specific needs of Black and other non-white employees in the areas of housing, health care, transportation and recreation.

- Evaluate methods for utilizing existing, expanded or newly established in-house medical facilities or other medical programs to improve medical care for all non-whites and their dependents.

- Participate in the development of programs that address the educational needs of employees, their dependents, and the local community. Both individual and collective programs should be considered, in addition to technical education, including such activities as literacy education, business training, direct assistance to local schools, contributions and scholarships.

- Support changes in influx control laws to provide for the rights of Black migrant workers to normal family life.

- Increase utilization of and assist in the development of Black and other non-white owned and operated business enterprises including distributors, suppliers of goods and services and manufacturers.

With all the foregoing in mind, it is the objective of the companies to involve and assist in the education and training of large and telling numbers of Blacks and other non-whites as quickly as possible. The ultimate impact of this effort is intended to be of massive proportion, reaching millions.

PERIODIC REPORTING

The Signatory Companies of the *Statement of Principles* will proceed immediately to:

- Report progress on an annual basis to Reverend Sullivan through the independent administrative unit he has established.

- Have all areas specified by Reverend Sullivan audited by a certified public accounting firm.

SULLIVAN CODE (Cont.)

- Inform all employees of the company's annual periodic report rating and invite their input on ways to improve the rating.

APPENDIX VIII

THE
AFRICAN NATIONAL CONGRESS
FREEDOM CHARTER

The ANC Freedom Charter, first presented in 1955, has now been updated and modified. The "Constitutional Guidelines for a Democratic South Africa" remain relatively general but offer what a good many South Africans feel is at least a basis for beginning discussions.

The *Weekly Mail* asked a wide range of organizations to comment on the guidelines for its 7 October 1988 issue. Following are, first, the Guidelines, then some of the comments made by representatives of various other political parties:

The ANC's "Constitutional Guidelines"

THE STATE

A.   South Africa shall be an independent, unitary, democratic and non-racial state.

B.   Sovereignty shall belong to the people as a whole and shall be exercised through one central legislature, executive, judiciary and administration. Provision shall be made for the delegation of the powers of the central authority to subordinate administrative units for purposes of more efficient administration and democratic participation.

C.   The institution of hereditary rulers and chiefs shall be transformed to serve the interests of the people as a whole in conformity with the democratic principles embodied in the constitution.

D.   All organs of government, including justice, security and armed forces, shall be representative of the people as a whole, democratic in their structure and functioning, and dedicated to defending the principles of the constitution.

FRANCHISE

E.   In the exercise of their sovereignty, the people shall have the right to vote under a system of universal suffrage based on the principle of one person/one vote.

F.   Every voter shall have the right to stand for election and to be elected to all legislative bodies.

NATIONAL IDENTITY

G.   It shall be state policy to promote the growth of a single national identity and loyalty binding on all South Africans. At the same time, the state shall recognise the linguistic and cultural diversity of the people and provide facilities for free linguistic and cultural development.

BILL OF RIGHTS AND AFFIRMATIVE ACTION

H.   The Constitution shall include a Bill of Rights based on the Freedom Charter. Such a Bill of Rights shall guarantee the fundamental human rights of all citizens, irrespective of race, colour, sex, or creed, and shall provide appropriate mechanisms for their protection and enforcement.

I.   The state and all social institutions shall be under a constitutional duty to take active steps to eradicate race discrimination in all its forms.

J.   The state and all social institutions shall be under a constitutional duty to take active steps to eradicate speedily the economic and social inequalities produced by racial discrimination.

K. The advocacy or practice of racism, fascism, nazism or the incitement of ethnic or regional exclusiveness or hatred shall be outlawed.

L. Subject to clauses I and K above, the democratic state shall guarantee the basic rights and freedoms, such as freedom of association, thought, worship and the press. Furthermore, the state shall have the duty to protect the right to work and guarantee the right to education and social security.

M. All parties which conform to the provision of I and K above shall have the legal right to exist and to take part in the political life of the country.

ECONOMY

N. The state shall ensure that the entire economy serves the interests and well-being of the entire population.

O. The state shall have the right to determine the general context in which economic life takes place and define and limit the rights and obligations attaching to the ownership and use of productive capacity.

P. The private sector of the economy shall be obliged to cooperate with the state in realising the objectives of the Freedom Charter in promoting social well-being.

Q. The economy shall be a mixed one, with a public sector, a private sector, a co-operative sector and a small-scale family sector.

R. Co-operative forms of economic enterprise, village industries and small scale family activities shall be supported by the state.

S. The state shall promote the acquisition of management, technical and scientific skills among all sections of the population, especially the blacks.

T. Property for personal use and consumption shall be constitutionally protected.

ANC FREEDOM CHARTER (Cont.)

LAND

U.   The state shall devise and implement a land reform program that will include and address the following issues: abolition of all racial restrictions on ownership and use of land; implementation of land reform in conformity with the principle of affirmative action, taking into account the status of victims of forced removals.

WORKERS

V.   A charter protecting workers' trade union rights, especially the right to strike and collective bargaining, shall be incorporated into the constitution.

WOMEN

W.   Women shall have equal rights in all spheres of public and private life and the state shall take affirmative action to eliminate inequalities and discrimination between the sexes.

THE FAMILY

X.   The family, parenthood and children's rights shall be protected.

INTERNATIONAL

Y.   South Africa shall be a non-aligned state committed to the principles of the Charter of the OAU and the Charter of the UN and to the achievement of national liberation, world peace and disarmament.

Reactions to the ANC Constitutional Guidelines

INKATHA (Oscar Dhlomo, Secretary General)

"There is a striking resemblance in the way the African National Congress has introduced its Constitutional Guidelines and the way the National Party normally introduces so-called constitutional reform.

"Both parties apparently subscribe to the 'top-down' approach, whereby the ruling clique unilaterally decides on the proposed constitutional reforms and then invites the rest of the population to comment on them.

"As someone who subscribes to the 'bottom-up' approach in constitutional affairs, I feel I must state this reservation from the beginning. The 'top-down' approach in constitutional affairs is manifestly undemocratic and can never yield a broadly acceptable constitutional settlement.

"The ANC apparently favors a strong centralised state which would not allow for maximum devolution of powers to lower lines of government....

"The idea of a rigidly centralised state arises out of the belief that it is such a state that is able to effectively tackle the inequalities in our society and eradicate remaining pockets of apartheid. Whilst this is a noble idea worthy of support it is likely to lead to social conflict. At worst it could lead to less and not more participatory democracy.

"I support the principle of universal suffrage based on the principle of one man/one vote. This is the universal demand of the black majority. However, I hope the ANC is aware of other possibilities in this regard should it be called upon by concerned minorities to consider alternative options. I have in mind such voting procedures as proportional representation.

"In the Bill of Rights section of the Guidelines, I have problems with clause K. It is quite clear that under this clause ANC rulers could conduct a witchhunt against those organisations they disapprove of....

"If the ANC claims it supports a multi-party democracy then it should allow all parties to operate freely and trust the electorate as ultimate judges. Interestingly, nothing is said in clause K about the advocacy of revolution to overthrow a legitimate future ANC state. If there is need to outlaw anything I would have thought the advocacy of revolution would be the principle candidate.

"Once again the ANC envisages far reaching and unrestrained state intervention in the regulation of economic life. There is, however, a welcome change in the ANC's economic thinking in that nationalisation, as a mechanism for the redistribution of wealth, has been dropped. One appreciates this state intervention will be aimed mainly at affirmative action and not at stifling private initiative.

"Whilst I appreciate the victims of forced removals need to be considered first in any land reform exercise, I feel it is also important to consider the case of peasant farmers. Land reforms in countries like Zimbabwe have demonstrated how peasant farmers, if given adequate land, resources, and know-how, can be a vital factor in the country's economy....

"I support clause V without any reservation.

"The guidelines are too scanty for any detailed and effective evaluation. There are, nevertheless, a few vital omissions:

- The geographic boundaries of the ANC state are not defined. Is it assumed the unitary state will include the "independent" states of the TBVC axis? If so, how will these states, with their reasonably well-equipped and trained armies be brought back into the unitary state?

- Whilst recognition is accorded to linguistic rights, nothing is said about the official language(s), the name, the flag, or the anthem of the new state.

- It would also have been interesting to observe what titles are envisioned for senior state leaders. Are we talking about a republic with an executive president or a government headed by a prime minister with a ceremonial president?

- With reference to the franchise clauses, no indication of voting age is given.

- It is not clear whether the ANC's version of a 'unitary state' actually excludes the federal option. There is a school of thought in politics that would argue a federal state can in fact be regarded as unitary.

- ANC publicity director Thabo Mbeki is on record as saying the ANC would consider a federal option provided the federal units (or states) were geographically, and not racially, designated....This has been Inkatha's position for over ten years."

NATIONAL DEMOCRATIC MOVEMENT (Wynand Malan)

"The African National Congress's Constitutional Guidelines for a Democratic South Africa represent a significant advance on the Freedom Charter in that they open up a wider debate. Yet there are elements of prescription which are truly worrying.

"To be applauded is the intention to promote a national identity and yet to recognise the cultural and linguistic diversity in the country. What is lacking here is a provision that this diversity will be protected....

"What is worrying about the ANC's guidelines is a certain similarity between them and some aspects of National Party thinking. Both groups think in prescriptive fashion and in concrete terms look to a strong central government which will take all or almost all decisions....This amounts to a delegation of power, and not a true devolution – and is not, particularly in a diverse society, democratic....

"What economic system people desire is the result of voting, during which a preference for the policy of this or that political party is expressed – and the winning party will determine the economic course until the next election....

ANC FREEDOM CHARTER (Cont.)
Reactions to the Guidelines

"Certainly the fact that the document is available inside South Africa and can be discussed is a contribution to normalising the internal situation, i.e. that a constitutional debate is not conducted without one of the major players, in the form of the ANC, being able to put its case."

NATIONAL PARTY (Dave Steward, Bureau for Information)

"In direct contrast to its revolutionary and violent nature, the ANC in the recent past has increasingly emphasised political initiatives. It has even shown a willingness to negotiate with the South African government — albeit only to negotiate the government's surrendering of power.

"The ANC's Constitutional Guidelines are part of this change in style. They can create the impression that the ANC has now adopted a liberal stance and even altered its course.

"The question arises: Are the recent ANC initiatives not merely tactical moves to attain the objective of a total take-over of power more rapidly?....

"Just as Gorbachev frankly declared that *glasnost* and *perestroika* do not mean he is departing from his basic ideology but that through these strategies he is actually attempting to pursue it more effectively, so the ANC's new strategy does not mean it is turning away from terrorism and violence....

"The real voice of the ANC is not represented by the honeyed words in its new political initiative; it may more accurately be heard in the bomb and limpet mine explosions in South Africa's cities."

PAN AFRICANIST CONGRESS OF AZANIA (Information Dept)

"The Pan Africanist Congress does not have the mandate or the time to debate a document the origin and authenticity of which remains unknown....

"The PAC ... is averse to clever talk or quibbling....

"These 'guidelines' do not help ameliorate the self-defeating disunity and dangerous bickering among the oppressed and exploited which the Freedom Charter triggered and continues to perpetrate, thus delaying our freedom.

"We shall continue to say: 1) Settler/colonialism can never be reformed — it must be eradicated. We cannot afford to appease the enemy. And 2) the vehicle for change in Azania is and shall always be the oppressed and exploited African majority and not the settler regime. We cannot afford to marginalise the workers in this regard.

"... Robert Sobukwe said, 'Watch our movements keenly and if you see any signs of 'broad-mindedness' or 'reasonableness' in us, or if you hear us talk of practical experience as a modifier of man's views, denounce us as traitors to Africa.'

"The so-called constitutional guidelines therefore leave us cold."

PROGRESSIVE FEDERAL PARTY (Zach de Beer)

"... There are phrases and sentences...which one can welcome warmly.... On the other hand, the preamble also contains a reference to 'rapid and irreversible redistribution of wealth.'

"Now it is easy to understand and to sympathise with the feeling behind this proposition, but we would not be able to support a programme which stopped or reversed the process of economic growth, since that would be contrary to the interests of all the people of our country.

"... Our party is committed to federation in its normal sense, that is a geographical decentralisation of certain government powers to states or provinces, as in the United States, Canada, or Australia.

ANC FREEDOM CHARTER (Cont.)
Reactions to the Guidelines

"...*prima facie*, we could not agree to the guidelines. But... it is clear that what is sought is 'extensive and democratic debate' about them. In that we could certainly participate.

"What is more, I think the present South African government should be prepared to participate also.

"I conclude by repeating what we have often said: Jailed and banned leaders should be set free, peaceful political activity should be permitted, and genuine negotiations on the future constitution of South Africa should take place."

TRANSVAAL INDIAN CONGRESS (Cassim Saloojee & Firoz Cachalia)
"...Our response to the ANC's Constitutional Guidelines will ...be different in substance and tenor from the others, because it comes from 'within.'

"...The old order in South Africa is disintegrating and we have entered a transition period, the outcome of which is uncertain. This has made it vital to visualise the nature of post-apartheid society more concretely and to advance practical proposals.

"In this context, we welcome the ANC's intervention. Its guidelines situate the organisation more clearly in the political spectrum and provide the framework for debate.

"...The strong element of centralism in the proposals is necessary to encourage the formation of a national identity....A strong, non-racial state will be a creative instrument of national reconciliation.

"...The new post-apartheid South Africa can only be built on the basis of recognition of rights to cultural and linguistic expression.

"...The concept of group rights is rejected — implicitly, not explicitly — in the ANC proposals. Cultural forms... cannot and should not form the basis of claims to special privilege and powers.... We see no reason why Afrikaans churches, schools and cultural organisations should not continue to exist, provided only that access to them is not limited by racial criteria.

"...The guidelines envision a state which is both national and democratic.

"...It is not clear, however, whether the ANC sees the Bill of Rights as embodying 'fundamental rights' or how such rights would be enforced. There is no mention also of 'due-process' rights, which should be included in a Bill of Rights.

"The key challenge we are facing is to ensure that change takes place without destroying our productive infrastructure, indeed that it takes place in a way that facilitates further development.

"...We are hopeful that the forms of economic restructuring contemplated in the guidelines will make it possible for us to harness our national material and human resources effectively to achieve developmental political and ethical goals.

"...It is neither feasible nor desirable to attempt to subsume all economic activity under a central plan. On the other hand, the market is no panacea.

"...To the extent that [the guidelines] make the construction of viable compromises possible, they improve the prospects of peaceful transition to a non-racial democracy."

ANC FREEDOM CHARTER (Cont.)
Reactions to the Guidelines

CONSTITUTIONAL LAW EXPERT
(Tony Matthews, University of Natal)

"It is good to see recognition being given to the independence of the courts...but there are two important things we do not know yet: One is that we do not know the 'exclusions' or the circumstances under which rights can be suspended.... The second issue is what jurisdiction the courts will have.

"...*Groups* will be politically salient for a long time and will have to feature in a constitution through protection of minority groups in some way if there is to be full freedom.... We cannot simply wish away the existence of groups — the chief example of the futility of trying to do so is Northern Ireland.... Allowing everyone the vote does not solve the problem."

APPENDIX IX

KWA ZULU/NATAL BILL OF RIGHTS[1]

Adopted July 10, 1986

On July 10, 1986 the KwaZulu/Natal Indaba adopted a bill of rights as a tentative step towards a new provincial constitution for their combined territories. The bill did not necessarily reflect unanimity among delegates regarding its aims. No mention was made of protection of group rights. Interestingly enough the Nationalist government, which for years has resisted a bill of rights, shortly afterwards indicated that it no longer rejected the idea outright.

1. HUMAN DIGNITY AND EQUALITY BEFORE THE LAW

1.1 All human beings are born free and equal in dignity and rights.

1.2 Everyone is equal before the law, and shall be entitled to equal protection by the law, without any distinction on the basis of race, colour, language, sex, religion, ethnic or social origin, property, birth, political or other opinion, or economic or other status.

2. RIGHT TO LIFE

2.1 Everyone's right to life shall be protected by law, and no one may be deprived of his life intentionally save in the execution of a sentence of a court following his conviction of a crime for which this penalty is provided by law.

2.2 Deprivation of life shall not constitute a contravention of this article when it results from the use of such force as is absolutely necessary and justified in the circumstances:

---

1   This Appendix is quoted in its entirety from *Usuthu! Cry Peace!*, pp. 155-161.

2.2.1 in defence of any person against unlawful violence;

2.2.2 to effect a lawful arrest in order to prevent the escape of a person lawfully detained for a serious offence;

2.2.3 in action lawfully taken for the purposes of quelling a riot or insurrection.

3. PUNISHMENT

No one shall be subjected to torture or to inhuman or degrading treatment or punishment.

4. RIGHT OF LIBERTY

4.1   No one shall be held in slavery or servitude.

4.2   No one shall be required to perform forced or compulsory labour, provided that this does not include:

4.2.1 any normal work required to be done in the ordinary course of detention under the provisions of subsection 4.3 or during conditional release from such detention;

4.2.2 any service of a military character in terms of a law requiring citizens to undergo military training;

4.2.3 any service exacted in case of emergency or calamity threatening the existence or well-being of the Province;

4.2.4 any work or service which forms part of the normal civic obligations imposed by law.

4.3   Everyone has the right to liberty and security of person and no one shall be deprived of his liberty save in the following cases and in accordance with a procedure prescribed by law which does not deny his basic rights to physical and mental health and integrity:

4.3.1 the lawful detention of a person after conviction by a competent court;

4.3.2 the lawful arrest or detention of a person for non-compliance with the lawful order of a court;

4.3.3 the lawful arrest or detention of a person effected for the purpose of bringing him before a competent legal authority on reasonable grounds of having committed an offence or when it is reasonably considered necessary to prevent his committing an offence or fleeing after having done so;

4.3.4 the lawful detention of a person for the prevention of spreading of infectious diseases, of a person of unsound mind, an alcoholic or drug addict;

4.3.5 the lawful arrest or detention of a person to prevent his effecting an unauthorised entry into the Province or of a person against whom action is being taken with a view to deportation or extradition.

4.4 Everyone who is arrested shall be informed promptly, in a language which he understands, of the reasons for his arrest and of any charge against him.

4.5 Everyone arrested or detained in accordance with the provisions of subsection 4.3.3. shall be brought promptly before a judge or other officer authorised by law to exercise judicial power and shall be entitled to trial within a reasonable time or to release pending trial, which may be conditioned by guarantees to appear for trial.

4.6 In the determination of his civil rights and obligations or of any criminal charge against him, everyone shall be entitled to a fair and public hearing within a reasonable time by an independent and impartial court established by law; judgment shall be pronounced publicly but the press and public may be excluded from all or part of the trial in the interests of morals, public order or national security in a democratic society, where the interests of juveniles or the protection of the private life of the parties so require, or to the extent strictly necessary in the opinion of the court in special circumstances where the publicity would prejudice the interests of justice.

4.7 Everyone charged with a criminal offence shall be presumed innocent until proved guilty according to law.

4.8 Everyone charged with a criminal offence shall have the right:

4.8.1 to be informed promptly, in a language of his choice which he understands and in detail, of the nature and cause of the accusation against him;

4.8.2 to have adequate time and facilities for the preparation of his defence;

4.8.3 to defend himself in person or through legal assistance of his own choosing or, if he has not sufficient means to pay for legal assistance, to be given it at no cost to himself when the interests of justice so require;

4.8.4 to examine or have examined witnesses against him and to obtain the attendance and examination of witnesses on his behalf under the same conditions as witnesses against him;

4.8.5 to have the free assistance of an interpreter if he cannot understand or speak the language used in the court, or if he so requests.

4.9 Everyone who is deprived of his liberty by arrest or detention shall be informed promptly in a language of his choice which he understands, and in detail, the reasons for his arrest and detention, and shall be entitled to take proceedings by court, and to be released if the detention is not lawful, provided that, if he has not sufficient means to pay for legal assistance, he will be given it at no cost to himself.

4.10 Everyone who has been the victim of unlawful arrest or detention shall have an enforceable right to compensation.

4.11 No one who is tried for a criminal offence shall be compelled to give evidence at the trial.

4.12 No one who shows that he has been tried by a competent court for a criminal offence and either convicted or acquitted shall again be tried for that offence or for any other criminal offence of which he could have been convicted at the trial for the offence, save upon the order of a superior court in the course of appeal of review proceedings relating to the conviction or acquittal.

4.13 No one shall be found guilty of any penal offence on account of any act or omission which did not constitute a penal offence at the time when it was committed.

5. RIGHT TO ADMINISTRATIVE JUSTICE

5.1 All administrative tribunals, public authorities and officials shall follow rules of fundamental fairness in coming to their decisions and they shall, unless inappropriate, be required to furnish reasons for such decisions.

5.2 Delegated legislation shall be drafted with a reasonable allowance for public comment and participation.

5.3 Everyone who has suffered damage as a result of unlawful action by public authorities shall have an enforceable right to compensation.

6. RIGHT OF PRIVACY AND PROTECTION OF THE FAMILY

6.1 No one shall be subjected to arbitrary interference with his privacy, family, home or communications, nor to attacks upon his honour and reputation.

6.2 The widest possible protection and assistance shall be accorded to the family, which is the natural and fundamental group in society, and the care and upbringing of children are recognised as a natural right of, and a duty primarily incumbent on, the parents.

South Africa: Land of Hope?

7. RIGHT OF PROPERTY

7.1 Everyone has the right to lawfully own and occupy property anywhere in the Province.

7.2 No one is to be deprived of his property without due process of law, and expropriation may only be authorised in terms of a law if it is for the public benefit and if equitable and fair compensation is promptly paid.

7.3 Land and natural resources shall not be expropriated except for the common good and in accordance with laws providing for equitable compensation.

8. ETHNIC, RELIGIOUS, LINGUISTIC, CULTURAL AND EDUCATIONAL RIGHTS

8.1 A person belonging to an ethnic, religious or linguistic group shall not be denied the right to enjoy his own culture, to profess and practise his own religion or to use his own language.

8.2 Everyone shall have the right freely to participate in the cultural life of the Province, to enjoy the arts, to share in scientific advancement and its benefits, and to the free and full development of his personality.

8.3 In all proceedings involving customary law followed by persons in the Province, such law may be applied except insofar as the court finds that it has fallen into disuse or is contrary to the principles of natural justice and morality.

8.4 Every person shall have the same right to public education in an institution that will cater for his interests, aptitudes and abilities and the Province shall make provision for this right without discrimination: provided that, notwithstanding the provisions of section 1.2, it may, in providing facilities, distinguish between persons on grounds of language or sex.

9. FREEDOM OF MOVEMENT

Everyone lawfully present in the Province shall be entitled to freedom of movement and residence within the borders of the Province.

10. FREEDOM OF THOUGHT, CONSCIENCE AND RELIGION

10.1 Everyone shall be entitled to freedom of thought, conscience and religion and to change his religion or belief, to manifest his religion or belief in worship, teaching, practice and observance, whether alone or in community with others, in public or in private.

10.2 No one shall be compelled against his religions convictions to render military service involving the use of arms but shall be required to perform national service as required by law or in lieu thereof.

11. FREEDOM OF OPINION AND EXPRESSION

11.1 Everyone shall be entitled to freedom of opinion and expression, which includes the freedom to hold opinions without interference and to seek, receive and impart information and ideas.

11.2 Any advocacy of national, racial or religious hatred and aggression between groups that constitutes incitement to discrimination, hostility, violence or political animosity is prohibited.

12. FREEDOM OF ASSOCIATION

12.1 Everyone shall be entitled to freedom of peaceful assembly and to freedom of association with others, including the right to form and to join trade unions for the protection of his interests, and no one may be compelled to belong to an association.

12.2 Everyone shall be free to form or to join political parties in order to participate in periodic and free elections, which shall be held by secret ballot or by equivalent free voting procedures.

13. FREEDOM OF WORK AND FREEDOM OF CONTRACT

13.1 Everyone shall be entitled to equal work opportunities and to free choice of employment.

13.2 Everyone with legal capacity shall have freedom to contract and to conclude agreements with others in the voluntary exercise of his rights and freedoms and generally for the promotion of his interests.

14. RESTRICTION OF RIGHTS AND FREEDOMS

14.1 The rights and freedoms recognised, under the provisions of the Bill of Rights, may be restricted by a law of the Provincial legislature which has general application, for reasons which are necessary in a free and democratic society in the interests of public safety, for the prevention of disorder or crime, for the protection of health and morals, for the protection of the rights, freedom and reputation of others, for maintaining the authority and impartiality of the judiciary and for the social, moral and economic well-being of all the inhabitants of the Province.

14.2 Everyone's exercise of his rights and freedoms shall be subject to such limitations as are legally determined for the purpose of securing due recognition and respect for the rights and freedoms of others; and groups which, by reason of their aims and the behaviour of their adherents, seek to impair or abolish the free democratic order or to endanger the security of the Province, are prohibited.

14.3 A fundamental right and freedom protected in this Bill of Rights may not be abolished or in its essence be encroached upon by a law of the Province.

15. ENFORCEMENT OF RIGHTS AND FREEDOMS

15.1 The rights and freedoms protected in this Bill of Rights are binding on the legislature, the executive, the judiciary and all government institutions in the Province insofar as they fall within the purview of and flow from the powers and functions devolved on the Province and any person may forthwith apply to the Supreme Court or to other competent authorities provided for in the Constitution by appropriate proceedings or by petition to enforce these rights and freedoms.

15.2 The Supreme Court shall have the power to make all such orders as may be necessary and appropriate to secure to the applicant the enjoyment of any of the rights conferred by the provisions of this Bill of Rights: provided that if at the commencement of this Constitution there are laws in existence in the Province which fall within the purview of the powers and functions bestowed on the Province and which are inconsistent with this Bill of Rights, such laws may, after the lapse of one year after the commencement of this Constitution and on application to the Supreme Court be declared void to the extent of such inconsistency.

Bibliography

BIBLIOGRAPHY

Books

Adam, Heribert and Kogila Moodley. *South Africa Without Apartheid*: *Dismantling Racial Domination*. Berkeley: University of California Press, and Cape Town: Maskew Miller Longman, 1986.

Arkin, Marcus, editor. *South African Jewry: A Contemporary Survey*. Cape Town: Oxford University Press, 1984.

Berger, Peter and Bobby Godsell, editors. *A Future South Africa*. Cape Town: Human & Rousseau Tafelberg, 1988.

Butler, Jeffrey, Richard Elphick, and David Welsh, editors. *Democratic Liberalism in South Africa*. Middletown, Connecticut: Wesleyan University Press, 1987.

Cloete, Stuart. *Against These Three: A Biography of Paul Kruger, Cecil Rhodes and Lobengula, Last King of the Matabele*. Boston: Houghton Mifflin Company, 1945.

Crisp, Robert. *The Outlanders: The Men Who Made Johannesburg*. London: Peter Davies, 1964.

de Kock, Wessel. *Usuthu! Cry Peace!*. Cape Town: The Gallery Press (Pty) Ltd, 1986.

de Villiers, Marq. *White Tribe Dreaming*. New York: Viking, 1988.

Elphick, Richard. *Khoikhoi and the Founding of White South Africa*. Johannesburg: Ravan Press, 1975.

Harrison, David. *The White Tribe of Africa*. London: British Broadcasting Corporation, 1981.

Louw, Leon and Frances Kendall. *South Africa: The Solution*. Bisho: Amagi Publications, 1986.

Bibliography
(Continued)

Books

Maré, Gerhard and Georgina Hamilton. *An Appetite for Power: Buthelezi's Inkatha and the Politics of 'Loyal Resistance.'* Johannesburg: Ravan Press, 1987.

Mutwa, Credo. *Let Not My Country Die*. South Africa: United Publishers International, 1986.

Paton, Alan. *Save the Beloved Country*. Melville, South Africa: Hans Strydom Publishers, 1987.

Rive, Richard. *Writing Black*. Cape Town: David Philip, 1981.

Sunter, Clem. *The World and South Africa in the 1990s*. Cape Town: Human & Rousseau Tafelberg, 1987.

Treverton, Gregory, editor. *Europe, America and South Africa*. New York: Council on Foreign Relations, 1988.

Wilkins, Ivor and Hans Strydom. *The Super-Afrikaners*. Johannesburg: Jonathan Ball Publishers, 1978.

Newspapers

Business Day, Johannesburg
The Argus, Cape Town
The Cape Times, Cape Town
The Citizen, Johannesburg
The Daily Dispatch, East London
The Daily News, Durban
The Natal Mercury, Durban
The Natal Witness, Durban
The Sowetan, Soweto
The Star, Johannesburg
The Weekly Mail, Johannesburg

Bibliography

(Continued)

Periodicals

Black Enterprise, Johannesburg.
Foreign Affairs, New York: Council on Foreign Relations.
National Geographic, Washington, D.C.: National Geographic Society.
South Africa Foundation Review, Johannesburg: South Africa Foundation.
South Africa International, Johannesburg: South Africa Foundation.
South African Panorama, Pretoria: Bureau for Information.
South Africa Profile, Pretoria: Bureau for Information.
Style, Johannesburg.

Newsletters

Race Relations News, Johannesburg: South African Institute of Race Relations.

South Africa Foundation News, Johannesburg: South Africa Foundation.

Articles

Nyati, Eugene. "Groundswell: Threat to the Struggle?." *Tribute Magazine*, (April 1988).

Relly, Gavin. "Towards a Non-Racial Democracy in South Africa." *South Africa Forum*, (April 1988).

Simpson, Carol and Edgar, and Helen and Harry Weldon. "Report to the Canadian Junior Chamber/Jaycees and the Canada JCI Senate of the Fact Finding Mission to the Republic of South Africa, February 1 to February 20, 1987." Ottawa: 1987.

Bibliography

(Continued)

Articles

Sullivan, Rev. Leon. "Statement of Principles of U.S. Firms with Affiliates in the Republic of South Africa." Philadelphia: International Council for Equality of Opportunity Principles, Inc., 1977.

Thomashausen, André. "The Dismantling of Apartheid, The Balance of Reforms, 1978 - 1988." Pretoria: Sigma Press (Pty) Ltd, 1987.

INDEX

A

INDEX

B

INDEX

('C' Cont.)

INDEX

('D' Cont.)

Dismantling of Apartheid, 118, 128, 186, 311, 313.
Durban, 87, 165.
Dutch in South Africa, 3, 5-6, 58.

Dutch Reformed Church, 39, 131, 172, 187.

E

Early Afrikaners, 209.
Economics, 35-36, 48, 56, 60, 73, 110-111, 118-119, 122, 128-129, 137, 139, 142-143, 155, 159-160, 166-167, 170, 175, 177-178, 180, 182-184, 187-188, 193-195, 197-198, 201, 211, 222, 228, 235, 238, 243, 246, 248, 255, 263, 267-271, 273, 277, 328-329, 331, 333.

Education, 16, 19-20, 27, 32, 34, 51, 56, 73, 95, 97, 102, 117-118, 122-123, 130, 153-157, 164, 168, 171, 185, 221, 241, 271.
English in South Africa, See: British in South Africa
English-Speakers, 111, 155, 218, 240.

F

Farmers, 60-61, 83, 99.
Federation, 33, 38, 56, 95, 110, 127, 134, 139, 215, 242, 329, 331.
Five Freedoms Forum, 115.
Foreign Affairs, 141.
Foreign Affairs Committee, British Parliament, 245, 257.
"Freedom Charter," 8, 59, 102, 120,

131, 253, 263, 307-308, 311, 323, 329.
Free Settlement Areas, 50.
Friedman, Steven, 176.
Funda Art and Culture Centre, 109.

G

Gavender, Gladys, 107.
Gavin, Relly, 184.
GaZankulu, 31.
Gcaba, Milicent, 92.
General Motors South Africa, 200.

Gerdener, Theo, 157.
Goodwill, 49, 65, 89, 92, 97, 102, 113, 127, 129, 139, 147, 172, 283-284.

INDEX

('G' Cont.)

INDEX

J

K

L

INDEX

M

N

INDEX

('N' Cont.)

Non-Violence (Cont.), 277.
Nothnagel, Albert, 157, 159.

Ntsanwisi, Professor Dr HWE, 31.
Nyati, Eugene, 140.

O

Omar, Ismail, 160.
"101 Ways to End Apartheid,"
115.
, 19, 33, 51-52,
73, 91, 95, 113, 121, 127, 129, 134,
137, 173, 238, 261, 327.
One Man/One Vote/One Time,
113, 137.

Opinion, 170.
Oppenheimer, Harry, 121.
Overpopulation, 20, 22, 34, 44, 46,
60, 96, 122, 128, 130.
Owen, Ken, 163.
"Own" and "General" Affairs, 41,
46, 51.

P

Pacaltsdorp, Cape Province, 154.
Pan Africanist Congress of
Azania, 330.
Parliament, 60-61, 156-157, 168,
196, 215, 222, 271.
Parsons, Raymond, 197.
Partition, 169, 235.
Paton, Alan, 215, 217, 229, 240, 242,
253, 260, 262, 265-266, 273, 275,
278, 284.
PFP, 47, 52, 108, 110-111, 126, 131,
157, 174, 222, 235, 240, 307, 331.
Pick 'n Pay, 172, 183.
Pietersburg, 19.

Political Parties, 113, 157, 235, 240,
284, 305.
Pope's Visit, 163.
Population Groups, 303.
Population Registration Act, 3,
311.
Port Elizabeth, 156, 200.
Posselt, Ekhart, 16.
Power-sharing, 37, 50, 101, 213,
243, 247-248, 265, 270, 284.
President's Council, 45, 53, 169.
Pretoria, 2, 13.
Pretorius, Professor Jan, 19, 22.
Progressive Federa Party
See: PFP
Pym, Lord Francis, 142.

INDEX

Q

Qualified Vote, 91, 133, 215.

Questions, 293.

R

S

South Africa: Land of Hope?

INDEX

('S' Cont.)

Shaw, Percy, 82.
Shell South Africa, 178.
Shrire, Dr Robert, 174.
Singh, Adhir, 87.
Small Business Development
    Corp, See: SBDC
Smuts, Gen. Jan, 104, 126.
Sobukwe, Robert, 331.
Socialism, 113-114, 119-121, 132,
    182, 187, 228, 240, 268-269.
Solidarity Party, 157, 307.
Somtunzi, Headman, 75.
South Africa Foundation, 170, 180
South Africa Foundation Review,
    168, 177.
South Africa International, 171,
    176, 180.
South Africa Map, viii.
South Africa: The Solution,
    See Louw and Kendall
South Africa Without Apartheid,
    See: Adam and Moodley
South African Blacks, 3, 5-6, 21,
    25, 27-28, 32-33, 38, 40, 45, 47, 56,
    60, 68, 72, 84, 89, 91-92, 94-95,
    97-98, 102, 104, 112, 114-115, 120,
    123-124, 126-127, 130, 132-133,
    141, 154, 159, 164, 166, 172,
    177-178, 181, 193-196, 201,
    211-212, 215, 221, 227-228, 232,
    237, 243, 246, 248, 261, 268-270,
    273, 281.
South African Black Taxi
    Association, 182.
South African Coloureds, 231.
South African Council of
    Churches, See: SACC
Souith Africa Foundation, 180

South African Institute of Race
    Relations, See: SAIRR
South African Jewry, 103.
South African Newspapers, 283.
South African Panorama, 64.
South African Police Dept, 13.
South African Press, 110, 117-118,
    134, 164, 221, 252.
South African Realities, 211.
South African Whites, 4, 6, 35, 40,
    47, 49, 55, 63-64, 84, 91, 95, 102,
    114-116, 120, 123-124, 126,
    158-159, 164, 171-172, 174, 181,
    183, 228-229, 241, 243, 261-262,
    265, 275, 281.
Southern Africa Forum, 184.
Soweto, 44, 66, 108, 116-118, 125,
    130, 153, 268, 311.
"Spear of the Nation," 127.
Spicer, Michael, 121.
Sport, 118, 153, 165.
Stadler, Herman, 13.
Stamelatos, George, 66.
State of Emergency, 56, 59, 97,
    124, 133, 212.
"Statement of Principles of US
Firms with Affiliates in the
Republic of South Africa,"
    See: Sullivan Code
Steinkuehler, Franz, 194.
Stellenbosch, 37.
Steyn, Jan, 168.
Strauss, Jaco, 54.
Strydom, Hans, 218.
Students, 17, 22, 25, 52, 54, 93, 97,
    109, 124, 140, 154-156, 168, 226.
Style Magazine, 171.
Sullivan Code, 8, 32, 71, 123, 141,

INDEX

('S' Cont.)

T

U

South Africa: Land of Hope?

INDEX

('U' Cont.)

University of Fort Hare, 84.
University of Stellenbosch, 49, 54,
   57, 156, 187, 226.
University of the North, 25.

University of the Witwatersrand
   See: Wits
Unterhalter, Dr Beryl, 131.

Urban Foundation, 168, 268.
US Congress, 15, 21, 51-52, 56, 66,
   69, 71, 167, 175, 177, 181, 195, 201,
   207, 213, 271-272.
Usuthu! Cry Peace!
   See: deKock
UWUSA, 244.

V

van der Merwe, Stoffel, 171.
van der Spuy, Carla, 54.
van der Walt, André, 159.
van der Watt, Professor Philip,
   131.
van Dijk, Evert, 25.
Van Zyl Slabbert, Frederik, 47,
   137.
Venda, 75.
Verwoerd, Dr Hendrik, 197, 307
   278.
Victims Against Terrorism, 137.
Vigilantes, 20.

Violence, 22, 47, 53, 59, 64, 89-90,
   92-94, 101-102, 113-114, 120,
   124-127, 134, 137, 139, 142,
   158-159, 164, 168-170, 173,
   176-177, 194, 201, 212, 237-238,
   241, 243, 246-247, 249, 251-252,
   257, 261, 271-272, 277, 279, 330.
Voting, Unitary State, 5, 28, 48, 99,
   112, 127, 129, 139, 156, 213, 242,
   261, 281, 284, 328.
Vrye Weekblad, 57, 165.

W

Webb, Denys, 164.
Weekend Argus, 157.
Weekly Mail, 8, 164-165, 170, 173,
   177, 179.
Welfare, 21, 47, 60, 97, 128, 167.
Westfalia Estate, 27.
White Tribe Dreaming,
   See: de Villiers, Marq
Wilkins, Ivor, 218.
Williamson, Margaret, 62.
Williamson, Neville, 80.

Wits, 52, 128, 175.
Women, 28, 37, 50, 62-64, 66, 89, 91,
   94, 96, 117, 128.
Women for Peace, 141.
Women for South Africa, 117.
Worrall, Dr Denis, 157, 306.
Writers, 133-134.
Writing Black,
   See: Rive

Page 362

INDEX

X

Xhosas, 38, 59, 82, 92, 94, 114, 210, 262.

Z

Zimbabwe, 125, 163, 267, 328.
Zion Christian Church, 262.

Zulu Wars, 5.
Zulus, 38, 87-89, 92, 114, 210, 238-240, 258, 262.

About the Author

Taffy Gould McCallum brings a broad background and wide-ranging interests to her research and interviews. A former computer programmer and teacher of French and mathematics, she branched into public relations and interviewing during her years with Public Television. In 1977, she travelled to ten countries (among them, South Africa), interviewing American women married to foreign nationals.

Ms McCallum's business background stems from her involvement in real estate development and property management; her cultural interests have been heightened by years as a volunteer for the arts. Since the early 1980s, she has written a weekly newspaper column and, in recent years, added a daily radio talk-show to her résumé. She has travelled through forty-one countries, speaks French and Spanish, and is studying Afrikaans. Her work-in-progress focuses on the rôle and influence of women in South Africa's diverse societies.